# MONEYWOOD

WILLIAM STADIEM

# MONEYWOOD

## HOLLYWOOD IN ITS LAST AGE OF EXCESS

ST. MARTIN'S PRESS ≋ NEW YORK

MONEYWOOD. Copyright © 2012 by William Stadiem. All rights reserved.
Printed in the United States of America. For information, address St. Martin's Press, 175 Fifth
Avenue, New York, N.Y. 10010.

www.stmartins.com

Library of Congress Cataloging-in-Publication Data

Stadiem, William.
  Moneywood : Hollywood in its last age of excess / by William Stadiem.—First edition.
     Pages   cm
  Includes bibliographical references and index.
  ISBN 978-0-312-65689-8 (hardcover)
  ISBN 978-1-250-01407-8 (e-book)
   1. Motion picture industry—California—Los Angeles—History—20th century.   2. Motion
picture producers and directors—California—Los Angeles—History—20th century.
3. Hollywood (Los Angeles, Calif.)—History—20th century.   I. Title.
  PN1993.5.U65 S73
  791.43'09794'94—dc23

                                                                    2012038502

First Edition: January 2013

10 9 8 7 6 5 4 3 2 1

# CONTENTS

# MONEYWOOD

# CHAPTER 1
## CAPITAL HILL

WITH THE EXCEPTION of the McCarthy witch hunt, the public face of Hollywood had never before seemed as Republican as it did on the night of January 19, 1981. The scene was the ball celebrating the next day's inauguration of America's first "Hollywood" president, Ronald Wilson Reagan. Reagan had been California's first Hollywood governor. His way had been paved by the state's first Hollywood senator, song-and-dance man (and, incongruously, Yale man) George Murphy. Reagan in turn would pave the way for California's second Hollywood governor, strong-and-death man Arnold Schwarzenegger. Both Murphy and Schwarzenegger were, coincidentally, also Republicans.

But that was California, which was on the cutting edge, and this was America, which for all its fascination with the silver screen was always wary of liberal, Jewish, bleeding-heart, foreign-seeming, and overwhelmingly Democratic Hollywood. Ronald Reagan had overcome the country's prejudices by repackaging himself as the nativist, conservative, *Knute Rockne, All American* version of the Hollywood dream. He was the pioneer, and the master, of channeling celebrity for right-wing political purposes, just as John F. Kennedy had done it for liberal ones, albeit without having been a member of the Screen Actors Guild, of which both Reagan and Murphy had been president.

A major sign of the new times was that Reagan's inaugural gala was being staged by the same man who had staged JFK's glamorous kickoff exactly twenty years before, none other than Frank Sinatra. In 1961, Ol' Blue Eyes, who at forty-five wasn't all that old at the time, assembled a dream team of superstars to create the very first Hollywood inaugural. He had everyone from Sir Laurence Olivier to Louis Prima, Bette Davis to Keely Smith, Fredric March to Milton Berle, not to mention a phalanx of black talent that included Ella Fitzgerald, Nat King Cole, Harry Belafonte, and Sidney Poitier. The most conspicuously absent black superstar was Sinatra's fellow Rat Packer Sammy Davis Jr., who had been barred from the event by Big Daddy Joe Kennedy for marrying the Aryan Swedish goddess May Britt. Even Democrats had their limits. Now Ol' Blue had become Ol' Red, a Republican converso. With his new affiliation came a new appellation, Chairman of the Board, more appropriate to his new political party and to his seniority of sixty-five years. To Kennedy he brought Mahalia Jackson; to Reagan he brought Mister T.

Bloated and crowned with one of the worst toupees in a lifetime of cover-ups, the superstar introduced the television star of *The A-Team,* who looked like a psychedelic version of a sommelier in Brazzaville. In a foreshadowing of Reaganomics, Sinatra quipped that "if he decides to melt down all his gold chains, he could wipe out the national deficit." Mister T bowed to Mister S and recalled that he had last been to the White House to play Santa Claus for Jimmy Carter, and now he was back. "Where else but in America," he exulted, "can a black man from the ghetto play a white man from the North Pole?" He brought down the house of millionaires.

The big evening, held in a basketball arena in Landover, Maryland, home of the Washington Bullets, was like an extended television special, a middling night on Ed Sullivan. Johnny Carson co-emceed with Sinatra, but he wasn't swinging for the fences. There was Rich Little, a Republican favorite for his impressions of Richard Nixon, who was surely having the last laugh tonight, though not here. There were Donny and Marie Osmond and Debby Boone and Mel Tillis, the stuttering country singer who had turned his impediment into stardom.

In addition to Mister T, there were numerous other awkward nods to black power, Republican style: Donny Osmond tried, in vain, to channel Chuck Berry by not quite duckwalking the stage and singing "Ronnie B. Goode." Charley Pride channeled Hank Williams, after expressing his deep gratitude to "Miz Nancy" for inviting a poor Delta boy to this Holy Land. Ben Vereen, channeling Stepin Fetchit, put on a kind of minstrel show, covering his visage with a seemingly superfluous layer of blackface while singing (cringe) "Waitin' for the Robert E. Lee."

The only duplication from the Kennedy gala was Ethel Merman, unsinkable at seventy-three and way above and beyond party, belting out "Everything's Coming Up Roses." Old Hollywood was represented, sparsely, by Charlton Heston, channeling Moses; by Bob Hope, still game at seventy-eight; and by James Stewart, then seventy-three, who had become a brigadier general in the U.S. Air Force Reserve. Stewart stood proudly beside a real supergeneral, Omar Bradley, at eighty-seven the last of the five-star commanders. Dean Martin was in the front row, drunk. The press was not kind. One critic compared the show to *Hee Haw* (meow).

Here, in all its Republican lack of glory, was Hollywood taking over Washington. But whose Hollywood was it, anyway? Not the New Hollywood of Spielberg, Lucas, and Coppola, whose blockbusters were the only hope of rescuing a moribund feature film industry. Those auteurs were all Democrats, as were the so-called baby moguls, a bunch of ex–student radicals turned studio executives who were green-lighting offbeat fare like *Animal House* and *Airplane!*

No, the Hollywood that conquered Washington was the Hollywood of the second chance, the Hollywood of television, which was the new cash cow of entertainment. Look at Reagan himself. A basic B-actor turned TV presence was now commander in chief. It was big-time for Bonzo. The same thing was happening in the entertainment business: TV was taking over. B-actors and -actresses, finding themselves irrelevant on the big screen—which was itself in danger of becoming irrelevant unless it became even bigger—were getting remarkable resurrections on the small. Television was the reanimator. What F. Scott Fitzgerald had written about there being no second acts in American life was totally wrong. TV was the miracle. Ronald Reagan was Exhibit A.

The hunky heartland sportscaster had beaten long odds once to get a Warner Brothers contract, but then, despite entering the movie lexicon as "the Gipper," he never became the Gable-level star he wanted to be, ending up on the tube in *Death Valley Days.* Furthermore, he was eclipsed, if not emasculated, by his first wife, Jane Wyman, who had won an Oscar for *Johnny Belinda* in 1948 at a time when Ronnie could barely get a role and ended up co-starring with a monkey. They divorced that year. Wyman, like her ex, would wind up on television on her own show, *Jane Wyman Presents The Fireside Theatre,* and ultimately on *Falcon Crest,* where she, too, was resurrected and won a Golden Globe.

Not even television could salvage the career of Nancy Reagan, who had re-created herself as a Republican social lioness. Quickly rebounding from Wyman, Reagan had remarried, in 1952, Nancy Davis, a Chicago society girl and a Smith College Seven Sister who had her own insuperable struggles in the thespian game. Before marrying security and class in her stepfather, a prominent if fanatic right-wing neurosurgeon, Nancy's mother, Edith, was a struggling actress herself, who had abandoned Nancy to her sister so she could go on the road and chase her dream, which Nancy also inherited.

Using her mother's showbiz connections, Nancy was able to get a screen test through Benny Thau, MGM's resident casting gatekeeper and master of the quid pro quo. How much *quid* Nancy had to surrender for Benny's *quo* cannot be known, but they did go out a lot. In the end, it came to naught but a few minor roles. Nancy was coming into the business in the early 1950s, a time when gentlemen preferred blond bombshells like Marilyn Monroe and Jayne Mansfield. No match for Grace Kelly or Eva Marie Saint in the social ice goddess department, Nancy was dismissed as a poor man's Dina Merrill. Ironically, the best Dina Merrill, the genuine Post Toasties heiress, could do was marry Cliff Robertson, the man who played JFK (in *PT 109*), while Nancy's husband would succeed JFK and make Nancy, the lost lady of Hollywood, the First Lady of America. The country liked comebacks and they liked winners, and the Reagans were providing it in spades.

Frank Sinatra had long ago made his comeback, from washed-up singer of novelty ditties with dogs ("Mama Will Bark") to 1954 Oscar winner in *From Here to Eternity*. Now he was making his turnaround. No one could have ever been a bigger and better Democrat than the underdog, up from nothing Italian Hoboken crooner and civil rights champion whose mother, Dolly, had been a ward heeler. Sinatra liked to take credit, among his friends, for having done more to get his buddy John F. Kennedy elected (as well as laid) than anyone except maybe Sam Giancana, who was said to have "fixed Chicago" for JFK. Ah, that toddlin' town.

But what one Kennedy giveth, another taketh away. Blue-stocking Bobby, as much as he might have liked Marilyn Monroe, whom he had met through Sinatra, couldn't stand the stain of Ol' Blue's gangland ties, particularly with Giancana. Although Sinatra had redecorated his Palm Springs estate to turn it into

JFK's informal western White House, Bobby put the nix on his brother's travel plans and arranged for John to stay instead chez Bing Crosby. Crosby was Sinatra's idol as well as his rival, and the unkindest cut of all was that he was also a Republican. Then again, so were a lot of stars, and not just John Wayne. Many of the giants were Republicans—Gable, Grant, Stewart, Mitchum, Holden, Hudson, plus Crosby's *Road* partner, Hope, and Lucy and Desi, and even Elvis the King.

The great moguls who built the studios, Warner, Mayer, Goldwyn, despite their immigrant roots, had all eventually become Republicans. Ronald Reagan himself had been a Democrat until 1962. Then he switched, and he quickly rose to governor. Sinatra had always looked down on Reagan as tedious, boring, and second-rate, a classic "B." This was no star; there was no shine. Nor did Sinatra have lust in his heart for Nancy, which was rare for the serial Lothario. He had made fun of her fat ankles, which were no match for the magnificent gams of his almost wife, South African dancer Juliet Prowse. Now Nancy was the First Lady of California, and where was Juliet Prowse? Ronnie had begun a trajectory that would make him the biggest star in the world. The list of Republicans, and the success of Reagan, was enough to get Sinatra thinking.

Sinatra thought even harder in the aftermath of his humiliating 1968 breakup with hippie Mia Farrow, who was rumored by gossip queen Rona Barrett to have cuckolded the master by having an affair with his long-term black servant, George Jacobs. Sinatra equated hippies—who were not buying his records, like "Something Stupid"—with Democrats, and as for Black Power, he fired Jacobs for seeming to have taken it a step too far. Jacobs denied the whole non-affair.

The Farrow divorce sent Sinatra careening to the opposite end of the romantic spectrum. He began to pursue the recently widowed

Edie Goetz, as daughter of Louis B. Mayer the most eligible woman in Hollywood and acknowledged by all to be the film industry's hostess with the mostest, the preeminent party giver for celebrity Democrats (despite the fact that Daddy was a Republican). Wags in show business immortalized her by paraphrasing the show-stopper from *Damn Yankees*: Whatever Edie wants, Edie Goetz. No matter that Goetz was a good decade older than her pursuer, a man who was three decades older than Farrow. She had class, and she was the ultimate in the Establishment that Sinatra had longed to belong to all his life. Alas, Goetz mocked his courtship. "I don't date the *help,*" she declared, deflating the famous heartthrob.

It wasn't long after this rejection that the man who was supposed to be able to get any woman on earth found himself in the less vaunted arms of the ex-showgirl ex of Zeppo Marx, the Marx Brothers' straight man who later became a talent agent. Sinatra also found himself arm in arm with his new best friend in politics, Vice President Spiro Agnew. Having fled the Farrovian love children and longhairs of the Sunset Strip for the Lacosted golfers of Palm Springs, Sinatra became part of a billionaire party circuit dominated by Walter Annenberg (heir to the *Daily Racing Form*) and Armand Deutsch (heir to Sears, Roebuck), who would both become key members of Reagan's "kitchen cabinet." President Eisenhower's obsession with golf had put Palm Springs on the Republican map. This was Valhalla for rich conservatives, and some of its political stardust must have rubbed off on its still preeminent celebrity, Mister S, the one even the billionaires were in awe of, Edie Goetz notwithstanding.

That billionaires would envy (indeed, covet) show business stars was a sign of the times. With the launch of *People* magazine in the mid-seventies, and CNN in 1980, America was entering its never-ending age of celebrity, with television serving as both the cause and the effect. Although there were far fewer, and far worse, movies than ever before, there were more celebrities than ever. The bar for a star had been lowered but the audience vastly expanded. It was hard to compare Erik Estrada with Cary Grant, or Farrah Fawcett-Majors with Katharine Hepburn, but the legions of TV fans in the seventies dwarfed the number of movie fans in the forties, and they loved their idols just as ardently, and even more profitably for the advertisers of their shows.

It was also the dawning of the age of money. In 1980, the Whitney Museum bought Jasper Johns's *Three Flags* for $1 million, the first time a living artist had hit seven figures. The commerce of art, whether that art be painting or music or film, became more interesting to the public than the art itself. The 1958 hit and classic of the year *Bridge on the River Kwai* had a then whopping annual domestic gross of $18 million. Two decades later, *Star Wars* grossed more than $200 million in America alone, not to mention the vast foreign market. The numbers became the news, and the public began following the business of culture as much as if not more than the reviews.

Aside from the blockbuster "event" movies like *Jaws,* what the fans of the era seemed to like most of all were soap operas, particularly the nighttime ones. *Dallas,* which was a monster hit, was replicated by *Dynasty* and *Falcon Crest* and *Knots Landing. Dynasty* had its debut just following the Reagan inaugural. Its creator, Aaron Spelling, became the Cecil B. DeMille of the small screen simply by giving a huge and vicarious public an *à clef* and only slightly racier and more florid (though in some cases much tamer) version of the lives of the Reagan kitchen cabinet who were Spelling's real-life neighbors in Holmby Hills and other Southfork-like estates throughout Greater Los Angeles. Low art was imitating high life, with spectacular ratings, both for the low artists and the high livers.

No viewer of *Dallas,* even in Dallas, could have been more obsessed with the real-life soap opera that was Hollywood than the tycoons and trophy wives of Reagan's kitchen cabinet. For all their social triumphs and business successes and political clout, an inordinate number of the group had been, earlier in their lives when failures become indelible, failed producers or failed starlets, like Nancy Reagan herself, as well as Nancy's mother. Ronnie's daughter by Jane Wyman, Maureen, had sought the screen, too, acting with Elvis in *Kissin' Cousins*. And now Nancy's daughter, Patti, was trying to become an actress. And son Ron wanted to be a ballet dancer. The beat went on and on, the endless wail of the show business siren.

Because of the way one's ego is put on the line, Hollywood dreams seem to die hardest of all. The "kitchen" group, who would be running interference for the Gipper in running the country, had a huge amount of unfinished business in Hollywood. They simply couldn't get over the place, and their deep-seated, unspoken obsession with the world of entertainment would, in the decade ahead, become a communicable virus that would infect the entire nation, and the world, in a way that showbiz, for all its magic, had never done before. How different these people were from their predecessors, the peanut farmers from Georgia. And how the public was delighting in living through the glamorous lives of this new First Family and their First Friends. After Jimmy Carter, the country was being born again, in the most secular way.

Take Alfred Bloomingdale, husband of Betsy B, Nancy Reagan's best friend and style icon. Despite his family's fame in retailing in their eponymous New York emporium, and despite his having made his own name as chairman of the Diners Club credit card colossus, what Alfred Bloomingdale really wanted to do was be a producer, which is exactly what he set out to do after flunking out of Brown in 1938. He had all the obvious qualifications: he was rich, connected, grandiose, extravagant, tall, dapper, and obsessed with beautiful women. He was made for the movie business, but Broadway got its hooks into him first. Holding court at the Stork Club, which he used as his preliminary casting

couch, Alfred began producing flops. His first, *Your Loving Son,*
closed after three performances; his fourth, *Sweet Charity* (no re-
lation to the later Bob Fosse hit), closed after eight. A witty script
doctor of the time, called in to rescue another of Alfred's efforts,
suggested that Alfred close the show and keep the store (Bloomie's)
open nights.

But Alfred's pockets were too deep and his libido too stoked to
let him give up. He decided to cut to the chase, which was his
main motivation in any event, and focus on musical revues, where
he could cast the most leggy chorines. He did *High Kickers* with
George Jessel, where he met his first wife, a chorus girl named Barbara Brewster; then *Early to Bed,* which actually had a good score
by Fats Waller; and finally, in 1943, a minor hit revival of the *Zieg-
field Follies.* But Alfred's glory was short-lived. His next extrava-
ganza, *Allah Be Praised,* set in a Persian harem, was such a total
disaster that it drove Alfred, whose flop marriage had lasted barely
longer than his flop shows, completely out of town, to Hollywood
and the waiting arms of ogre mogul Harry Cohn. Cohn, one of
the seminal figures in sexual harassment, saw a kindred spirit in
Alfred and offered the heir an office on Cohn's Columbia lot.

Hollywood proved to be an even tougher nut to crack than
Broadway. Alfred couldn't get a single movie off the ground. He
did, however, find a wife, another tall chorine type and wannabe
actress (who in L.A. was not?) named Betty Lee Newling. Exactly
Alfred's type, Betty Lee, who was the daughter of an Australian-
born, Harvard-trained orthodontist to the stars, had expectedly
great teeth as well as great legs. She had been living the fast life on
the Hollywood circuit, having been one of Gloria Vanderbilt's
bridesmaids at her eyebrow-raising wedding to Hollywood agent-
stud Pat DiCicco, who had a second, darker life as the right hand/
black hand of supermobster Lucky Luciano. DiCicco was also the
first cousin of producer Albert "Cubby" Broccoli, who would later
bring the world the James Bond series. The Hollywood world was

small and infinitely surprising, and Betty Lee wanted in desperately. She got her big break when she was introduced to Alfred by Freddy De Cordova, who would go on to great fame as Johnny Carson's producer on *The Tonight Show*. But when he befriended Alfred, Freddy was a director of B pictures, most notable of which was *Bedtime for Bonzo,* starring Ronald Reagan and the chimp.

Betty Lee's parents had done their best to take their daughter out of the loop of Hollywood temptation. They had sent her to the most exclusive finishing school in town, the no-Jews, no-stars Marlborough. From there they sent her east to horsey Bennett Junior College up the Hudson in Millbrook, New York, where proper young ladies were prepared less for careers than for their debuts. Nonetheless, Betty Lee remained hell-bent on getting into pictures, but, alas, even with those legs and those teeth, and all her dad's connections, she still couldn't get a studio contract. There was no other option but to marry a millionaire, and fortunately, Freddy De Cordova, who couldn't get her a part even in his lowest B pic, put her in romantic harm's way. Alfred fell hard and fast for Betty Lee and quickly proposed. In a trade-off, he converted from his neglected Judaism to his new bride's Catholicism, while Betty changed her name to Betsy, which Alfred found to be less rustic and *plus chic*. The new Mrs. B also gave up her thespian ambitions. The would-be Hollywood star would have to be content to be a Hollywood wife. Arguably she would become *the* Hollywood wife of her generation.

Jackie Collins would have been hard-pressed to conjure up the tribulations Alfred put Betsy through. Once a player, always a player, Alfred was a mainstay of the many madams who thrived in the film capital. Even before the expression "MAW" (model actress whatever) was coined, everyone knew that the oldest profession was actually the only profession, or means of support, for the countless homecoming queens and beauty pageant winners who came west only to have their celluloid dreams dashed on the cold, closed gates of Fox and Paramount and Universal. One of these MAWs, Vicki Morgan, a towering blond inferno who for a while had been in the globe-trotting harem of rogue financier Bernie Cornfeld, so entranced Alfred in submitting to his ever-escalating Felliniesque S&M orgies that she became his main mistress for over a decade, the very decade where Alfred's support was key in putting Ronald Reagan in the Governor's Mansion and then the White House.

Vicki was tall and leggy, just like Alfred's two wives. Alfred looked for the same qualities in his mistresses that he did in his wives, minus the inhibitions that come with being a permanent trophy like Betsy. Alfred paid Vicki over $20,000 a year, which was a major payday in the 1970s, though he always held out the vastly bigger payday of his leaving Betsy and making an honest woman out of Vicki. Then, in his mid-sixties, Alfred, a heavy drinker and smoker, got esophageal cancer and died, leaving Betsy to fight off one of the most embarrassing palimony suits Hollywood's top divorce lawyer Marvin Mitchelson ever filed.

Betsy had thought the height of embarrassment came in 1976, when she was arrested and convicted of a felony for deceiving customs officials by seriously undervaluing two Christian Dior dresses at Los Angeles International Airport en route from Paris, all to save about $600. The rich are indeed different. That contretemps was nothing compared with the Vicki Morgan scandal-fest. In the midst of Mitchelson's suit, seeking $5 million in lifetime payments to Vicki from Betsy herself, word began circulating that Vicki had a cache of sex tapes that featured not only Alfred but other august fellow Reagan right-wingers participating in S&M orgies with other nubile MAWs—ménages à droit, so to speak—that could bring down any house, including the White House. While Nancy and her court of rich, perfect, but aging blond socialites were at the Bistro Garden in Beverly Hills having lunch, Alfred and his multimillionaire golf buddies were allegedly somewhere very, very far off the course. This was the real Hollywood, the Hollywood Babylon of *Confidential* magazine, trying to smash through the Reagans' very un-Hollywood prim façade.

With all this getting too close for Republican comfort, Vicki discovered that Mitchelson was invited for dinner at said White House. Suddenly, Vicki had to get herself another lawyer, Beverly Hills barrister Robert Steinberg, who was nowhere in Mitchelson's big league. Still, Steinberg insisted he had the tapes, evidence that would incriminate a nation. *Hustler's* Larry Flynt was offering millions for them. The gossip mills were in an overdrive that made the future Clinton-Lewinsky scandal seem like something from behind the gym at a high school prom.

The next twist in the very twisted tale found Vicki, having sold the Mercedes and baubles Alfred had bought her, taking in a roommate to pay for her downwardly mobile Studio City address Alfred was no longer alive to foot, a gay man named Marvin Pancoast who had met Vicki years before when both were at the same mental hospital being treated for depression. Three weeks after moving in together, Pancoast, with no prior criminal record, took a Louisville slugger and batted Vicki to death.

The tapes suddenly disappeared. Pancoast quickly confessed, was quickly convicted, and died of AIDS in prison a few years later. Conspiracy theorists had a field day, asserting that Pancoast had as much motive to kill Vicki as Jack Ruby had to kill Lee Harvey Oswald and was silenced in the clink the same way Ruby was, so that the awful political truth would never emerge. This, they screamed, was a major kitchen cabinet cover-up. The only slight justice here was a posthumous jury award of $200,000 to Vicki's estate for money Alfred promised and never paid. The unsinkable Betsy Bloomingdale returned to the best-dressed list and a seat of honor at White House functions, and the "bad" Hollywood was successfully swept back into the celluloid closet.

The grandest of the Reagan kitchenites were the Baron and

Baroness of Palm Springs, Walter and Lee Annenberg, who had one of the great French Impressionist collections in America and whose parties were considered the most lavish in the country. Spending a lot of time in L.A. for his magazine *Screen Guide,* the precursor of cash cow *TV Guide,* Walter Annenberg had also been something of a player as a young man on the make in Hollywood, but compared with Alfred Bloomingdale he was a Franciscan monk. However, Walter had his own share of scandals, especially the high-profile fall from grace of his father, Moe, who died shortly after he was released from two years in prison on tax evasion charges, and the suicide of his son, who overdosed on sleeping pills while a student at Harvard.

Moe Annenberg's past was tainted well before his incarceration. As Chicago circulation manager for William Randolph Hearst's yellow press, Moe was a master of using violence to outsell the competition, from beating up newsboys to burning newsstands. He later joined forces with Lucky Luciano in New York to build circulation, physically, with Mob muscle, for Hearst's *New York Daily Mirror.* Eventually Moe made his own fortune with the bookie bible, the *Daily Racing Form,* then went legit by buying the *Philadelphia Inquirer* and turning it into a publishing empire. In 1939, young Walter was indicted with his father, but Moe cut a deal to plead guilty if his son was spared. Walter redeemed the family by rising from Moe's ashes, first in the 1940s by launching *Seventeen* magazine, then in the 1950s with *TV Guide* and a chain of TV stations.

Like his dear friend Alfred Bloomingdale, Walter was an Ivy League dropout (Penn '29). In his Hollywood-Broadway wild oats period, he romanced Ginger Rogers and Ethel Merman (which, given their enduring friendship, might explain Merman's performance at the Reagan inaugural). When Moe died, Walter settled down, wedding a retail heiress from Toronto. By 1950 that union was asunder, and Walter got back deep into the Hollywood swing by marrying showbiz royalty, Leonore "Lee" Cohn, the niece of Harry. Lee's father, Maxwell, had been a producer at Columbia Pictures, which his brother had founded and ruled like a dictator. When Lee's mother died young, Harry took her in and had her raised by his servants. Spoiled but not rotten, Lee studied hard and graduated from Stanford, then made a series of big-buck unions, first to Belden Katleman, the son of a parking lot king, then to Lewis Rosenstiel of the Schenley liquor dynasty, and finally to Walter.

The Annenbergs grandly divided their time between a Main Line estate in Philadelphia, a palatial ski lodge in Sun Valley, and Sunnylands, the barony in Rancho Mirage rivaled in Palm Springs lore only by the nearby Sinatra compound. This was where Richard Nixon retreated after Watergate, where Sinatra married Barbara Marx, where Prince Charles liked to spend his American weekends, and where Ronnie and Nancy would celebrate New Year's. Nixon had appointed Walter to the plum post of ambassador to Great Britain, over the catcalls of the British press, who mocked Walter as a Jewish philistine arriviste. Walter had the senatorial look—Republican senatorial, that is—that huge money could buy. But the snooty Brits saw through the laundered façade. They looked at Walter and they saw Papa Moe. However, when Reagan appointed Lee Annenberg his first chief of protocol, no one said a word about the bona fides of this genuine Jewish American princess, who became Nancy's role model for style and class. The English tended to revere Hollywood as they did their own royalty.

That Lee Annenberg style, that class, became one of the signatures of the Reagan era. One way to describe it would be Bistro Garden Stepford Wife. So many of the wives of Reagan's kitchen cabinet looked so much alike—bleached blond, dieted thin, coiffed by the same hairdressers, and coutured by the same designers—that the maître d' at the Maison Blanche in Washington, *the* power restaurant of the administration, kept a photographic cheat sheet at his dais so he could tell who was who. And even then he had trouble.

The style of "les girls" was an iteration of the Holiday Inn ad campaign of the period: "The Best Surprise Is No Surprise." The Reagan look was classic country club, be it Hillcrest or LACC. They had their privileged Cal-chic Bev Hills look, their formal state dinner Washington look, their ranchy Palm Springs look. Reagan red was the color of the party, and the parties. Tinier than Jackie Kennedy, Nancy Reagan was five four and a perpetual size 2, and her female friends toed the same thin line.

The women had all been shoppers in their youth at the Beverly Hills temple of conservative chic, Amelia Gray, a dress shop that was showcasing the work of a young Philadelphia-born, Jersey-bred, but Paris-trained Greek American designer named James Galanos. Galanos would become the Reagan world's designer-in-residence, the "count of chiffon," his signature fabric. While Betsy B and Lee A couldn't live completely without their Diors and Chanels, by and large the Reagan girls anointed the L.A.-based American Republican Galanos as their main man, turning couture into an act of patriotism. They might also turn to the all-American Bill Blass, to Adolfo, who may have been Cuban born but was a U.S. citizen and a navy man to boot, or to the naturalized Oscar de la Renta. Shopping with Givenchy, Jackie Kennedy's go-to, seemed practically un-American.

The one accessory Nancy and her clique could not do without was the "walker" Jerry Zipkin, who became both grand vizier and court jester of the First Lady and her ladies-in-waiting. Dubbed "the Social Moth" by *Women's Wear Daily,* the flamboyant, effeminate Zipkin, basically John Wayne turned inside out, may not have fit the staid Republican image but was pure Hollywood, albeit of the Fred and Ginger *Gay Divorcee* era, not the current one of *Raging Bull.* Introduced to Nancy by Betsy Bloomingdale,

Jerome Robert Zipkin, as a rich and privileged New Yorker, had a lot in common with Alfred Bloomingdale, except the latter's rampant heterosexuality, though it could also be said that Jerry was infinitely more interested in women than Alfred ever was.

Jerry, who lived with his mother until she died in 1974 (he was sixty-four) in the Park Avenue apartment house built by his real estate developer father, was also an Ivy League dropout (Princeton '36). After leaving Princeton in a cloud for shoplifting an art tome from its bookstore, Jerry finished his education at gentleman-C Rollins College in Florida, where he liked to joke that he majored in canoeing. He returned to New York, where he continued to joke that he spent the war years doing intelligence for the OSS "at the Stork Club."

After the war, Zipkin's father died and he began accompanying his mother on clothes- and antiques-buying sprees to Europe, where he developed the keen and ruthless eye for fashion and décor that would endear him to Nancy and company, who were nowhere as sure of their style as he was. Zipkin, as hard-core Republican as Walter Annenberg, adored Hollywood, where he became the intimate of decorator to the stars Billy Haines and the over-the-top high-camp Ross Hunter, the big producer (*Imitation of Life, Pillow Talk*), as well as the canasta partner of such stars as Joan Bennett, Claudette Colbert, and ZaSu Pitts, who was also a close friend of Nancy Reagan's mother. It was just a matter of time until Jerry met Nancy, and once they did, nothing could tear them asunder.

Another of the look-alike Stepford Reagan wives and a Zipkin fan was Lee Annenberg's best friend and fellow Jewish dream girl, Harriet Deutsch, wife of Sears heir Armand "Ardie" Deutsch. Lee owed Harriet big-time, for Harriet was the one who introduced her to Walter. Again, it was all the Hollywood six degrees of separation game. Another thwarted actress and actual fashion model, New Yorker Harriet Berk had become film-adjacent by marrying prolific B-director S. Sylvan Simon, whose biggest credits were

*Abbott and Costello in Hollywood* and *The Fuller Brush Man,* starring Red Skelton. But things were looking up for Simon when Harriet befriended Lee Cohn, who introduced her to Uncle Harry. Harry took to Simon and made him producer, though not director, of the Judy Holliday comedy hit *Born Yesterday.* Simon might have become a major Columbia producer had he not succumbed to an untimely coronary at forty-one in 1951, which put widow Harriet back on the market.

Harriet's own Dolly Levi was Fran Stark, wife of super-A-producer Ray Stark and daughter of comedienne Fanny Brice, whom Ray would immortalize with Barbra Streisand in *Funny Girl.* The Starks introduced Harriet to Deutsch, a playboy producer who had recently divorced his Broadway actress–dancer wife, Benay Venuta. Demonstrating *comme le monde est petit,* Venuta was the best friend of Walter Annenberg flame Ethel Merman, whom she had understudied as Reno Sweeney in *Anything Goes* and then co-starred with in *Annie Get Your Gun.* Ardie Deutsch was him-self a B-producer of such forgettable A-talent fare as *Ambush* with Robert Taylor and *Carbine Williams* with James Stewart. Still, he met the stars, and he was so rich and charming that the stars were happy to come out to play with him.

Deutsch's main claim to fame was that he was supposedly the original target of the kidnap killers Leopold and Loeb. He was spared only when his chauffeur picked him up from school for a dental appointment, forcing the plotters to kidnap and murder schoolmate Bobby Franks in his place. Deutsch never ceased to dine out on the tale. Still another Ivy League dropout (Dartmouth '35), like Bloomingdale, Annenberg, and Zipkin, he became great friends with everyone from Bogart and Bacall to Burns and Al-len, from William Holden to Jack Benny. Deutsch knew Nancy Reagan from her days as a role-seeking MGM starlet, though she and Ronnie were able to join the Deutsch A-party list only after Ronnie's emergence as a political star.

As good as Harriet's parties were, though, they were never considered as good as those of Edie Goetz, such as her World Series party with a television set at every table while a French chef–prepared gourmet dinner was served, or the memorable occasion when she introduced Mae West to Greta Garbo. Harriet and Edie were superficially effusive but fierce rivals, even if their husbands were best friends and business partners in financial ventures. Unlike the rest of the Reagan entourage, the Deutsches, like the Goetzes, were staunch Democrats. Eventually, Ronnie got so successful that it would have been unseemly, if not un–American, for the Deutsches not to switch parties.

Lest one think that for a Jew to be in Reagan's inner circle, he had to be a major heir, like Bloomingdale, Annenberg, or Deutsch, look at Charles Z. Wick. Wick was totally self-made, including having Scrabbled the letters of his original name Zwick, changing the Z to a middle initial to make himself seem more WASPy. Wick, who held degrees in both music and law, had begun his career doing band contracts for Tommy Dorsey. He worked in New York as a William Morris agent, representing Benny Goodman and Peggy Lee, then moved to California, where he made his first serious money in a field diametrically opposite show business— nursing homes.

Flush with that elder care money, Wick tried his hand at producing. His singular film credit was the 1961 *Snow White and the Three Stooges,* which even the dour Reagan got a huge laugh making fun of. In fact, the tiny Wick was considered the jester of the Reagan court, entertaining the men the way Jerry Zipkin entertained the women. Wick played piano, told jokes, and flaunted his gorgeous, rangy WASP wife, Mary Jane Woods, who had come west from Minnesota to become a Goldwyn Girl but, like the rest of the Reagan wives, got no further, at least on-screen. Mrs. Wick was the actual flypaper that got her husband into the august Reagan circle.

Nancy had met Mary Jane manning a hot dog booth at a carnival for the John Thomas Dye School, a junior Eton for the Bel-Air set, where both the Wick and Reagan children were enrolled. Nancy was so captivated by Mary Jane's charm and their shared actress roots that it was the beginning of an unlikely friendship that would see Ronald Reagan appoint Wick to the directorship of the U.S. Information Agency, making the world safe for Republicanism. The bottom line was that Ronnie was more comfortable around Wick than he was around the heirs and the tycoons. Two midwestern boys who tried to make it in pictures but made it even bigger in something else, they spoke the same language, Hollywoodese.

Ethel Barrymore had once joked that the definition of Los Angeles society was "anyone who had finished high school." Nonetheless, Los Angeles had an impermeable WASP elite and a sharp line of demarcation drawn between show business, which was seen as "Jewish" (in the most pejorative sense), and big business, which was not. The social high temple of Hollywood society was the Hillcrest Country Club, on Pico Boulevard right behind the Fox lot, which had, as its symbol of wealth, its own working oil well. Its fifties clubhouse looked like something out of the Sinatra compound in Palm Springs. On the other side of the Fox lot was the Los Angeles Country Club, which was the big business redoubt. They didn't *need* an oil well to show off. Their members, the Dohenys, the Sinclairs, and the like, had endless oil wells of their own. The clubhouse at LACC looked like Tara in *Gone with the Wind,* though that was about as close to showbiz as the LACC was going to get. The genius of Ronald Reagan was that in his inner circle he was able to blend the two constituencies and make them peacefully coexist. As in most things Republican, the common denominator was money, but even for the WASPs, there was also at play here an atavistic call of the Hollywood wild.

Of all the kitchen cabinet, only über–Ford dealer Holmes Tuttle and über–corporate lawyer William French Smith were defiantly untouched by the entertainment business. Tuttle, a part-Chickasaw Oklahoman farmboy, had ridden a boxcar to California in the 1920s and married a plain schoolteacher. His big Hollywood moment was having sold Ronald Reagan a car right after the war. But Tuttle never saw Reagan again until the ex-Democrat reimagined himself as a golden-tongued savior of the Right. Unlike the pure heartland Tuttles, the Smiths were American aristocrats. William French Smith was a proper Bostonian Yankee, a *Mayflower* descendant, and a very square Harvard man. His wife, whose family owned the city's first lumber mill, was a third-generation Los Angelino, which is *Mayflower*-like in these climes.

Like Tuttle and Smith, no Reaganite could have seemed as un-Jewish and unshowbiz as the "top chef" of Reagan's kitchen cabinet, Earle Jorgensen, except for the fact that his life was the stuff of films. The son of a Danish ship captain, Jorgensen as an eight-year-old had fled the 1906 San Francisco earthquake to the safety of his father's schooner, from where he watched the city burn. By sixteen he had sailed the South Seas and begun a scrap metal business, armed with no education but with a scrap of a magazine in his wallet with three words that would become his motto: "Hustle, that's all." Hustle, he did, until he became the Steel King of the West, the chief supplier of the explosive postwar Southern California aerospace business that made him a billionaire.

No vulture capitalist, Jorgensen believed in giving back. Inspired by his Danish mother's volunteer work making bandages for the wounded in World War I, Jorgensen became a chief benefactor of the Red Cross, creating one of the world's biggest blood banks during World War II. That charity brought him into the arms of another of its benefactors as well as the founder of "Bundles for Britain," the ultraglamorous Marion Bren, and, indirectly, into the arms of Hollywood.

Marion Newbert herself was a Chicago industrial heiress; her

Irish immigrant grandfather produced the wheels for America's freight trains, and her own family fittingly traveled in its private railway car. Marion's parents had moved to Los Angeles, where she attended Marlborough some classes ahead of the future Betsy Bloomingdale. She got her pilot's license at seventeen, which shocked her family, but not as much as when she eloped with a young man who had crashed her 1930 debutante party at the Ambassador Hotel (where Bobby Kennedy was later shot by Sirhan Sirhan). The man, Milton Harold Bren, had the double whammy curse of being both Jewish and a film producer, which was terra incognita for Marlborough girls.

The son of a St. Louis dry goods salesman and grandson of a Confederate infantry captain, Bren had come to Los Angeles to star on the University of Southern California track team and then to be in the movie business. He had begun his career as Irving Thalberg's office boy. Eventually he would produce ten undistinguished films, the best known of which was *Topper Takes a Trip,* a sequel to the original ghost comedy but minus its star Cary Grant. More a social lion than a mogul, Bren, an accomplished yachtsman and sailboat racer, made his big money in real estate, developing office towers. He did direct one film, the 1952 Pullman farce *Three for Bedroom C,* starring Gloria Swanson past her expiration date. By then Bren and Marion had divorced, and Bren had remarried actress Claire Trevor, who had won an Oscar as Edward G. Robinson's moll in *Key Largo.* Trevor would share mothering duties with Marion for Marion's two sons with Bren, the oldest of whom, Donald, had his dad's knack for property and would become, pre-dot-com, the richest man in California, owning much of the prime real estate in booming Orange County.

After the split with Bren, Marion went on to marry insurance heir Tom Call, whose father, Asa, had teamed up with *L.A. Times* publisher Norman Chandler to propel Richard Nixon's political career. When that Republican union didn't work, Marion was game to try another, to Jorgensen, which did. They became one of the premier power couples in Southern California, as well as perhaps the most generous, to a long list of causes, from the Boy Scouts to Caltech, from gardens to hospitals. The closest Marion came to entertainment after the Bren divorce was her trusteeship of the Los Angeles Music Center and Washington's Kennedy Center. Still, through politics, she became a key mentor to Nancy Reagan, in blondness and in chic, just as her husband was bankrolling Nancy's husband's run for the governorship.

The most successful actress in the Reagan political elite was Bunny Wrather, wife of real estate and TV syndication tycoon Jack Wrather. As Bonita Granville, she had been the star of the Nancy Drew girl detective series and was the only kitchen cabinet wife to get that holy of holies, a star on the Hollywood Walk of Fame. She was also in a Milton Bren–produced comedy, *Merrily We Live,* with Constance Bennett, and she co-starred with Ronald Reagan in the 1939 Dead End Kids comedy *The Angels Wash Their Faces.* Such are the roots of Republicanism. Bunny was nearly the same age as Nancy and also from Chicago. Thus she was a major inspiration for the future First Lady, particularly when at thirteen she got an Oscar nomination for her role as the evil child in *These Three,* based on Lillian Hellman's *The Children's Hour.*

It was hard, however, for Bunny to make the transition from child star to adult one. Fortunately, her child stardom still was an aphrodisiac to Jack Wrather, a handsome oil-rich Texan marine commander who had come to play in Hollywood and produced some of her later, lesser films. He would soon make two fortunes, one in syndicating old TV shows like *The Lone Ranger* and *Lassie* and another in real estate, owning such iconic properties as the Disneyland Hotel in Anaheim and the Balboa Bay Club in Newport Beach. The Wrathers lived down the block from the Bloomingdales in Holmby Hills. It was all so cozy and clubby.

Oil exploration magnate Henry Salvatori, one of the most right-wing of the Reagan circle, also had a would-be actress wife, Grace. A young beauty from Oklahoma, Grace had won a contract with MGM that provided the sizzle that got her married. That union took her more places in her husband's global empire than any starring screen role. Still, there was that "what if" fairy tale that haunted her, just as it haunted Nancy.

Jane Dart, wife of drugstore colossus Justin Dart, actually had a real acting career that she gave up to marry her millionaire. Warner Bros. had discovered the beauteous Jane O'Brien, an L.A. lawyer's daughter, and took out the O, renaming her Jane Bryan when they put her under contract in 1936. She had made twenty films by the time Dart swept her off the screen in 1939, getting rave reviews opposite Bette Davis in *We Are Not Alone* and making new friends with her co-stars Ronald Reagan and his then wife, Jane Wyman, in the hit military school comedy *Brother Rat* and its sequel, *Brother Rat and a Baby*. Keeping the show business connection going, the Darts' son Stephen married Linda Gosden, daughter of Freeman Gosden, the co-creator and classic voice of both Amos and Kingfish on the long-run smash radio and TV hit *Amos 'n Andy,* which was indirectly part of the homage to Hollywood's golden age of racism that Ben Vereen was criticized for paying on inauguration eve.

While Sinatra was the symbol behind the big show, the actual producer of the spectacle was Charles Z. Wick, who hadn't had so much fun, and so much publicity, since he teamed up Snow White with the Three Stooges. What Wick lacked in subtlety, he more than made up in heavy-handedness, saturating the American television audience with every second of what he viewed (as did the country) as the glory and glamour of it all. For all his days of wandering in the Hollywood wilderness, Wick had finally come up with the blockbuster that dominates every producer's fantasies. Here was a real-life soap opera of the American Dream, about an actor who couldn't rule Hollywood, so he comes to rule the world. Call it *Mr. Reagan Goes to Washington* or simply *Hollywood President.* Think of the trailer. It was all about comebacks, and winning, and romance, and big money and power, and rich twisted friends, and rebellious children, and the most conspicuous consumption since Marie Antoinette. Plus, and the biggest plus of all, patriotism.

It was way beyond Frank Capra and way beyond *Dallas.* It was also higher concept than the soon-to-come *Beverly Hills Cop, Lethal Weapon, Die Hard,* and other blockbuster franchises that would create a new generation of brash, hustling, shameless moguls who would make the Goldwyns and the Mayers spin in their marble mausoleums. Just as television gave new life, and endless power, to Ronald Reagan, these bad-boy wild-men impresarios, aided by a Reagan-spawned, movie-mad, and equally shameless Wall Street, would supercharge a crumbling feature film business to an undreamed-of bottom line. Hollywood would become Moneywood, but at a cost of its art and soul.

# CHAPTER 2
## DOWN AND OUT IN CENTURY CITY

AND I HAD THOUGHT Forest Lawn was in Glendale. But I was wrong. Forest Lawn was *everywhere*. The whole idea of Hollywood, of glamour and glory and glitz, seemed dead, from the gone-to-seed Grauman's Chinese Theatre to the sterile generic skyscrapers that had turned most of the Twentieth Century Fox lot into the Century City office park. If L.A. was a great big freeway, as Dionne Warwick had sung, Hollywood was a great big cemetery. The year was 1972, and I was having my first professional encounter with show business as a summer clerk in the law firm of Mitchell Silberberg and Knupp, which sounded more like a real estate outfit in Fargo or somewhere in the pioneer West than a hot shop of entertainment law in the heart of big-moneyed West Los Angeles.

Although 1972, which saw the release of *The Godfather* and *Cabaret,* may seem like a vintage year for movies, such masterpieces were few and far between. The seventies as a decade, notwithstanding the emergence of auteurs like Scorsese and Coppola, De Palma and Ashby, were one of the dark ages of American cinema. Most films were bad, and most people were staying home and watching television, which may have been even worse, but at least it was free.

Not that this mattered to me. I was at Harvard, home of the Brattle Theatre, famed for its Bogart revivals, and the Orson Welles Cinema, the best repertory house in the country. I wasn't reading the gloom-and-doom stories in *Variety*. I was reveling in the past magic of movies. I avoided typical Hollywood fare like *Blacula* and *Conquest of the Planet of the Apes* and saw lots of art films like *The Discreet Charm of the Bourgeoisie*. I was a fan, and money was no object. Blissfully unaware that Hollywood was going under, I dreamed of going there and being in show business. Whatever that was.

One of the greatest perks of attending Harvard was having access to wonderful summer jobs. I was in the new and very special twenty-student joint program of Harvard Law School and Harvard Business School. We were considered the elite shock troops of capitalism, and all the big firms and big investment banks came after us. At that innocent stage of our lives, we tended to judge firms by the company they kept (that is, their clients) and not so much by the (hideously tedious) work they all did. So in the first of my three summers before I got my two degrees, I worked in a London solicitors office, Macfarlanes, which represented Mary Quant (miniskirts) and Mark Birley (exclusive nightclubs). Seeing Jean Shrimpton at Annabel's was definitely cool Britannia, but drafting default provisions about fabric and filigree was straight out of *Bleak House*. In my second summer I went to Wall Street to Willkie Farr & Gallagher, which represented Major League Baseball. But no number of Yankees box seats could outbalance the boredom of proofreading. And in my third summer, I decided to go Hollywood.

I had no idea until that summer what second-class citizens lawyers could be. Lawyers in Hollywood were, more than anywhere else, "the help." It was thus amazing to me that a mere decade later, 1980s Hollywood would come to be dominated by lawyers, who had shaken off their shackles, locked in an uneasy symbiosis with a producer corps of con men, wild men, and hucksters whom these same lawyers would have been too ashamed to represent without those blockbusters under their Hermès belts.

Mitchell Silberberg, as the firm was known (no one knew how to pronounce Knupp), was located right over the Beverly Hills city line in a Century City tower referred to as the Hamburger Hamlet building because of the luxe ground-floor eatery, the platonic ideal of a coffee shop chain that took California casual to its ne plus ultra and served some of the world's best charcoal-grilled prime burgers. The top-floor offices overlooked the Pacific to the west as well as the golf course of the no-Jews, no-stars Los Angeles Country Club. The firm was heavily Jewish, and there were lots of jokes about being as close to the LACC as we were going to get. Every office was equipped with an elaborate stereo system, something I had never seen before in a law firm, as a nod to the firm's large music practice. Once, I turned it on as background for my proofreading. I was amazed at how a little rock helped ease the pain, but my solace was brief. A neighboring partner chastised me for, in effect, whistling while I worked and warned me the console was to be activated only if I were on a record deal.

Having trod the high-propriety, sacrosanct boards of firms in the City of London and on Wall Street, I found it a tad incongruous and un-Californian to be working in the Hamburger Hamlet building and overlooking a golf course and the blue Pacific while still being required to wear a suit and tie and toiling in rockless silence. The operative descriptive of Southern California was "laid-back," and Mitchell Silberberg was anything but.

There was one exception, a tall, gangly man with scraggly long hair who sported cutoff jeans and a Mickey Mouse T-shirt. I thought he might be a messenger on the Disney route, but I was informed that he was none other than Abe Sommer, the head of

the music department and someone whose stereo was always
on. How come he wears Mickey Mouse and I'm stuck in Brooks
Brothers? "Because he went to Hebrew school with Herb Alpert," I was told summarily. Alpert had built his Tijuana Brass into
the music colossus A&M Records and turned to his fellow *yid-
dishe bucher* to do his legal work. Sommer also represented, among
many other legends, the Rolling Stones. Music, which was booming, was a far bigger source of revenue for the firm than movies,
which were dying. Abe could wear whatever he wanted. That
summer, he never once spoke to me or to any of the five other interns. We were way too unhip for him.

Even though I thought I was going to be an entertainment
lawyer for the summer, I not only didn't get a music assignment,
I didn't get any movie work, either. Instead, all I was given was
some incomprehensible corporate filing work for the firm's biggest client, its cash cow, Occidental Petroleum, whose chairman,
the global tycoon Armand Hammer, was close friends with the
firm's senior corporate partner, Arthur Groman. On the bench of
every bus stop in Los Angeles was an advertisement for Groman
Mortuaries, a big business of death, shades of *The Loved One*,
founded by Arthur's family. This inspired me to joke to some
other underlings at the firm that Arthur had gone from one life-
less profession to another. No one laughed. Even though Groucho
Marx was reputedly a client, Mitchell Silberberg was no laughing
matter. No music, no mirth. It was as if, to rebut any presumptions of Lotuslanding, the firm was out to work harder and be
even duller than the sweatshops on Wall Street.

Standing beside Arthur Groman as the firm's other twin tower
was the head of the entertainment department, Eddie Rubin. Neither man was much over five feet, but each cast a huge shadow in
the L.A. sun. While Arthur "had" (lawyers are notoriously pos-
sessive) Armand Hammer, Eddie had Howard Hughes, not to
mention Steve McQueen, Paul Newman, and Warren Beatty, as

well as Columbia Pictures, where the firm kept an office on the lot (where we boys of summer were never taken). Eddie also was close to then president Richard Nixon. The two had been classmates at Duke Law School. The firm was as "in the loop" as any law firm could be, but I never got any frisson of power or privilege the way I did at the old white-shoe New York and Washington outfits like Cravath or Sullivan & Cromwell or Covington & Burling. Maybe it was the Hamburger Hamlet location that eliminated the gravitas.

But that summer I wasn't looking for power; I was looking for stars, and it didn't look as though I were going to meet any. One day Arthur Groman, himself a Yale Law man, huddled with the three summer interns who came from Harvard and explained the facts of life to us. "Only sons of clients with law degrees get to do entertainment work," he told us. "You Harvard guys do Oxy. It's much more challenging. Anyway, you're way too smart for the other stuff. You didn't come here to wipe stars' asses."

Somehow, I had the heretic thought that it might be more fun doing bedpan duty for, say, Faye Dunaway than Armand Hammer, whom I also never met, but I bit my tongue. I found some solace from one of the privileged entertainment lawyers, Jonathan Goodson, the son of game show king Mark Goodson of *The Price Is Right, What's My Line?,* and *To Tell the Truth.* Jonathan, who had gone to Yale Law, lived in an architectural house in Westwood filled with expensive modern art and was a gourmet with a wine cellar full of noble vintages. His beautiful wife was a judge, the youngest judge I'd ever met. The sons of the rich were different indeed, and Beverly Hills seemed to be the world capital of nepotism. I mean, how do you say no to movie stars or studio heads or game show kings, and once you had said yes to all of them, what was left for mere mortals like me? "It's just as boring as what you're doing," Jonathan consoled me. He insisted that his entertainment work was pure drudgery, the only difference being the famous names on the filings. He was just biding time until Big Daddy brought him into the family business.

Jonathan also warned me about the dead-endedness of being an entertainment lawyer. "You're Bob Cratchit for life," he declared. Invoking Dickens seemed to be the most common theme of life at the bar. "You leave the firm and go to a studio, but they stick you in legal affairs or business affairs. And you keep shuffling papers. Plus you never make any real money. What you really want to be is a producer." Producers indeed. They were the ones who lived the life. They created the projects, they went on location, they slept with the stars, they lived in palaces. I had never met a producer, but I had the images of one from the lordly Cecil B. DeMille (who also directed) to the glam Robert Evans, who had made *Rosemary's Baby* and was now running Paramount and taking credit for *The Godfather*.

Neither DeMille nor Evans nor any other big producer I knew of had gotten to be one by going to Harvard. The right school could get you law jobs and bank jobs, but that was all indentured servitude. Getting freedom required something else. Family money seemed the preferred mode of advancement. Like Jonathan Goodson, Evans came from big money, specifically his brother Charles's major Seventh Avenue fashion house Evan-Picone. It was rumored that the real secret of Evans's success was his access to fashion models whom he fixed up with his boss Charles Blühdorn, founder of Gulf+Western, the conglomerate that owned Paramount. Lawyers were just the backstreet boys, and I chafed at what I now realized was the myth of social mobility in a Hollywood that was just as stratified as feudal England.

One lawyer who did catch my attention that summer was a dapper, confident young man whom older Mitchell lawyers would point out with envy at Beverly Hills restaurants where they would take the summer associates to lunches that were tax-deductible. The man was Peter Guber, and the lawyers saw him as "one who escaped." Possessed of a J.D. and an LL.M. from NYU, Guber was the rara avis of an attorney who did not practice, either in a firm or in the legal affairs department of a studio. No, Guber was an executive at Columbia, a guy who picked movies to make and actually oversaw their production. He had been involved with such hits as *Shampoo* and *The Way We Were*. He was "creative." Was "creative lawyer" an oxymoron? Didn't matter. Guber had made the Great Escape from the Dickens grind and was a Hollywood player.

It occurred to me, over and over, that if Guber could do that with those degrees from NYU, just think what I could accomplish with my Harvard sheepskins. But then I was brought back down to earth. I was informed that what set Guber apart was not his education or even his brains and drive. It was his wife. Her name was Lynda Gellis. Her family owned the Isaac Gellis kosher delicatessen empire. She was deli royalty, and in West Los Angeles, that was as good as being a Romanoff in czarist Russia. Isaac Gellis was an invaluable asset in a Hollywood escutcheon, much more so than any Harvard diploma. As we will see, this was only the beginning of the Guber juggernaut, the salami express.

Of course, this being America, there was another way to make it into the showbiz inner sanctum, and that was the sheer chutzpah and backstabbing aggression immortalized in Sammy Glick. The antihero of Budd Schulberg's Hollywood antinovel *What Makes Sammy Run?* was said to be inspired by the producer Jerry Wald, who made *From Here to Eternity* and other huge hits at Twentieth Century Fox. It wasn't lost on me that Schulberg's father had also been a studio head, and that Wald's son Robby, whom I met that summer, was a rising young agent and a prince of this city. I, on the other hand, with my fellow lawyers, was a serf, as opposed to a Malibu surfer, which was a princely pursuit. That the serfs and the Sammys would revolt and take over this declining kingdom a decade hence was again inconceivable to me

while I shuffled my papers in the Hamlet building, as melancholy
as the great Dane himself.

Perhaps sensing my dissatisfaction at not getting a shot at entertainment work, and probably seeking a way to cure me of this foolish desire, Eddie Rubin called me into his corner office overlooking
what was left of the Fox lot and told me that I was going to get a
showbiz assignment. Wow, I exulted to myself, notwithstanding
Jonathan Goodson's warnings that entertainment law was still law
and not entertainment. I had visions of playing golf with Cary
Grant, or dining at Chasen's with Elizabeth Taylor, or maybe being
flown to Switzerland to go over some deal points with Audrey
Hepburn. None of the above. I was going to be working for Doris
Day, one of the firm's biggest clients, who was in an epic lawsuit
with her late husband's business partner for embezzling her out of
over $20 million.

That sounded like fireworks and lots of juicy scandal. But that
wasn't what I was getting. Instead my task was to write a contract
for a dog on the Doris Day television series. I spent weeks on the
contract. I never met Doris Day. I never met the dog. I never
met the trainer. I never went to the set or to the kennel. I just kept
drafting that contract, over and over. *That* was entertainment. *Que
sera, sera!*

One night the three Harvard musketeers (we all roomed together in a tacky lanai complex under the bleachers of the Uni
High football field) decided that if the firm would not send us
to Chasen's, the most famous restaurant in Hollywood, then we
would take ourselves. My cohorts were a student body president
from the University of Michigan who had an encyclopedic knowledge of old movies and a student radical from the University of
Wisconsin who had an encyclopedic knowledge of pop music. The
other two boys of summer, one from UCLA Law and the other
from USC, both L.A. natives, seemed smart but dull, which appar-

ently was how this firm, and most others, liked its lawyers. Neither showed any interest in hanging with the Harvard guys.

Then again, Harvard didn't seem to have the magic status value it had on the East Coast. We noted that the *L.A. Times*, in doing profiles, almost never mentioned where someone went to school, often because most of its success stories hadn't gone anywhere of note. Maybe that was the difference between traditional East and pioneer West. Out here, they didn't care where you had gone, only where you were going. So much for our credentials. As it turned out, the dull UCLA guy, Alan Levine, went on to become president of Columbia Pictures in 1989, proof that lawyers had come a long way, baby.

For all the absence of the expected movie glamour, we still felt pretty exclusive, having gotten what was perceived back in Cambridge as dream summer jobs. Most of my generation was movie-mad, though few of them were aware of what doldrums the movie industry was in. There was immense competition for these jobs at Mitchell, as well as for the few slots at the tiny cartel of entertainment law powerhouses: Wyman, Bautzer; Kaplan, Livingston; Pacht, Ross; Gang, Tyre & Brown; O'Melveny & Myers. We may have felt like Rodney Dangerfield, but compared with our brethren sweating it out on Wall Street for the summer, we were in paradise and had ample cause to celebrate our good fortune. We booked at Chasen's, using the firm's name, got dressed up, and drove over to Beverly Boulevard and Doheny Drive to the plantation-white temple of celebrity gastronomy. This was the place that had air-freighted its chili to Elizabeth Taylor in Rome as a gastrodisiac for her and Richard Burton while they were bankrupting Fox with *Cleopatra*. What an eyeful we got. At separate red leather banquettes, we quickly spotted James Stewart, Gregory Peck, Joseph Cotten, Roddy McDowall, and Governor Ronald Reagan. We *had* arrived.

But not for long. The imperious Mexican maître d' hustled us out of the celebrity sight line around the bend to a walled-off Siberia, and even there to the very worst table in the restaurant, the end of the line, next to the swinging doors of the kitchen. They wouldn't even serve us the famed chili, which the arrogant Mexican waiter said was not on the menu, though we were certain we saw the governor spooning it up. Instead we had the equally famous hobo steak, desultorily sautéed in butter tableside by the waiter, who clearly was just going through the motions for these three nobodies. The meat was tough and greasy, and we were sure it came from the tourist refrigerator, as opposed to the star larder. We left deeply depressed. As with the entertainment work, we were learning our place, and our place clearly was not here.

Toward the end of summer, Arthur Groman announced a big outing for the summer associates. He was going to take us to see the famous art collection amassed by his friend and client Edward G. Robinson. Then we would lunch at the Hillcrest Country Club. This was all pretty thrilling. To meet Robinson, Little Caesar himself, Mr. *Double Indemnity,* that would have been a blast even without the Renoirs and the Matisses. And to enter the pearly gates of Hillcrest, that was a ticket to heaven. Hillcrest was the golf course of the stars, most of whom rarely even played. It was the only club where Groucho Marx, who famously vowed that he wouldn't want to join any club that would have him, was thrilled and proud to be a member. Hillcrest was as important a landmark on this fan's Map of the Stars as Chasen's, Perino's, Forest Lawn, or Nate 'n Al's deli, except you couldn't get into Hillcrest, or even near it. Hillcrest was to Jews and stars what the L.A. Country Club was to socialite WASPs.

Now that Arthur was taking us to Hillcrest, we thought he was God. On the appointed sunny day, Arthur packed us into his white Rolls and drove us to Robinson's estate in Beverly Hills. He warned us on the way that Robinson had been ailing with cancer and that we were not allowed to address him, even if he tried to engage us in conversation. This made for a very awkward situation, especially since Little Caesar himself was full of energy and immense charm and kept asking us what we thought of his French Impressionists.

All we could do was smile and nod. Where was Marcel Marceau when we needed him? Robinson must have thought we were idiots, but we were following Arthur's orders, and Arthur was not one to be disobeyed. After a half hour of fine art, we drove on to Hillcrest. We could have walked there from the Hamlet building in ten minutes, but if nobody walked in L.A., certainly nobody walked into Hillcrest. The parking lot lived up to expectations. There were far more Rollses, Bentleys, and Aston Martins (and little else) than in the parking lot of Spago in its heyday to come.

In our dark law-suits, we must have looked like a raiding party from the IRS. Golfers in their Lacostes and Gucci cleats stared hard until they saw Arthur shepherding us, then they smiled in relief. A small army of black attendants in crisp white jackets virtually bowed as Arthur walked in. This was still the age of Rochester, the star valet, and we couldn't forget that Rochester's cheapskate boss, Jack Benny, was a Hillcrest man. The club itself was very fifties Palm Springs desert pastel, call it Annenbergian or Sinatraesque (both were members). The main club dining room opened out to the first tee, which was dominated by an adjacent working oil well, which was both a status symbol and a source of wealth. Not that Hillcrest needed it; its dues were reputedly the highest in the country.

But money wasn't the point here. Celebrity was. Our first sighting was Fred Astaire. Second was Danny Kaye, just walking through, larger in life than any screen image we had ever known. Then we were totally blown away when we passed the Comedians' Round Table, every bit as renowned as the Algonquin Round. There was a circle of legends: Benny himself, George Burns,

George Jessel, Milton Berle, Sammy Davis Jr., Jack Lemmon. Only Groucho was missing. We all felt like "made men," a point Arthur used as an incentive over lunch. He told us that if we were invited back to the firm, worked like dogs for a decade, and made partner, Mitchell had a "special relationship" with Hillcrest that could allow us to join this Valhalla someday.

Then the lunch. The Pullman-style waiters presented us with huge and daunting menus. Arthur cut to the quick. "The food's the best in town, boys," he said, preening, "but if you want something special, I'd get the hamburger. I'd go so far as to say it's the best hamburger on earth. I wouldn't miss it, if I were you." This, in the burger capital of the world. It was an offer we could not refuse. One by one, each of us placed our bets. "Hamburger. Hamburger. Hamburger . . ." The courtly waiter stood by Arthur. "I'll start with the Scotch salmon, and then I'll have the broiled Canadian lobster," he declared with a straight face. Off the record, the burger didn't compare with the half pounder at the Hamburger Hamlet. Then again, you didn't see Astaire at the Hamlet.

While we were eating, two stunning blondes in tennis whites exploded into the dining room. They were West Coast country club versions of Brenda Patimkin in *Goodbye, Columbus*. "That's my daughter," Arthur said, leaping up from his leviathan lobster. As he greeted the girls, they looked over at our table and, within earshot, asked Arthur who we were. "Nobody," he said. "Just some kids from the firm." Our hearts collectively sank. Those dream dates weren't going to happen. Worse, our dream memberships at Hillcrest seemed much more a campaign promise than a lifetime guarantee.

So we went back to the firm and kept grinding it out until summer's end. I worked just as hard as I had on Wall Street the previous summer, albeit with fewer fringe benefits. I spent one entire weekend doing an SEC filing for Occidental, and on the Saturday night I treated myself to a tempura dinner at Yamato, an esteemed Shinto shrine of a restaurant in the Century Plaza Hotel that looked like an old set from *Sayonara*. The following Monday morning the managing partner, a Harvard College grad who went to law school at Berkeley and somehow developed a nasty chip on his shoulder against the Ivy East, came into my office and threw down the dinner receipt I had submitted to accounting. "When you work overtime for a client, you can go down to the Hamlet and order the small hamburger, the quarter pounder, *not* the half pounder, and a small Coke, not a large," he snarled. "Oxy, any client, will pay for that. Anything beyond that is out of your own pocket. Where the hell do you think you are, Wall Street?" Actually, yes, I replied. He didn't like the answer. "Harvard," he sneered under his breath, and stormed out.

In the few hours I wasn't Cratchiting away, I tried to get into the groove of 1970s Los Angeles. I went to the most expensive store in Beverly Hills, a Carnaby-ish emporium of trend named Eric Ross, and tried to atone for my Brooks Brothers sins by purchasing an after-hours wardrobe that was intended to make me feel like Clark Kent turned Superman. The striped pants and psychedelic shirts were a fusion of Capri and Woodstock, and suffice it to say I was deeply ashamed to wear any of this once I got back to preppy Cambridge. What was I thinking? I guess I bought the clothes to impress a beautiful blond Jewish surfer girl I met in an all-night Safeway who thought lawyers were way uncool. I did lots of other foolish L.A. things, going to hear Eagles-knockoff bad bands at the Troubadour, getting poisoned on pork tacos in the Mexican Grand Central Market in downtown L.A., nearly getting sun poisoning watching Wilt Chamberlain play volleyball with two teams of beach bunnies on the sands of Marina del Rey.

A matchmaker of a partner even fixed me up on a blind date

with a genuine heiress, the daughter of a client construction magnate who was bulldozing the charming old Spanish apartments of
Wilshire Boulevard and putting up bland Manhattan-style high-
rise apartments. I suspect the partner knew my celluloid ambitions
and was providing me with a shortcut, if not an only hope. As it
happened, my ticket to paradise turned out to be as massive as her
father's edifices and no more inviting. Expecting Cybill Shepherd,
I got Brunhilde. I had planned to take her for a seafood dinner in
Santa Monica and then a walk on the beach, but I changed di-
rection and took a tatami room in Little Tokyo that would better
accommodate her. The partner had told me that her family was
"big in Hollywood." I later learned what a closet jokester he was.

By late August, I decided that entertainment law and I were
probably not made for each other. However, my love for movies
was undiminished, and I had even developed an affection for Los
Angeles and all its sybaritic tinsel. Nowhere else in summer was
the living as easy. Thus, I tried to figure out a way to come back
after I graduated the next year without being a lawyer, short
of betrothing myself to a deli heiress. My M.B.A. was worthless,
unless I was willing to become a studio accountant, which was
even more deadly than the law.

I looked around to see who was having fun, which was what
Hollywood was supposedly about. I rejected the idea of being an
agent. William Morris ruled the town back then, but those guys
were too scary, men in black and even more corporate than the
gray flannel men of Madison Avenue. William Morris's rival,
CMA, which would soon shuffle its letters and become ICM, was
less of a monolithic hit squad. But its star agent, Sue Mengers, was
so aggressive that I knew I could never rise, or fall, to her standard. This barely five-foot-tall roly-poly ball of fire was famous
for flashing herself, à la Sharon Stone in *Basic Instinct* but minus
the allure, at crucial moments of negotiations to gross studio executives into capitulating to her terms.

What I came up with finally was to go into publicity. Was I crazy? Of course it lacked the cachet of the law, but the only people I saw consistently enjoying themselves were the PR people. They went to all the best restaurants and best parties. They dressed well. They traveled the world with the stars. They seemed sophisticated. And they didn't have to proofread, which took up most of any young lawyer's days and nights. On a lark, I rang up the preeminent Hollywood publicity firm Rogers & Cowan to set up an interview. I thought that as a Harvard J.D.-M.B.A. willing to pass up the great Mitchell Silberberg to work for them, my overqualification for the task would be doing them a huge favor. Was I ever wrong. I can't remember exactly whom I spoke with, probably the head of personnel. Whoever it was, he gave me the best lesson I had yet learned in the realpolitik of the film business. He dismissed my credentials and my pitch like water off a duck's back. It made zero impression on this man. "Listen, kid," he told me in a gravelly sidewalks-of-New York accent. "If we don't *already* know you, we don't *want* to know you. So go fuck yourself!" He slammed down the phone.

To cite Bob Dylan's "Just Like Tom Thumb's Blues," I decided that I was "going back to New York City, I do believe I've had enough." Hollywood seemed like a completely closed shop. Whatever it was I had to sell, nobody here was buying it. The Establishment may have wanted me, but not the Disestablishment, whose siren call had brought me to the West. So back I went to the open arms of Wall Street. No more Rodney Dangerfield. I didn't realize that my best path to Hollywood glory was precisely the unlikely road I was choosing by default.

# CHAPTER 3
## OFF THE MENU

IF A RESTAURANT can be a leading indicator for the future economic state of the entertainment industry, then Ma Maison boded spectacularly and incongruously well for a Hollywood that seemed permanently mired in a slough of despond. Ma Maison, which opened in the depths of Hollywood's miseries in 1973, would within two years become the coolest, most exclusive restaurant in the entire world, sort of what Café Royal was to the London of Oscar Wilde or of Delmonico's to the New York City of Diamond Jim Brady, or of Le Pavillon to the chic clique of Cole Porter and Babe Paley. At Ma Maison, it seemed as if Hollywood were wholeheartedly embracing the Epicurean philosophy of eat, drink, and be merry, for tomorrow we die, for things on the big screen were that bad.

These restaurants of the gods always have an entertainment connection. The original Le Pavillon leased its space from Harry Cohn, who owned the Columbia Pictures building above it on Fifth Avenue. On Cohn's first visit, the imperious patron Henri Soule exiled the mogul to his French Siberia, behind a potted palm, which may have been the genesis of Hollywood's deep complex about either having an A-table or better starving to death. You *are* where you sit. No such problem at Ma Maison, where every table was an A, because virtually every diner was a star or a mogul who employed the stars. One of the bestselling books of the 1970s was *Winning Through Intimidation*. Ma Maison was dining through intimidation.

It started with the unlisted phone number and continued in the parking lot, where the restaurant itself was obscured by a murderers row of Rollses, Bentleys, Aston Martins, and Ferraris. Porsches and Mercedes sedans seemed to need not apply, and God forbid if you showed up in a rental Mustang, as I did on my first visit, out from New York, in 1976. I parked two blocks away, hid my car on a side street, and slunk over. Even at lunchtime, there was a small army of paparazzi lying in wait outside, but they didn't even look up as I walked by. They had a sixth sense as to who was famous and who was not, and not an ounce of energy was to be wasted on the no ones. If we don't already know you, we don't want to know you. That was the mantra out here. I was glad to be meeting my son-of-fame friend Jonathan Goodson; at least I was getting in.

In a tour de force of reverse chic, the restaurant was housed in what looked like a former garden supply shop on then torpid Melrose Avenue. The cinder block outside was painted a hideous shade of yellow, while the inside garden dining area was carpeted with AstroTurf and hideous, mismatched lawn furniture. Still, it was seventy-five degrees in January, and soft, warm Santa Ana breezes wafted through the patio. But you didn't go to Ma Maison for the climate. You came for stars, and you saw stars.

My eyes were spinning. The first stars I saw were Sean Connery and Michael Caine, who had just finished *The Man Who Would Be King,* directed by John Huston. At another table was the director's daughter, Anjelica Huston, dining with beau Jack Nicholson. Across the room was Steve McQueen. On the other side was Faye Dunaway. With only about twenty tables, there was no Siberia, only Valhalla. There was a small dining room inside what was once either a house or a toolshed, but there was only one diner there. It was Orson Welles, hugely fat and wearing a cape, but still Orson Welles. The other lawn chairs at this garden party of legends were filled with agents and producers and moguls, but the only one I recognized was a pre–*Indecent Exposure* David Begelman, the dapper, superconfident, table-hopping studio head of Columbia Pictures. I had seen him at Elaine's in New York, but Elaine's was a little sideshow of arcane literati compared with this cavalcade of stars.

Stars were only half the story of Ma Maison. The other half was the food, and its pedigree. Ma Maison was considered Tour d'Argent West, because its owner, Patrick Terrail, was the nephew of Claude Terrail, the dashing proprietor of Paris's then three-star preeminent culinary shrine, with the world's most iconic views over the flying buttresses of Notre Dame. The Tour, as it was known, was most famous for its *caneton,* whose beyond-rich sauce was created by crushing its bones and innards in a silver duck press.

Sinatra and his Rat Pack dubbed the Tour "the duck joint," and it became Hollywood's favorite foreign restaurant. The connection was further strengthened when Claude Terrail married the daughter of Jack Warner and himself became a member of the film colony until their divorce, and even afterward, with affairs with Ava Gardner, Rita Hayworth, and Jayne Mansfield, among other stars to whom a great meal was the ultimate turn-on. Barbara Warner, who fled America to Europe right after graduating from Sarah Lawrence, seemingly thought she could stick it to her flagrantly philandering mogul father by marrying an even bigger philanderer than Daddy. Claude Terrail was famous for his orgies in his private apartment right under the Tour d'Argent penthouse, erotically catered by Europe's top procuress, Madame Claude herself. Claude and Claude, king and queen of the Paris *partouze.* No one expected the glamorous union of gastronomy and cinema to last long, and it did not.

After his divorce in the 1960s, Claude Terrail stopped coming to Hollywood. He didn't need to. By then *le tout* Hollywood was coming to him. The name Terrail became synonymous with sybaritism and sophistication, so it was easy for Patrick Terrail to get endless mileage out of it. No one knew that Claude Terrail couldn't stand his brash nephew, a Cornell Hotel School grad who Claude felt was taking his name in vain. The name was great any way you took it, and Patrick took it straight to the bank.

But Ma Maison couldn't live by local sourdough bread alone. It also had the best food California had ever seen, at least south of the also just opened Chez Panisse in Berkeley. The chef was a pudgy, bubbly young Austrian who had cut his culinary teeth at the Michelin shrine L'Oustau de Baumanière in Provence, as well as at Maxim's, the Tour's chief rival in Paris for the palates of the rich and famous.

His name was Wolfgang Puck, and he knew exactly how to cook for stars. However, he was obsessed with coming to America and ended up so deep in the heartland that he almost couldn't get out. Puck had taken an odd turn cooking at a pompous restaurant on a bank rooftop in Indianapolis. He thought the city had to be a great place because of the Indy 500, which he naively equated with the Monte Carlo Grand Prix, a passion of his from his Provençal days. Eventually he escaped by transferring to another top-of-the-money pomposity in downtown L.A., whence Patrick Terrail sagely discovered and rescued him. I'll never forget my foie gras and the duck by Puck, which would have been treats even in Paris but were epiphanies in this desert of burgers and tacos.

When I returned to Ma Maison five years later, in 1981, the restaurant was still doing vastly better than the movies whose stars continued to jam the place. This was the dawn of the Reagan era, and no power lunch anywhere could seem as powerful as lunch at Ma Maison, whose out-of-the-way location, before sleepy Melrose became the King's Road of L.A., proved to be one of its key assets. Perfectly situated between Warner's and Fox, down the street from Paramount, a zippy Ferrari slalom from William Morris in Beverly Hills, Ma Maison was never more than twenty minutes from anything that mattered in L.A.'s entertainment universe. Dinner, compared with the celebrity circus of lunch, was a low-key affair, with very little of the cliché Hollywood after-dark show-and-tell of gold-chained producers dripping with blond starlets. In fact, there were few starlets at Ma Maison either night or day. There were only stars. It wasn't becoming to be "becoming." It was essential "to be." And the time to flaunt your being was lunchtime, in the California sun-time, where you *were* whom you ate with.

For all the tribulations of the big screen, there were new signs of life. With the rise of the hipster neo-auteurs of the 1970s—Coppola, Scorsese, De Palma, Ashby, et al.—the movies had definitely gotten better. With the rise of the neo-DeMilles Spielberg and Lucas, the movies had also definitely gotten bigger, much bigger. But when *The Deer Hunter*'s wannabe neo-auteur Michael Cimino tried to become a neo-DeMille, the result was *Heaven's Gate* and a major debacle for Hollywood, which became the whipping boy and laughingstock of Wall Street and the press. *Heaven's Gate* had just self-destructed, and John Lennon had just been shot, when I came out to Hollywood that March, when L.A.'s springtime never seemed to stop and New York's winter never seemed to end.

This time I was coming not as a tourist, but as a player, albeit of the most minor sort. It should nonetheless be noted that even the most minimal player in Hollywood still develops a megalomaniacal self-image, best captured in the Rolling Stones' "Under Assistant West Coast Promo Man": "Well, I'm waitin' at the bus stop in downtown L.A. . . . sittin' here thinkin' just how sharp I am . . ." I thought I was pretty sharp, too, sitting here with Claude Fernand-Cook, Madame Claude, the most famous madam in Paris, in the world. She was to celebrity sex what the Tour d'Argent, and now Ma Maison, was to celebrity dining. I had chucked my brilliant legal career and decided that what I wanted to be was talent. But what talent? I couldn't sing, dance, paint, sculpt.

I did, however, like to write. My New York law firm had chided me that my memos were way too entertaining. To them, boredom equaled seriousness. But I took that as a sign, a sign to get out. I had quickly forged a new career and even had a global bestseller with a book I did with Marilyn Monroe's maid, who had gone to work post-MM for the billionaire father of a college friend who was in gambling straits and in dire need of a big finder's fee to avoid the wrath of his father, and the Mob. It wasn't Saul Bellow, but as the go-to guy for insiders who needed a mouthpiece, I knew I was having more fun.

Icon after icon stopped by our table to kiss the lady's hand. The superagent Swifty Lazar, resplendent in yachting blazer and boutonniere, spoke to her in Brooklyn French. George Peppard, resurrected by *The A-Team,* tan and glowing, and having played a gigolo in *Breakfast at Tiffany's,* seemed to know precisely where Claude was coming from. Orson Welles lumbered over. Charles Bronson was much smaller than I would have imagined from *Death Wish.* Walter Matthau mumbled something funny, probably naughty, in French that brought the rare smile to this tiny blond, Chanel-clad, fiftyish Frenchwoman who was as serious as a banker and undoubtedly richer. She had begun her professional life selling Bibles door-to-door, and now she had gone to the other extreme, selling luxury sin.

A tall, feral casbah type stopped by the table with the beauteous Jacqueline Bisset on his arm. That's what Claude girls were supposed to look like. But no, it couldn't be . . . or could it? Claude wouldn't say. Who was the guy? I asked. He was a rising Moroccan jeans mogul, washed ashore in L.A. in the wake of the Guess? empire of the Moroccan Marciano brothers. L.A. was full of rising jeans moguls then. Jeans were bigger than movies. But what kind of magic denim could win the heart of the famously T-shirted queen of *The Deep*? How did he do it? I asked the queen of unfree love. *"Le plus gros casquette du monde,"* she said, referring not to the jeans but to the artillery within. Yes, I was in Hollywood.

What I was trying to do was get Madame Claude to collaborate with me on a memoir called *Sex and Power*. I saw it as the ultimate tell-all. In the course of a dozen meals at Ma Maison and other power spots (she ate only where the big boys were), she would share amazing stories of a clientele that included Picasso and Chagall, Lord Mountbatten and the shah, Rockefellers and Rothschilds, every Greek tycoon in the Aegean. And of course a *Who's Who* of Hollywood, arrayed before us at every meal. Doing my best to keep up with her machine-gun staccato of gossip in my North Carolina high school French, I was exhausted but exhilarated. She told me tales of Agnelli and Onassis and JFK and of how she helped the CIA line up dates for an unaware Henry Kissinger to bolster his confidence during the Paris peace talks. And clueless Henry had thought that power was the aphrodisiac.

Madame Claude was in exile in L.A., having run afoul of the administration of Valéry Giscard d'Estaing supposedly because he had a Claude mistress who could be a political liability. I was introduced to her by a Wall Street friend who was part of the Persian Jewish diaspora to L.A. after the fall of their patron, the shah. If Moroccan jeans moguls were big in L.A., Persian real estate moguls were even bigger. En route to the coast, my friend's family lived in Paris for a while, where his rich father got to know Claude, and smelling one of those big finder's fees, he had brought us together.

Claude was seeking to get an American green card in return

for agreeing to appear as a key witness in a gargantuan palimony action against the estate of Darryl F. Zanuck, the cigar-chomping, polo-playing, epic-making mogul who more than anyone else embodied in-your-face Old Hollywood sass and glamour. The cigars had killed Zanuck, giving him jaw cancer, though it might be argued that his excesses with Madame Claude's *filles de joie* might have contributed to his demise at seventy-seven, in 1979. Originally from Wahoo, Nebraska, Zanuck had begun his film career writing scripts for Rin-Tin-Tin and parlayed that dog's life into the ownership of Twentieth Century Fox, which he left in 1956 to live in Europe, produce gigantic films like *The Longest Day,* and, with Claude's aid, pursue the most beautiful young women on earth.

I had recently met Zanuck's last consort, a stunning fringe French actress named Genevieve Gilles, who lived palatially, courtesy of Darryl Z, in an apartment at the Dakota in New York, close to that of the now late John Lennon. Gilles had come to me wanting to do a memoir of her involvement with Zanuck, but I had turned her down because it was all so chaste. She claimed that they were never lovers and that Zanuck had met her at a convent school while scouting *Longest Day* locations and had taken a strictly paternal interest in her. Where was the love? I asked her. Not in the boudoir, she insisted, and I said au revoir.

In interviewing Madame Claude, I found that she had an altogether different recollection. If believed, Claude's testimony about Gilles could have been the coup de grâce to Gilles's claim to the Zanuck millions. The goal was that the grateful heirs would then use their immense clout to get Claude a green card so she could evade the long arm of the French tax collectors d'Estaing had unleashed on her.

Claude pointed out Zanuck's number one son, Richard, across the room, who was the rare person in the garden who did not come over to kiss the madam. The tiny, wiry bronze Zanuck was there with his dearest friend, the handsome, bushy-browed Alan

Ladd Jr., son of Shane. Talk about Hollywood royalty and Hollywood dynasty. Darryl Zanuck had made Richard, who had grown up grandly riding elephants in his Bev Hills estate, head of production at Fox at age twenty-seven. But Richard was no brat. He had gone to Stanford, then teamed up with old-time producer David Brown, husband of *Cosmopolitan*'s Helen Gurley Brown, to win Oscars for *The Sting* and to break the bank with *Jaws*.

What young Zanuck was to Spielberg, having produced his first feature, *The Sugarland Express,* young Ladd (or "Laddie," as he was known about town) was to George Lucas. Championing Lucas's *American Graffiti* to a town of naysayers, Laddie, as president of Fox in the 1970s while still in his thirties, had green-lighted *Star Wars* when no one else would, mainly because Lucas pitched the sci-fi epic in terms of the swashbucklers of Laddie's youth, like *Captain Blood* and *The Sea Hawk.* Laddie, now a major independent producer, was just about to win his first Oscar for *Chariots of Fire.*

I would later meet Laddie, who for all his power and connections was very charming and self-effacing. He liked to tell a story about being a teenager on location with his father in the Canadian Rockies for the film *Saskatchewan* in the early 1950s. As it turned out, there were actually three westerns being shot at the same time in Banff, and all the stars were staying in the same resort. It was a Hollywood location version of *Grand Hotel.* In addition to *Saskatchewan,* starring Ladd père and Shelley Winters, there was *Thunder Bay,* with James Stewart and Joanne Dru, and *River of No Return,* with Robert Mitchum and Marilyn Monroe.

Suffice it to say that the person in the mix whom the ragingly hormonal sixteen-year-old Laddie wanted to get to know was Marilyn, whose room was tantalizingly next to his own. But there was another star that Laddie, who was more a baseball fanatic than a sex maniac at the time, wanted to meet even more, and that was Marilyn's then husband, Joe DiMaggio, the pride of the

Yankees and the idol of Laddie. Through his father, Laddie had
no problem getting to Marilyn, but he may have been the only
straight teen on earth for whom she was not obsession number
one. He kept importuning her to meet Joe when he came to visit.
Sure, kid, she told him, if you get me that bottle of peroxide.
Countless bottles of peroxide and countless errands later, the
Clipper finally arrived in Banff. But Marilyn either forgot to introduce them or she was too ashamed to. She and her slugger
were fighting mightily, and the closest Laddie got to his idol was
hearing the cacophony of bangs and crashes through their common wall.

The fights in Banff had a double bill, with DiMaggio versus
Monroe as the main event but with Mitchum versus Winters filling out the slate. The two thespians had apparently despised each
other since making *Night of the Hunter* together in 1955. They
were one of Hollywood's big hates, and their rage played out in
screaming curse-fests in the hotel lobby. "Just wait till Vittorio
gets here. He's going to kill you," Winters threatened Mitchum,
referring to her hunky Italian stallion of a husband, the dashing
Vittorio Gassman.

Laddie witnessed the showdown in the lobby when Gassman
arrived, resplendent in the Canadian wilds in his Via Condotti
white linen suit. Mitchum jumped him before he could throw the
promised punch, strangling him around the neck and snarling, as
scary as anything he did as the Holy Roller psychopath in *Hunter,*
"Now who's gonna kill who?" All continental aplomb even in the
face of death, Gassman managed to ask Mitchum where he got the
idea that Gassman was after him. "Your fucking wife," Mitchum
growled.

"Oh, how can you listen to that crazy cunt?" Laddie recounted
Gassman saying with his Italian accent, breaking Mitchum up
and defusing his rage. It was the beginning of a beautiful friendship, though never between Shelley and Bob.

Never disillusioned enough by the madness he saw backstage to scare him away from his father's business, Laddie followed the conventional path to power, college at USC, an agency stint at CMA representing Redford and Beatty, the sixties decade as a producer in swinging London making films with Taylor and Burton, Richard Attenborough, and Michael Caine, and forging a friendship with a young British producer named David Puttnam that would result in Laddie's Oscar. Once he was properly prepared in England, the next step in this perfect career was Laddie Come Home. In 1973, Laddie was summoned to Fox and took his place at the executive high table over which he soon would preside. So this was how the son of Shane grew up, at ease and at home in a Hollywood that was clubby and cozy and where moguls from rival studios would call each other and work it out over croquet instead of stabbing each other in the back. The eighties decade that was just beginning would soon see an end to all that.

Notwithstanding the simmering emergence of the "baby moguls" from the sixties generation, Zanuck and Ladd, then in their forties, were still considered kids in a Hollywood dominated by the ancient grandees like Lew Wasserman and Jules Stein. Stein would die that year but his ghost ruled on. Zanuck and Ladd were both low-key, almost retiring. With nothing to prove, they had more than proven themselves. The more typical Hollywood producers of the soon-to-obsolesce old guard were embodied by a table in the center of the garden at which were seated a gang of four swaggering, charismatic, totally self-created fifty-something ex-agents off the sidewalks of New York—David Begelman, Freddie Fields, Elliott Kastner, and Sidney Beckerman, who were sometimes described as the Four Horsemen of the Hollywood Apocalypse. Each of them tried to outdo the others for bragging rights to first pick of the Madame Claude litter, but that was just their style: flat-out gusto, big blondes, big food, big films.

And often big lies, which is what it could take to close the big deals. Nobody in the business could lie like David Begelman. It started with his education. Begelman was a Yale man through and through, not only Yale College, but also Yale Law. He was that rarity in pre-1980s Hollywood, an Ivy Leaguer. How could you not trust him? Of course, it was all a huge lie. The closest Begelman had gotten to Yale was doing some basic training on a base outside New Haven during World War II. But he was a genius in knowing what he could get away with. Nobody in Hollywood checked anything. That was why it was the world capital of reinvention. That was how Begelman became the town's Ivy pillar of rectitude.

Fresh out of "Yale," Begelman had become an agent at Jules Stein's octopus MCA and charmed his way into representing Judy Garland, on the downhill slope. It seems that Begelman embezzled the singer out of hundreds of thousands of dollars, which Begelman, a compulsive, addictive gambler, took to play in Las Vegas. He even took for himself a Cadillac convertible that was given to Garland as compensation for an appearance on the Jack Paar TV show, of which the drunken, distracted Garland was never aware. Begelman thus rode in high style, just as he dressed in high style. Small wonder he didn't rep Pierre Cardin.

Begelman joined with Fields in leaving MCA and scrambling the initials to form their own agency, CMA, in 1960. They had everyone, Streisand, Fonda, Peck, Woody Allen, Peter Sellers, the whole town. Begelman was rewarded for his gutsy risk-taking style by being made president of Columbia Pictures in 1973, where he packaged his former clients into such hits as *Shampoo* and took the risks that led to *Close Encounters of the Third Kind* in 1977. That same year, Begelman got one signature too close when he was caught forging the John Hancock of Cliff Robertson on a $10,000 check. It may have seemed like small potatoes, but Begelman wanted *it all,* and he took it.

The wages of sin were paltry. All Begelman got from the

courts was community service, and what he got from the studios, after being fired by Columbia, was being made the new president of MGM. He had the magic touch, the magic Rolodex. He had relationships, the lifeblood of Hollywood. He was the key man. Plus he was a social lion. His latest wife, Gladys, had previously been the spouse of Manhattan real estate giant Lewis Rudin. She was a major bicoastal hostess, a worthy successor to Edie Goetz. Who said crime didn't pay?

In fact, Columbia—under pressure from such all-powerful Begelmaniacs as Ray Stark, Barbra Streisand, her agent, Sue Mengers, Columbia's banker, Herbert Allen, and even Woody Allen—had initially refused to fire the self-admitted forger and embezzler. This was how business in Hollywood gets done, this was the cost of blockbusters, was the message. However, an outraged press, decrying how this was the most flagrant example ever of Hollywood playing by different rules from the rest of us, turned the affair into Begelgate and shamed Columbia into letting their loved one go. What, I wondered, would that same press make of deducting Madame Claude as a necessary entertainment expense? When I saw Begelman at Ma Maison, he looked like a lord of the realm, not a convicted felon.

Begelman's former partner, Freddie Fields, didn't dress as well as Begelman (nobody did) and he may not have gone to Yale (nobody here did, either), but he was considered the greatest agent the business had ever known, and that included fellow Maisonite Swifty Lazar. Freddie Fields was born Fred Feldman, and he was also born into show business. His father ran a Borscht Belt resort in the Catskills that booked such stars as Al Jolson and Eddie Cantor. His brother became the big-band bandleader Shep Fields, whose greatest hit was the Bob Hope trademark "Thanks for the Memory," which Fields introduced in Hope's first film, *The Big Broadcast of 1938*. As a boy agent, Freddie Fields handled such clients as Martin and Lewis. After several decades at MCA, repping the likes of Fred Astaire and Jackie Gleason, he founded CMA with Begelman, where Fields showed he could enter the New Age by launching the careers of the new Big Three—Lucas, Coppola, and Spielberg. Judy Garland, in full gallows humor, called Begelman and Fields Leopold and Loeb, but she never dismissed them, screaming allegations of defalcation notwithstanding. She knew how important it was to have killers as her agents.

In the 1970s, Fields left the agency world he ruled and founded an intimidating production company, First Artists, with Newman, Streisand, Poitier, Hoffman, and McQueen. It seems to have intimidated itself, since, notwithstanding all its star power, its only smash hit was Streisand's derided remake of *A Star Is Born*. Undeterred, Fields also produced *Looking for Mr. Goodbar* and had just wrapped *American Gigolo* when I saw him at Ma Maison, looking as if he had just stepped off the putting green, while Begelman looked as if he had just stepped off Savile Row. Fields had been married to singer-actress Polly Bergen and had topped himself by recently wedding a former Miss Greece and Miss Universe, whom, according to Madame Claude, he had met without her good offices, although that was the kind of match she was known to make. Here was the Hollywood dream in the flesh. How did you top that?

Elliott Kastner was such a whirling dervish, you couldn't hold him in your sight long enough to figure out what he was wearing. Elliott was tricoastal. You would see him in all the celebrity places, Elaine's in New York, Le Caprice in London, Ma Maison in L.A., often all in the same week. The Concorde was his second home. What made Elliott run? Investors. He was always looking for new investors, and he could seduce them with his packages of stars. The problem was that despite the galaxy of stars, all of Kastner's movies had fared dismally at the box office, most notoriously 1976's *The Missouri Breaks*, where even Jack Nicholson and Marlon Brando couldn't draw a quorum. Still, with catnip names like that, Kastner was always one potential blockbuster ahead of his next flop. And his ability to stay alive after his movies died made Kastner an industry folk hero, the Houdini of Hollywood.

The Brooklyn-born college dropout from the University of Miami had an uncanny knack for peddling "class," both to stars and to moneymen. After working his way up from the William Morris mailroom to MCA, where he met Begelman and Fields, he became an independent producer. For his first film, in 1965, he sweet-talked William Inge into adapting one of his plays into *Bus Riley's Back in Town,* starring Ann-Margret. Mortified at the product, Inge used a pen name in the credits.

Undeterred, Kastner made flops out of high-prestige properties by Iris Murdoch (*A Severed Head*), Vladimir Nabokov (*Laughter in the Dark*), Henry James (*The Nightcomers*, which snared Brando a first time), and three by Raymond Chandler, including *The Long Goodbye,* which was a classic but, true to Kastner form, unappreciated. Kastner's jealous detractors, who were legion, insisted he had never read a single book he had packaged and maybe not even the coverage. Kastner was even the focus of a classic Hollywood joke:

Question: How do you get more people into movie theaters?

Answer: Show Elliott Kastner movies outside them.

No matter. Kastner did better with pure commerce than with mislaid art. His biggest hits were *Harper,* with Paul Newman as a very cool detective, and *Where Eagles Dare,* a World War II action thriller starring Richard Burton and Clint Eastwood.

At Ma Maison, Kastner was basking in the failure of his latest opus, *The First Deadly Sin,* where he proved that Frank Sinatra and Faye Dunaway had lost their box office mojo. Always the packager, Kastner had signed Roman Polanski to direct, but the auteur had to flee the country, and the film, because of the child molestation charges he had accrued in Jack Nicholson's hot tub. Kastner replaced Polanski with his *Eagles Dare* director, Brian Hutton, who soon thereafter quit the film business to become a leading plumbing contractor in Beverly Hills, selling toilets to the stars. Kastner was as ebullient as ever. He must have hopped and stopped at every table in the restaurant garden.

Then there was Sidney Beckerman, a tall, ruggedly handsome former Golden Gloves champion who had subsequently entered the ring of New York agents and fought his way into becoming one of Hollywood's top producers. Following Kastner's lead, he teamed Brian Hutton with Clint Eastwood in another World War II action film, *Kelly's Heroes,* in which Eastwood, Telly Savalas, and Donald Sutherland, who was also in Ma Maison that day, rob German gold from a French bank. Beckerman had also produced the acclaimed hits *Cabaret* and *Marathon Man,* as well as the superflop *Portnoy's Complaint,* which served to spook Jewish Hollywood away from anything vaguely Semitic until Spielberg broke the curse with *Schindler's List.*

Although his pet project, shades of Kastner, was making a film of Malraux's *Man's Fate,* Beckerman had recently secured legend status by copying yet another page from the Kastner playbook, the Robin Hood approach of taking from rich investors and giving to yourself. Beckerman had just had a lunch at Ma Maison with Reverend Moon, the zillionaire Korean cult evangelist, to advise him on his pet project *Inchon,* about the crucial battle of the Korean War. It was the most expensive business lunch of all time. Beckerman got $300,000, plus the duck.

*Inchon* did get made the following year, starring Sir Laurence Olivier, arguably the world's most respected actor, as General MacArthur; Jackie Bisset as a military wife caught on the wrong side of the 38th Parallel; Ben Gazzara as her major husband; and *Shaft*'s Richard Roundtree as Gazzara's sidekick. The director was Terence Young, whose earlier credits included *Dr. No* and *From Russia with Love,* and the screenwriter was the bestselling author Robin Moore, who had written *The French Connection, The Green Berets,* and, just for fun, *The Happy Hooker.* Had they no shame? No way. Shame was not an operative emotion in Hollywood.

The Reagans' favorite astrologer-psychic, Jeane Dixon, had served as the Hollywood-mad Reverend Moon's adviser on the production. It was she who had steered Moon away from his original plan to do a cinematic epic on the life of either Jesus or Elvis. Dixon claimed she had reached the spirit of MacArthur. Even though he did not promise to return, the general did give his blessing to the project. The film, with a budget of over $50 million, was a bigger financial disaster than the previous year's top turkey, *Heaven's Gate,* but this time there was no studio to bankrupt, only a worldwide cult, the Unification Church, with seemingly deeper pockets than the Vatican. Beckerman's lunch tab was small change, and he got out without a film credit and with his reputation unsullied.

Beckerman achieved still another entry in the Hollywood Book of Fame for recently having turned the celebrity garden of Ma Maison into one of the boxing rings of his Golden Gloves youth. Beckerman had a strikingly pretty and stylish daughter, Janis, who was a rising young artist as well as a rising social lioness. She dated rock stars, movie stars, hot young directors, and flashy young agents. Her social life was a microcosm of Young Hollywood. She was not just in the loop, she *was* the loop. I had been fortunate to get on Janis's party list because her first husband (of three) was a fraternity brother at the University of Pennsylvania of a friend of mine from a summer at Oxford. The Ivy League did have some utility, and not only for David Begelman.

One of Janis's many ardent but frustrated suitors was a smooth British agent named Bobby Littman, who represented the likes of Nicolas Roeg and other arty Anglo types. One day at Ma Maison, Sidney Beckerman overheard Littman casting aspersions on his daughter. Or as Janis joked to me, paraphrasing Groucho Marx to

Margaret Dumont, "Daddy stood up for my honor, which is more than I ever did." Sidney coolly got up from his postprandial card game with Begelman, Kastner, and some real estate high rollers, went over to Littman's table, and beat the Brit to a pulp, leaving him writhing and bleeding on the Ma Maison AstroTurf. Then he coolly went back to his card game.

Because Beckerman was a far better customer than Littman, Patrick Terrail didn't call an ambulance until Beckerman played his final hand and went back to Paramount, where he had his offices. Littman sued everyone. Kastner provided the alibi. Beckerman, he swore, went over to Littman's table just to say hello. But with a guilty conscience over his calumny of Janis, Littman went for the knife. Beckerman acted solely in self-defense. As with all Hollywood litigation, the fracas was settled out of court and did not even make *Variety,* though the contretemps was the talk of the town for months. *"Quel Wild West,"* Madame Claude remarked on *l'histoire.*

Whenever Madame Claude and I didn't rendezvous at Ma Maison, she also liked to have lunch at Caffé Roma in a faux souk called Le Grand Passage in Beverly Hills. Roma was much more casual than Maison, but the food, cooked by two émigré Romans, was as authentically peasant Italian as Puck's food was authentically haute French. But Madame Claude wasn't there for the food, usually grazing on a plate of garden tomatoes and buffalo mozzarella. She was there for the business. Just because she wasn't in Paris didn't mean she couldn't set up fantasy dates for famous guys.

Directly across the Passage from Caffé Roma's deep al fresco patio was a chic St. Tropez-ian sportswear store called Georges Cibaud, which surely had the most spectacular salesgirls of any store on earth. Most, if not all, of these girls, invariably aspiring actresses, moonlighted for Madame Claude. The emporium sold more girls than clothes. These beauties were basically on display to the men of Roma, smoking their Havana cigars from Nazareth's, a luxury tobacconist also in the Passage, sipping their Amarones, nibbling their mortadella, and conjuring up the earthly delights that Claude would arrange for them in the hours and nights to follow.

Claude also had a revolving roster of visiting Euro-goddesses, slinky models from Milan; tony Sloane Rangers on a Beverly Hills shopping spree; downwardly mobile German aristocrats who could play for pay here in the outland and never be caught in flagrante by the *Almanach de Gotha* set; many pay-for-playgirls of her Paris stable. It was a sexual version of the Fruit of the Month Club, whores on tour. These girls just wanted to have fun, see Hollywood, and get paid for the pleasure of their company, usually upward of $500 an hour, when the going rate in Beverly Hills was $100. Madame Claude would get half. Caffé Roma was full of potential clients, stars and executives and agents, plus connected doctors and lawyers and property men and countless Euros, mostly sophisticated types who had seen the world and wanted real spaghetti alla vongole and real *Vogue Italia* cover girls.

The crowd at Caffé Roma included celebrities like John Cassavetes, Roy Scheider, and young Arnold Schwarzenegger, freakishly fit but newly hot from *Pumping Iron* and just signed to do *Conan the Barbarian*. That the bodybuilder was smoking a fat Nazareth stogie seemed out of character; still, he had a new career to celebrate. The mogul corps was represented by Dan Melnick, the supercool producer who had joined the club by marrying the daughter of composer Richard Rodgers, created *Get Smart* as a TV executive, headed production at MGM, and produced *All That Jazz* and *Straw Dogs*. He had worked under Begelman at Columbia, where he was nicknamed "Nathan Network," a subtle put-down that would remind him of his TV roots at a time when TV people in status-conscious Hollywood were still very much second-class citizens or, more accurately, illegal aliens with no class at all. Movie people had good reason to fear the all-encroaching tube and responded to it with their own kind of snobby nativism. Calling something "TV" was an all-purpose put-down.

"Nathan" Melnick was a ladies' man in the tradition of his predecessor at the helm of MGM in the early 1970s, James Aubrey, another TV man who still got the girls. Immune to all put-downs, Aubrey showed that breaking the "color line" between TV and features could indeed be done. Aubrey, who had cut a sexy swath through early network television at ABC with shows like *Maverick* and *77 Sunset Strip* and who later, as president of CBS TV, articulated his programming philosophy as "broads, bosoms, and fun," was the inspiration for the lead in Jacqueline Susann's megapotboiler *The Love Machine*. The elegant, studly Aubrey had a rare-in-showbiz Ivy'd pedigree from Exeter and Princeton that was also the inspiration for David Begelman, who was just assuming the MGM pinnacle. Who *wasn't* head of MGM, it seemed.

Both Melnick and Aubrey were mentors of Sherry Lansing, the pretty baby-mogul who in 1980 had just become the first female studio chief, at Fox, and at a mere thirty-five. She was one of the only females with any power in this clubby bad-boy sex-obsessed business, but not as much power as was wielded by Madame Claude, whose unlisted number was the treasure of the City of Angels. Claude knew exactly how much she was worth. To do the book I was proposing, she wanted big money, Jackie Susann money, a cool million advance. I assumed it would be no problem. A law school friend had become a junior partner in the firm of Mort Janklow, who had parlayed his undergraduate friendship with roommate William Safire at Syracuse University into the coveted position of literary agent for the Nixon White House and, after that, the triumvirate of blockbuster princesses Judith Krantz, Jackie Collins, and Danielle Steel, among everyone else. My friend thought the million would be merely a floor at which the strato-spheric bidding among New York publishers would begin.

I wrote a provocative proposal, in which I probably dropped more names than Elliott Kastner. Visions of sugarplums dancing in my head, I was brought down to earth by my law school friend, who called after reading my pitch. The tidings were grim. He told me that Mort Janklow either knew, or wanted to know, every person in the proposal. This was no way for him to win friends or influence people, and he already had all the money he needed. In other words, Madame Claude was too hot for him to handle.

How could anyone be too hot? I wondered, and began shopping around. Lots of other agents were not rich enough to walk away from this, but after making their queries, they all brought back the same message. The "sophisticated" editors and publishers who knew of Madame Claude were also often her clients and, as such, were terrified of being hoist by their own petards if they published the book. That French connection could come back to castrate them.

The other, less sophisticated editors and publishers had a know-nothing, so-what, "freedom fries" xenophobia. Who gave a damn about some old French hooker, went the chorus of nos. How do you sell that in Peoria? The way to sell it, they said, was to turn Madame Claude into an American household name, not households in Neuilly and Parioli. The way to do that was to get a feature done on her in *People* magazine, that bible of mass recognition. Madame Claude was appalled by the idea, and by *People* itself, which she saw as beneath her chic dignity. Besides, in her quest for a green card, she wasn't ready for that kind of notoriety, which could backfire into her deportation. An under-the-radar book deal was what she wanted. By the time the book came out, she would be safely green carded.

That green card proved elusive. For all their pomp and power, the Zanucks were unable to get Madame Claude what she wanted. It was harder than they thought. As a result, when called to testify if she knew Genevieve Gilles, and how, Madame Claude said, *"Je ne souviens pas."* I don't remember. Soon after that memory failed, her visa expired, as did my hopes of the ultimate bestseller. Breaking the horny hearts of half of Hollywood, she fled her rented home in Coldwater Canyon and went to the South Seas, to the Polynesian island of Vanuatu, where there wasn't even a modern version of Van Gogh to procure nubile natives for.

Eventually the French authorities caught up with Claude and sent her to prison, for procuring, for tax evasion, for flying too close to the sun. As for myself, unlike in my previous incarnation as a Dickensian Century City lawyer, as a writer I was suddenly loving Los Angeles. I never wanted to go back to New York. Madame Claude was a big fish, but I had lots of others to fry. Claude had provided an invaluable Hollywood education. I finally understood who the players were, and how they got there, and what made Sammy run. Sittin' here thinkin' just how sharp I was, I had a hot script in my back pocket and the spurious confidence that I, too, could get a table at Ma Maison.

# CHAPTER 4
## AGENTS PROVOCATEURS

"THE THREE CRUELEST WORDS in the English Language: Let's Be Friends." That was the signage on a massive billboard on the Sunset Strip promoting the book *Real Men Don't Eat Quiche*. By the same token, in eighties Hollywood, the three cruelest *letters* in the English language were indisputably CAA. Cruel letters, cruel outfit, cruel times. Creative Artists Agency was the locomotive, or perhaps the Batmobile, of the decade, an organization that took winning through intimidation to its outer limits. And Mike Ovitz, the leader of this pack, was one man who did not eat quiche. Mike Ovitz only ate stars.

While there have been agents as long as there have been artists ("creative" seems like a redundancy), Mike Ovitz was a different kind of agent, in that he reversed the master-servant relationship and made the tail wag the dog. Until Ovitz, being an agent was never seen as an end in itself, only the beginning of an end. After the first generation of moguls who founded the studios, most of the men who ran them had cut their teeth, or fangs, in the agencies. If your father owned the studio, like Richard Zanuck's, you didn't have to pay your agency dues. But everyone else did. Even Alan Ladd Jr. had been an agent for David Begelman, who himself had been an agent for Jules Stein. Barry Diller, who was running Paramount in the early 1980s, had gotten his start in the William Morris Agency mailroom, as had David Geffen, who would in time be running half the world. But what Ovitz did was to turn a stepping-stone into the Rock of Gibraltar. Or Alcatraz, depending on how you looked at it.

The way Ovitz came to power was in the great power vacuum of the film business in the seventies. At that point there were only two major agencies, William Morris and the Begelman-Fields CMA, which itself had come to exist in an earlier power vacuum created in 1961 by trustbuster Bobby Kennedy. RFK, for all his supposed lust for Marilyn Monroe, seemed to have an even bigger hard-on for Jules Stein, whom the highbrow New Frontiersmen were blaming for the decline and impending fall of American civilization. It had all begun when JFK's new chairman of the FCC (Federal Communications Commission—this was the age of initials), a brain trust lawyer named Newton Minow, gave a famous speech denouncing television as a "vast wasteland." The date of the speech, May 9, 1961, became known as Black Tuesday in Hollywood, because it was Washington's call to arms against the philistinism of the West Coast, a hostility that would last two decades, until Ronald Reagan alchemized the hate into love and once again made the world safe for Hollywood.

The emperor of the Minow-denominated wasteland was Stein himself, then the most powerful man in Hollywood, whose vertically integrated MCA (Music Corporation of America, from its band-booking roots) was behind more television than any other entity. Stein's right hand and designated successor, Lew Wasserman, was Ronald Reagan's agent. At the time, MCA was the biggest agency as well as the biggest producer, and RFK somehow equated bigness with badness. Stein made an effort to co-opt the Hollywood-mad JFK by offering to redecorate the main reception area of the White House with priceless eighteenth-century antiques from his wife Doris's formidable collection. Doris wasn't known as "the Empress" for nothing.

Although Jackie Kennedy was sorely tempted by the antiques, brother-in-law Bobby basically told the Steins to park their Chippendales where the sun didn't shine, and not in the White House, which was not for sale. Bobby then unleashed the antitrust dogs of the Justice Department on MCA. Within a year, the MCA agency division was gone, with Fields and Begelman picking up most of the pieces as well as the initials at CMA. Ironically, Stein had the last laugh on the Kennedys. Even without the agency, television kept getting bigger—and badder, with the MCA parent and its Universal Studios reaping all the rewards.

With the MCA agency out of the picture, William Morris became the number one agency, with CMA the challenger. And that was about it until 1975, when Begelman and Fields both began to weary of tending to the neuroses of the neurotic likes of Streisand and McQueen and decided to put CMA into stepping-stone mode. Begelman stepped up to the presidency of Columbia Pictures, while Fields stepped up to the bank, selling CMA to an ambitious television conglomerateur named Marvin Josephson, whose outfit was called IFM, or International Famous Agency.

The new entity was called ICM, or International Creative Management. For Fields, whom Josephson wanted to stay on as president, it was all one initial too many. He jumped at Barry Diller's offer of a rich indie-prod (independent production) deal at Paramount, leaving the new ICM in the hands of the town's most colorful agent, the tiny terror and Streisand tamer Sue Mengers, who in her old-fashioned cuddly Bronx flamboyance was both the pre-Ovitz and the anti-Ovitz.

In 1975, while Mengers was catering to the high and mighty, Ovitz was a faceless schlepper just a few schleps removed from the William Morris mailroom. His appearance was that of an unsmiling, intense, potentially malevolent version of *MAD* magazine's

Alfred E. Neuman. Except that Neuman's motto, "What, Me Worry?" did not apply. Ovitz seemed perpetually worried. Adrift in the firm's high-profit, low-prestige television department, Ovitz had his future to be worried about. His biggest client was Sally Struthers from *All in the Family.* The son of a liquor salesman who moved his family from Chicago to Encino, which was snootily derided as the Beverly Hills of the Valley (an appellation akin to the Park Avenue of Watts), Ovitz seemed likely to be marooned in the middle class. He was no Richard Zanuck.

But the Valley Boy desperately wanted to go "over the hill," and he did. He made it to Westwood, to UCLA, in the glory days of Lew Alcindor and John Wooden, and made it into the top Jewish fraternity, where the richest Bev Hills brats would gravitate. He thus got his first set of initials, ZBT, which, ignoring the Greek, everyone knew stood for zillions, billions, trillions. The "Heebs from Zeeb," as they were known, ate the best food and gave the best parties on campus, and even Lew Alcindor (pre-Karim) was known to drop by. Transcending his roots, Ovitz ran the frat show, got elected president of the chapter, class of 1968, dated, and would marry, Judy Reich, the prettiest blond Jewish girl on a campus of goddesses. He was known by the sobriquet of King Mike. Even though he was there in the heart of the 1960s, Ovitz did not follow in the druggy footsteps of another campus legend, Jim Morrison, UCLA '65. Ovitz was so straight and business-oriented, he seemed to be stuck in an Eisenhower time warp. When he heard the Doors' "Twentieth Century Fox," unlike every other kid in America, Mike Ovitz was thinking the studio, not the babe.

Without showbiz antecedents, getting into the William Morris mailroom was probably tougher than getting into Harvard Business School without a friend at Goldman Sachs. Barry Diller, the son of a Realtor, got in only because of a close Beverly Hills High School friendship with Terre Thomas, whose father, Danny, was a prized client and put in the fix. But once Ovitz did get in, he just as quickly decided to get out and go to law school, not at Harvard or even UCLA, but at Loyola, something of a local diploma mill. As indecisive as Hamlet, he found that law school didn't suit him, either, and begged William Morris to take him back. In those days, no one ever walked out on the Morris mailroom and expected to get a second chance. However, Ovitz miraculously managed to do so, which more than any of his actual accomplishments at Morris thereafter presaged well for his future.

At Morris, the king whom King Mike desperately wanted to be was Stan Kamen, who with the departure of Freddie Fields from agenting was the most powerful man in the 10 percent business. Kamen handled the likes of Warren Beatty, Steve McQueen, Jane Fonda, and Goldie Hawn. Growing up in Brooklyn, Kamen acquired an unlikely patina of southern charm by transferring from NYU to Washington & Lee and getting a law degree there. He developed a courtly style, combining Madison Avenue gray flannel with Old Virginia gentility. He was also gay, wittily engaging but deeply closeted. The combo Brooklyn-Dixie-homo-lawyer was a unique alchemy that worked. Kamen's clients loved him. Only Sue Mengers had a better list, but eventually her cash cow and glittering prize Streisand left her for, among many suggested reasons, putting the diva in the dud *All Night Long,* a comedy in a convenience store directed by Mengers's non-auteur husband. Streisand signed with Kamen, making his dominance of the field complete. Sick transit, to be sure.

Kamen's was the dominance Mike Ovitz fantasized about back in 1975 when he and four other television agents, sensing William Morris was a small-screen dead end for all of them, defected and started CAA. Although they couldn't steal any of Kamen's star clients, what they did appropriate was Kamen's buttoned-up, buttoned-down, Wall Street fiduciary persona. Most agents were all flash and no pan. The concept of the CAA man was to inspire confidence and never distract from the aura of the star. But what stars? In addition to Sally Struthers, the fledgling agency signed Meathead, aka Rob Reiner, comedian Carl Reiner's son and Struthers's *All in the Family* co-star, long before he became a major director and producer. They got Coppola's kid sister, Talia Shire. They got Chad Everett from the series *Medical Center.* They got Debbie Reynolds and Ernest Borgnine, long past their prime, or even prime time. They got Jack Barry, the disgraced host and producer of *Twenty-One,* the focus of the quiz show scandals of the 1950s. Perhaps they thought that Barry might pull a Begelman-like resurrection. In Hollywood, every disgrace had an expiration date.

The agency began to get some essential pizzazz only when they realized they needed a rabbi and in 1976 brought in the much older and wiser Marty Baum, a lovable Broadway Damon Runyon type who had partnered at a minor agency in New York and then worked at ABC's feature division before it went defunct. Baum also had a producer's credit on Sam Peckinpah's failed blood-fest *Bring Me the Head of Alfredo Garcia.* Now Ovitz charged the seemingly washed-up Baum to bring him the head of Paul Newman, and mirabile dictu, that was precisely what Baum did.

In his agent days, Baum had represented Joanne Woodward, along with Sidney Poitier and Julie Andrews, none of whom were currently burning up the cinemas. Baum promptly signed them all again for CAA and then went after Woodward's husband. The seduction took four years, but by 1980 it finally worked. That year Baum signed Paul Newman, and with Newman as flypaper, he got Dustin Hoffman soon thereafter, and after that Robert Redford. It was widely rumored but never proven that what ultimately lured the big names was CAA's willingness to halve the standard agency 10 percent commission, something that august William Morris would never do, for to them that would have been the unkindest cut of all. Whatever it took, CAA had now become a force to reckon with. It had the names, and in

Hollywood, sticks and stones could break bones, but names could break the bank.

It was around this time that I got my first look at CAA. I wasn't the slightest bit impressed or intimidated, though I did feel that I perhaps had stumbled into a cult, which were then all the rage in L.A. No, I was not on Marty Baum's hit list. My humble entrée came through a friend from college who was a junior associate at the most up-and-coming entertainment law firm, Pollock, Rigrod & Bloom. The firm was an oasis of ivy in the desert of palms, though no one seemed to wear a tie, as had been mandated at Mitchell Silberberg. This was new law for the New Hollywood, though my friend complained bitterly of all-night proofreading marathons and assured me that boilerplate for Fox was no more fun to lawyer with than boilerplate for Bethlehem Steel. At least the partners seemed to be having fun. Tom Pollock, the son of a very connected Beverly Hills doctor, had gone to Stanford and Columbia Law and had had the perspicacity to take on the struggling George Lucas before *American Graffiti* would lead to *Star Wars*. I'm not sure whom Rigrod had discovered, but he had gone to Cornell with Jake Bloom, who had had the perspicacity to take on the struggling Sylvester Stallone before *Rocky*.

By such contingencies is Hollywood heat generated. Pollock was wild-eyed and wild-haired and looked like a mad scientist. Bloom was dour and impassive and looked like a cross between an Indian chief and a pastrami carver at Katz's Delicatessen. When my friend took me in to meet Pollock, I must have sat there through a hundred phone calls without being able to get five words at a time in edgewise. I quickly saw that it was more efficacious to write a script than try to pitch it to the overwhelmed likes of Pollock. Oh, to be in Lucasville, when Pollock would tell his secretary to hold all calls. Yet somehow I couldn't imagine this mogul-to-be without a receiver in his ear, sort of like Groucho Marx without his cigar.

It wasn't Pollock, then, who sent me to CAA, but another junior lawyer in the firm who was in a karate class with one of Ovitz's junior agents. He told me this was the hot shop and I had a chance to get in on the ground floor of what was sure to be the town's next mogulrama. The ground floor I entered was the non-descript Tiger International building in dreaded Century City, which was owned by the Flying Tiger cargo airline and was just a few steps away from the Hamburger Hamlet building, where I had spent my summer of L.A. law. Upstairs there was little décor and absolutely no hint of the I. M. Pei splendor that would house CAA a decade hence. There were lots of young guys in dark suits padding about intensely and purposefully, but without a sound, a kind of pantomime version of *The Blues Brothers*. Joie de vivre? Forget about it. If this was show business, where was the show? Mitchell Silberberg seemed like vaudeville by comparison.

Aside from his dark business suit, the karate kid agent I met didn't fulfill any of the Stan Kamen prototype requirements. He was a blond California surfer, all hang ten yet laid-back, clearly not Jewish and as far from the Sammy Glick agent-hustler image of Hollywood as anyone could be. Obviously that was what Mike Ovitz wanted, to break the mold, and he had. The closest tie to the movies I could fathom was that the agent could have been an extra in *Animal House*, playing a member of the snobby Establishment fraternity that wouldn't have John Belushi (but CAA would, and did). There were no scripts on the agent's desk. The only reading matter I noticed was a slim volume of *The Art of War* by Sun Tzu, which I would later learn was Mike Ovitz's bible, an MSG Machiavelli, Dale Carnegie gone Zen. The agent didn't speak Holly-woodese, about deals, points, love ya, baby; rather, he favored est-ese, which was all about authority, respect, perception, and reality, the argot of the Buddhist-inspired, master-disciple human potential workshops that were the West Coast vogue in the early 1980s.

I had recently attended a party at the Malibu Colony beach home of the hottest young star of the day, Tim Hutton, who had won an Oscar for his suicidal son in *Ordinary People*. What stuck in my mind more than any of the rising stars or fawning models was the bartender, who was the most positive, assertive bartender I had ever encountered. You will have this margarita and it will be the best margarita you've ever tasted and it will change your life. That was the message, and I found out the messenger was the son of Werner Erhard, the founder of est (Erhard Seminars Training, in addition to the Latin "it is") and the region's hottest guru since Timothy Leary. The mixologist's positivism seemed genetic.

Erhard père, né John Rosenberg, had himself been a disciple of another hot guru, L. Ron Hubbard of Scientology, as well as the old positive-thinking warhorse Napoleon Hill. The former car salesman changed his name and changed his life, not to mention those of his countless followers who attended his expensive, intense (no bathroom breaks) seminars and made him rich. Erhard inspired lots of copycats, like Lifespring and Insight, whose founder, John-Roger, was heavily funded by author (and CAA client) Arianna Stasinopoulos. Stasinopoulos had a thing for such gurus. She also liked Werner Erhard and introduced him to Nancy Reagan walker Jerry Zipkin, hoping to get Erhard into the White House. Zipkin professed to be charmed, but the match never was made beyond that. All these self-actualization outfits seemed like cults to me, and having seen what Charles Manson and his cult had wrought in Los Angeles, I tended to give culty types a wide berth.

What really put me off wanting to join the cult of Ovitz was less nightmare visions of Charles Manson than nightmare visions of Aaron Spelling, CAA's new and immediately most important

client. Spelling was the biggest producer on television, becoming
Getty rich on shows like *Fantasy Island, The Love Boat, Starsky &
Hutch, Charlie's Angels,* and, most recently, that paean to Reagan-
world, *Dynasty.* I had never seen any of them. I had lived in New
York, where no one I knew ever watched television, which would
have been a terrible admission of defeat. It wasn't as if New York-
ers were just going out to La Côte Basque or Da Silvano or Studio
54 or Xenon, but in those days, there were a million more entic-
ing things to do in Manhattan than watch Hervé Villechaize and
Ricardo Montalbán on the tube. I hadn't watched TV since I was
a kid in North Carolina, and because we were in the Bible Belt,
most of what we could watch was "sacred" programming like Oral
Roberts. *The Life of Riley,* maybe *Gunsmoke,* was about as risqué as
it got. The big screen, all two of them in my tobacco road back-
water, was the great escape.

But it was TV that was instrumental in putting CAA on the
power map. The chief enabler here was New York super–book
agent Mort Janklow, who had gotten cold feet on my Madame
Claude project. I probably shouldn't have taken no for an answer,
given Mike Ovitz's experience in hounding an equally ambivalent Janklow into one of the most lucrative symbioses in the media. For all the commerce of his client list, Janklow was an elitist
who had married Hollywood royalty, the granddaughter of Warner brother Harry Warner and the daughter of mogul Mervyn
LeRoy, who had discovered Clark Gable, directed *Little Caesar,*
and produced *The Wizard of Oz.* Linda Janklow was also the sister
of the flamboyant Warner LeRoy, who owned Maxwell's Plum
and Tavern on the Green. If there was any agent Morton Janklow
would use in Hollywood, it would be Swifty Lazar and no one
else, not some Valley Boy in the Tiger International building.

Ovitz was nothing if not audacious. He did not know his
place. When CAA had just opened, Ovitz boldly pitched his new
agency to Janklow, asking him if he could handle the television

rights to some of Janklow's properties. What properties they were, at least in terms of mass market bestsellers. Janklow repped Sidney Sheldon, Judith Krantz, Jackie Collins, and Danielle Steel, the killer lineup of commercial publishing. Janklow laughed the upstart off, but the upstart had learned the power of persistence from his reading of Sun Tzu. At some point, the networks passed on one of these opuses, and with nothing to lose, Janklow gave the pesky Ovitz his shot, and Ovitz scored a bull's-eye, raising the dead. After all, Jackie Collins and Danielle Steel were born to be produced by Aaron Spelling. Mike Ovitz was the best matchmaker since Dolly Levi.

TV was thus CAA's bread and butter, and I should have known that was what they would be pushing. Still, I was hoping the Ovitzian I was meeting might have a plan to introduce me to some of those Ma Maison producers who were looking for scripts to develop. Instead he predictably exhorted me to immerse myself in network TV and write some spec episodes of television series he could then get to the likes of Aaron Spelling. That was where the money was. I had zero interest in the small screen. To me Hollywood was movies, but to the Ovitzian, movies were a luxury, an endangered species that was the province of the very few, the masters of the game. Make your name and fortune in easier-to-enter TV, he urged me, then come back and inflict your newly respected will on the world of features.

It turned out to be prophetic advice, but I felt as capable of writing for episodic TV as I did trying out for the Lakers. To know it was to love it, and I simply didn't know it, and didn't think I wanted to. I was still under Newton Minow's ether that TV was the wasteland and a terra that should remain incognita. But the surfer was right about the success part. Soon many of the biggest directors of features would come straight out of TV and CAA. Meathead (Rob Reiner) and Opie (Ron Howard) and Laverne (Penny Marshall) and Spock (Leonard Nimoy) and Louie De

Palma (Danny DeVito), the caricatured characters of the small screen, would become the giants of the large, not to mention others like Mary Tyler Moore creator and ICM client James L. Brooks. It seemed the only CAA founding client who didn't become an auteur was Sally Struthers.

I bade adieu to this agentary Adonis, who would evolve into one of the "foot soldiers" whom years from now Mike Ovitz would famously dispatch to destroy the careers of writers like *Basic Instinct*'s Joe Eszterhas, who dared to escape the cult of power that CAA would become. TV was clearly the future, but I suppose that what I wanted was the past. The main reason I wasn't very impressed with CAA and the sinisterly corporate, controlling Ovitz, or his model Stan Kamen, or even the blasphemous Sue Mengers, was that none of them could compare with the real giants of the agent field—dinosaurs, perhaps, but amazing creatures who still strode the fault-laced earth. I'd see them at Ma Maison, or sometimes at Nate 'n Al's, or most evocatively of all at the decaying Musso & Frank's in Hollywood, where clients of theirs like Fitzgerald and Faulkner, who didn't find the movies' glory days all that glorious, tried to drink themselves out of their misery.

Fitzgerald and Faulkner's agent, and Raymond Chandler's, too, H. N. Swanson—"Swannie" to them—was still holding court in his Algonquin-evocative paneled offices atop the Sunset Strip, where champagne at Ciro's had given way to cocaine at the Rainbow. Still dining out on his discovery of Elmore Leonard, Swannie was a big man with a big list. In the heyday of the studios, when Fox had 110 writers under contract, he represented 80 of them. Swannie was a smart Iowa farmboy who went to Chicago in the Al Capone era and founded *College Humor,* the Second City's answer to *The New Yorker.* Swannie then came out to Hollywood, produced a dozen films for RKO, and then became a lit agent. He was a good editor, too. He convinced a stubborn Fitzgerald to change the title of *Trimalchio in West Egg* to *The Great Gatsby.*

If Swanson's offices looked like the Algonquin, Paul Kohner's, down the Strip, resembled the Bauhaus. Emigrating from Prague in the twenties, Kohner came from a movie family. His father ran the *Photoplay* of Czechoslovakia, and Kohner got a big job at Universal after interviewing Carl Laemmle. He founded his eponymous agency in 1938. His clients included the greatest European names, Garbo, Dietrich, Chevalier, von Stroheim, Wilder. After the war, he picked up Henry Fonda, David Niven, Yul Brynner, John Huston, and Ingmar Bergman. He was married to a Mexican movie star, Lupita Tovar, and their daughter, Susan Kohner, had a huge career for a while. Susan had gotten an Oscar nomination for playing a mulatta in *Imitation of Life* but dropped out to pursue family life, dumping fiancé George Hamilton to wed fashion designer John Weitz. The Kohners were A-list top of the town; it was hard to imagine the not particularly social Mike Ovitz making headway against such a colossus, but time was not on Kohner's side.

For a pure writer's agent, no one had a better client roster than Evarts Ziegler, and no agent was less agency. He was known as Ziggy, just as his rival Swanson was known as Swannie, perhaps in a Hollywood effort to make its WASPs seem more Jewish, more accessible, less "other." Ziggy was as "other" as one could be. A Princeton man who learned the *real* agency business at the OSS during World War II, he shunned the Beverly Hills scene and lived a genteel, gentile existence "over the hill" in Pasadena. His mighty stable included the Dunnes, as Joan Didion and her husband, John Gregory Dunne, were known, William Goldman, Robert Towne, Mario Puzo, and Terrence Malick. But as he got older, the only way he could survive the Ovitz onslaught was to merge his agency with ICM, where the personal charm of his original operation was lost in the monolith. Bigger wasn't better, but it was better than extinction.

Going least gently into that good night was the seemingly timeless Irving Paul Lazar, who seemed to eat more luxury meals than

Craig Claiborne, food critic of *The New York Times*. Whatever
great restaurant you went to, be it in Los Angeles, New York City,
or Paris, Swifty Lazar seemed to be there, at the best table. Five
feet two, with a shaved head before it was chic to have one and
his trademark giant black-framed glasses, Lazar was an even tinier, scarier terror than his similarly ubiquitous size mate and
client Truman Capote. He handled everyone, Porter, Gershwin,
Lerner, Loewe, Rodgers, Hammerstein, Coward, Hemingway,
Hellman, Nabokov, even Richard Nixon and Joan Collins. Lazar
had started small, as a Brooklyn bankruptcy lawyer during the
Depression. But with his first bankrupt vaudeville client, the little
man was hooked, big-time. He got the "Swifty" moniker, which
he detested, from Humphrey Bogart, for making three deals for
Bogie on the same day.

Lazar was a pathological snob and a pathological hypochondriac,
not necessarily in that order. He would air-freight his shirts to
London to be laundered, perhaps by Jeeves himself. A clean freak,
he would have his sheets washed after even a brief nap. He covered
his Ritz and Claridge's suites with wall-to-wall towels to avoid any
lingering germs. God knows what he'd do after (or during) a ses-
sion with a Madame Claude girl. More a star fucker than a star
signer, he was way beyond the Ovitz hustle and would get excited
only if a potential new client was an ex-president like Nixon.

Lazar stayed center stage with his ultracaste Oscar party, held
for years at the Billy Wilder–funded Bistro, famous for the scene
in *Shampoo* where Julie Christie gives Warren Beatty an under-
the-table blow job during an otherwise boring political fund-
raiser. In 1982, soon after Wolfgang Puck left Patrick Terrail to
open Spago, his own reverse-chic pizza shack in a former Armenian belly-dance dive across from Tower Records, Lazar, who had
a truffle hound's instinct for heat, switched allegiance to Puck for
his party venue and thereby put Spago once and forever on the
international map of the stars.

Puck had come to realize that Ma Maison had only half the equation right. Movie people loved casual, but the French food there was too fancy and formal. L.A. didn't have a single decent pizza restaurant. Further, Puck in his Baumanière days had watched the stars jam a simple restaurant called La Pizza in the old port of Cannes whose centerpiece was a wood-fired pizza oven. He had even spotted Lazar there at film festival time. Normally, Lazar would never eat anything less than three Michelin stars, specifically Le Moulin de Mougins, but La Pizza, Puck concluded, must have been doing something right and worth copying. Taking another page from Alice Waters in Berkeley, Puck went locavore on his designer pies, topping them with Santa Barbara shrimp and Chino Ranch baby vegetables and homemade duck sausage. Lazar brought the names, and it was the beginning of a beautiful friendship.

For me, the most exciting thing about being in Hollywood was to get the chance not only to meet the idols of my movie-obsessed youth but to actually get to work with them. One of my new friends was Ernest Lehman, the legendary screenwriter who had done the script for my favorite childhood movie, Hitchcock's *North by Northwest*. Another was Robert Wise, who had won Oscars for directing both *West Side Story* and the Lehman-scripted *Sound of Music,* which was the most despised movie of my childhood.

It wasn't that *Sound* was bad, notwithstanding Pauline Kael's killer three-word review, "Not for diabetics." It was that in my little town, there was nothing to do but go to the two movie theaters, which each changed features twice a week, Monday to Wednesday, then Thursday through Saturday. (Movies were never on Sunday in the Bible Belt.) But when *The Sound of Music* came out, the local church groups loved it so much that the theater held it over for the entire summer, thus eliminating one of my two sources of entertainment. Talk about an endless summer! Both Lehman and Wise were amused by how they had ruined this boy's summer vacation and tried to make it up to me by mentoring me in writing my first script, which eventually Wise offered to attach himself to as director. That bit of great fortune, I assumed, would turn this country boy into a made man.

The script, *Thirty Day Wonder,* was based on a true story I had come upon in New York about a nerdy advertising copywriter whose sister ran the "Bachelor of the Month" column in *Cosmopolitan* magazine. One month the upcoming stud got indicted for some unmentionable crime, and the editor, pressed for a last minute replacement, did a radical makeover on her dateless brother, fabricated a biography turning the acrophobe into a skydiver and stunt pilot, and made him the most eligible man in America overnight. The comedy was how this Cinderfella rose to the occasion, then turned into a pumpkin when the new issue hit the stands.

I got a lot of action, both meetings and money, off *Thirty Day Wonder,* which tapped into the just emerging vogue of media celebrity and may have seemed fresh at the time. It had the virtues of being a comedy, low-budget, and high-concept. High-concept was the thing to be in 1980s Hollywood, a notion pioneered at Paramount, which, as we will see, was the most TV-ish of all the studios, its big boss, Barry Diller, and his number two, Michael Eisner, both having risen to their studio headship through the ranks of the networks. High-concept was basically a *TV Guide* log line that summed up a movie in a very few words. My log line would have been something like "Press turns frog into prince." A great film like *Vertigo* could not be reduced to a log line. It was thus low-concept and would not get made were it not for its name director, Hitchcock, and name stars, Stewart and Novak. *They* were the high concept, not the story. Blockbusters like *Jaws* and *Star Wars* and *Animal House* were the highest-possible concept; their titles said it all.

What *Thirty Day Wonder* did not have was a bankable male lead. A young Woody Allen or Dustin Hoffman would have been just the ticket, but the star-making machinery wasn't spewing out antiheroes. The up-and-comers were handsome hunks like Tim Hutton and Rob Lowe and Charlie Sheen and Tom Cruise, guys who didn't need a *Cosmo* scam to help them get a date. Maybe John Belushi would have been funny in a totally preposterous way, but the comic OD'd at the Chateau Marmont in early 1982 before anyone could get him the script. The Adam Sandler nerd revival was over a decade away. Producers would option the project for a year at a time, then give up. The closest it got to a "go" was as a TV movie starring Bob Balaban, whose family had ruled Paramount but who still could not guarantee a green light from the networks. The Ernest Lehman–Robert Wise pedigree seemed to impress no one but me.

The ageism of the business was shocking. Both Lehman and Wise were only in their mid-sixties when I met them, but they were already considered as washed up as Norma Desmond in *Sunset Blvd.* (Gloria Swanson was only fifty when she played her, but seemed like a hundred.) Lehman, whose background as a Broadway press agent led him to co-script, with Clifford Odets, the nastiest of all showbiz films, *The Sweet Smell of Success,* and Wise, who had edited *Citizen Kane,* were considered at best historical curiosities, not founding fathers, by the CAA types like the culty surfer, who seemed to populate the studio suites I would visit. Don't bring me history, bring me Spielberg, was what they were thinking, if not saying. My biggest hero in the business, Billy Wilder, stiletto sharp at seventy-five, was put out to pasture after his *Buddy Buddy,* with Lemmon and Matthau, flopped. This was no country for old men, no second chances. They were all Rodney Dangerfields, no respect, like Buster Keaton being one of Wilder's extras in the card scene in *Sunset.* Now Wilder was in the same position, an elder statesman without the state.

I myself couldn't have been more thrilled and was frankly amazed that I could actually meet such legends. It is instructive to see how it's done. I met Ernie Lehman in France at a country weekend house party at the Norman cottage of Vicky Tiel, the only American dress designer in Paris. Vicky and her design partner, Mia Fonssagrives, the daughter of superphotographer Irving Penn and supermodel Lisa Fonssagrives, were the toast of Paris in the swinging sixties and beyond and very movie connected. They did the costumes for *What's New Pussycat?* while Vicky was the girlfriend of Woody Allen and later married the makeup muse of Richard Burton and Elizabeth Taylor, who helped finance Vicky's Rue Bonaparte Paris salon. Vicky became the doyenne of décolletage. All the big busty stars loved her got-it-flaunt-it gowns. Somehow it was easy to meet other Americans in Paris; oppressed minorities stuck together, and Vicky led to Ernie, who had put all those unforgettable lines in Cary Grant's mouth.

I met Bob Wise in Beverly Hills at the estate of Dr. William Kroger, one of the preeminent psychiatrists to the stars. Kroger had three daughters, the belles of Beverly High, and one of them I had met in New York, in a remarkable gesture of Southern (California) hospitality, had invited me to escape the East Coast winter and stay in their vast home on Lexington Road, right behind the Beverly Hills Hotel, one of the grandest streets in this grandest of zip codes. Shades of Norma Desmond, the *palacio* had once belonged to silent heartthrob Ramón Novarro, the original Ben-Hur, who sold it when he became obsolete and later died in a grisly gay ritual murder in Laurel Canyon in 1968. I ended up sleeping on Dr. Kroger's leather shrink couch in his home office for two months.

In addition to Wise, I met lots of celebrities at the Krogers', from Marlon Brando to Muhammad Ali to Kenneth Tynan, and countless producers, directors, writers, and executives. No agents, though. They must have all been with Werner Erhard. Kroger, then in his seventies but superfit, had begun his career as an OB-GYN. He was the father of medical hypnosis and had written the book on the subject, lecturing all over the world. He was famous for having used hypnosis to solve the Chowchilla, California, kidnapping and disappearance of a busload of students in 1977 and did many surgeries without anesthesia. Just down on the Sunset Strip was a nightclub that featured Pat Collins, "the Hip Hypnotist." Kroger turned a sideshow into a discipline, and the AMA bowed down to him, as did Hollywood's bad boys and girls. In a world with a million destructive habits to break, everyone came to Kroger to kick addictions.

The only blot on Kroger's estimable escutcheon was the 1977 death of his patient Freddie Prinze, star of the hit show *Chico and the Man*. Prinze like to play with guns, and Kroger convinced him he shouldn't and made Prinze give his top gun to him. However, the comedian somehow cajoled the hypnotist into giving him back his beloved gun, and he promptly killed himself with it. A huge scandal broke out that Kroger had enabled Prinze's suicide, but a jury concluded that the gun had gone off by accident, and Kroger was cleared.

I loved going out with Kroger at night, to the Polo Lounge and to Hernando's Hideaway (yes, it existed) at the Beverly Wilshire, both top haunts of the MAW (model actress whatever) species. The doctor was the greatest pickup artist of all time. No girl could resist his spell. I had never seen such a combination of focus and charm. I'm not sure what he said, but I think he hypnotized the aspiring beauties into believing that I was the second coming of Aaron Spelling.

The charismatic Dr. Kroger also attracted a coterie of young producers on their way up. One of these, David Permut, had spent his Beverly Hills youth earning spending money by selling maps to the stars' homes. Echoing the CAA karate kid, Permut, who would go on to produce *Dragnet* and lots of other high-concept moneymakers, was cutting his teeth on TV movies and urged me to cut mine as well. Kicking and screaming, I came up with a perfectly trashy miniseries idea called *Makeover*, about four Beverly

Hills women who have affairs with their un-Hippocratic plastic
surgeon. Permut thought it would be ideal for none other than
Aaron Spelling and set up a pitch meeting with Spelling's right-
hand woman, Lynn Loring, whom Permut told me was thought
to be the inspiration for Faye Dunaway's Oscar-winning network executive in *Network*. This was the big time, and I was
both abashed and excited, especially at the prospect of getting paid
something like $50,000 to develop this idea.

The old contract system, where writers worked for one studio
and were guaranteed a yearly income, usually negotiated by Swannie, was sadly over. Writers in Hollywood lived from pitch to
pitch, deal to deal. It wasn't even close to secure, but it was a bonanza if you connected, vastly more lucrative than the book
business, where most advances tended to be a fraction of (Screen)
Writers Guild minimums, mainly because there was no book
writers' union for collective bargaining, plus you usually had
to write a hundred pages of the book just to get anything. Here,
a half hour could make you a player, and a fat one at that. As Dire
Straits would sing, "Money for nothin' and your chicks for free."
Take that, Madame Claude.

Permut drove me in his old-school Cadillac to an old studio lot
in Hollywood where Spelling had his offices. I think it used to
belong to Republic Pictures, which made all the westerns. I conjured up the ghosts of Tom Mix and Bronco Billy and the recently
departed John Wayne. Those spirits were soon exorcised when I
met the dynamic Ms. Loring and saw where Ms. Dunaway may
have gotten it from. A brassy, sexy redhead, Loring had been a
child soap star for a decade on *Search for Tomorrow* and had made
her film debut as a teenager opposite Warren Beatty in *Splendor in
the Grass*. After a career on TV series such as *The FBI* in the 1960s,
she was one of the rare actresses (like Sherry Lansing) to make the
transition to the executive suite, producing such Spelling shows as
*The Return of the Mod Squad* and eventually leaving the master to

become president of MGM-UA TV. Her office was very de-signed, very power-feminine. This was no mere d-girl, as the development girls who took pitches for their bosses at the studios were derisively known, in a play on the b-girl of the dive bars of yore.

Permut hyperbolically presented me as a hot New York book writer, during which Loring politely stifled a déjà vu yawn, at which point I took my cue to do my pitch. Spinning my tale, I was more than careful not to put my foot in my mouth over any work Loring herself may have had done. Although this was just the dawn of the plasticine age in Hollywood, cosmetic surgery had instantly become big business. It wasn't a matter of did she or didn't she, but, usually, rather how much and by whom.

Somehow Loring managed to stay wide awake through the whole twenty-minute spiel and, at the end, seemed very enthu-siastic, so much so that she made numerous suggested tweaks to the story and invited us to return once I had worked them out. I realized I was dealing with an ex-actress, but afterward, Permut said he had been trashed by her before and that this was no act. She was one tough nut, he said, and this time we'd cracked the shell.

A few weeks later, we went back to Hollywood to see Loring. I had incorporated all her notes into a new pitch, and eastern man of words on paper that I was, I had memorialized it all into a five-page synopsis. Loring greeted us warmly. Somehow I dropped the synopsis on the floor, and once she realized what it was, she eagerly seized it from me and began reading. That seemed like a great sign. She's gotta have it! But once she had it, did I ever get it. She read it quickly, then looked up at Permut and me, steam coming out her ears, her face redder than her hair. "You gave me just what I asked for!" she snarled. That was the point. Why the snarl? "I could have written this myself," she declared. "What do I need *you* for?"

Loring then proceeded to rip up the synopsis slowly and me-
thodically, with a contempt I thought was reserved for high crimes
and misdemeanors. Then she threw the confetti of the synopsis all
over me and Permut, the reverse of a ticker-tape parade, a one-
way parade to Palookaville. "I want new! I want fresh! I want different!" she tiraded, pointing us to the door. Like *The Return of the
Mod Squad,* I thought, but was way too terrified to joke. Permut
apologized profusely on the long ride back. Live by the pitch, die
by the pitch, he said. This time we died. Tomorrow I might wake
up with *Jaws.* The idea, he exhorted me, was to learn to take a
punch and to get up off the canvas. Television might be show business's cash cow, but right then I just felt like a lamb to the slaughter.

# CHAPTER 5
## HAIR APPARENT

ONE OF THE HARDEST REALITIES that an aspiring screenwriter had to adjust to in the 1980s was that your target reader must be not Pauline Kael, but rather P. T. Barnum. Or Caligula. Your target reader was not a reader. Therein lay the great paradox of Hollywood creativity, intrinsic to the foundation of the movies themselves: The great passive pleasure was an alternative to reading. You went to a movie, or watched television, instead of reading a book. The "either" of the image was brutalizing, if not obliterating, the "or" of the word.

No people were less interested in reading than the moguls who ultimately determined the movies that would be made. To say that these were men of deeds rather than words would be the understatement of the century. Reading had become Hollywood's punishment, its forced labor imposed on its serfdom of story editors and d-girls, who would condense books and scripts to the briefest of "coverage" so that the rods and cones of the showbiz aristocrats would not be wasted on the page but would be left free to focus on the stage. Screenings, starlets, lunches, deals and more deals, these were the priorities of the eyes of the mogulocracy. If only

Twitter had existed for them. Small wonder movies seemed to have entered the direst of straits.

To try to comprehend the mind of the mogul (not necessarily an oxymoron) and the brevity of his attention span, it is instructive to chart the mogul's path to power. There were only four main roads to the top in Hollywood. The first was to be born to power, like Richard Zanuck or Alan Ladd Jr. Then there was the way of the agent, of Fields and Begelman and now Ovitz, of reflecting glory and then seizing it by the throat. The third path, now that a onetime family business was becoming big business, was to climb the corporate ladder. This was most pronounced at Paramount, now a division of Gulf+Western, the winner-eat-all conglomerate satirized by Mel Brooks as Engulf & Devour in his 1976 Fox film *Silent Movie*. Here Barry Diller and his hierarchical cadre of moguls-in-training dubbed the "Killer-Dillers" and led by Michael Eisner, who cut his teeth under Diller in the similarly hierarchical and corporate ABC, brought the Madison Avenue style of repressed ruthlessness to the palm coast.

But it was the fourth road, the hardest of all highways to heaven, that produced the most colorful characters and most outlandish success stories, as well as the most preposterous films, of a decadent decade. This was the Way of No Way. It wasn't paved. You had to cross impassable mountains and plunging crevasses. Its intrepid wayfarers started with absolutely nothing and ended up with treasures beyond anyone's wildest dreams. These were the Cortéses and Pizzaros of eighties moviedom, known as the independents, as in independent producer, which was a declaration of independence from the studios. At the same time it was a bit of bravado, because at the outset of the independents' unlikely careers, the studios would have absolutely nothing to do with them. If anything was the audacity of hope, this was it. One thing they all had in common was that they did not spend their time reading scripts.

The trailblazer, the Christopher Columbus, of the New World of Hollywood was a Hungarian émigré named Andrew Vajna. Born in Budapest in 1944, Vajna was the only child of a Jewish couple in a city that was only marginally more tolerant of Jews under communism than under Nazism. The family was thus deeply closeted. Vajna's father worked as an urban planner for the state. When that government was briefly toppled during the ultimately crushed 1956 revolution, the twelve-year-old Andy took the opportunity to flee the country, with his stay-behind parents' blessing and hopes.

Unable to get an American visa, and not speaking a word of English, he washed up in the subarctic frontier town of Edmonton, Canada, a place he still calls "the asshole of the world," his newfound freedom notwithstanding. There was a small Hungarian Jewish émigré community that took him in. After the Soviets retook Hungary, Vajna's parents escaped across the border to Vienna, where a Hungarian friend at the U.S. embassy did them a major good turn, getting them refugee status and dispatching them to, of all places, Beverly Hills. A newly passed congressional act reunited young Andy with his parents. When he saw the sun and the ocean and the palm trees, Andy felt he'd been reborn.

Finding that he had a gift for languages (anything was easy after Magyar), Andy was enrolled in Beverly Hills High School, with the likes of Rob Reiner, Richard Dreyfuss, Dino Martin, and other sons and daughters of the rich and famous, few of whom would bother to speak to him. He lived south of Santa Monica, very south of Santa Monica, in what were considered the slums of Beverly Hills. His father worked as a city-planning researcher at UCLA, while his mother stayed home and crocheted dresses for a clientele of fellow "slum" dwellers. Andy did well enough in high school to get into UCLA, where he took classes in cinematography. However, he found school was a luxury he couldn't afford. Driven by the financial imperative of the wealth that surrounded

him but that he lacked, he used his camera talents to open his
own photography studio on South Beverly Drive, specializing in
weddings and bar mitzvahs. He was doing extremely well until
he took a weekend off to go skiing in Big Bear and had a terrible
accident, badly breaking his leg. He was trapped in a cast for six
months.

Without that leg to stand on, Vajna's shutterbug career ground
to a halt. Ever resourceful, he got the brainstorm to go to a local
beauty school on Fairfax Avenue, around the corner from Canter's
Deli, a gathering spot for old pensioners and young rockers. The
course there was six months, perfect timing for his injury to heal.
Vajna loved the idea of the portability of this new profession that
would allow him to do hair all over the world. He also loved the
idea of winning the hearts of beautiful girls with his scissors and
blow dryer. The profession was much more heterosexual then. His
parents were appalled down to their old-world intellectual roots.
They had not come to America to see their only son work in a
beauty parlor.

Ah, but what a beauty parlor. Vajna's first job was gotten through
a friend who was working in the hottest hair shop in Beverly Hills
and, by that token, probably the world. This was the salon of Gene
Shacove on Rodeo Drive, right next door to the Luau, which was
a cross between Trader Vic's and Maxwell's Plum, a nonstop tiki
orgy. As if the Luau weren't party enough, Shacove, a hip and
handsome Jewish boy from Boyle Heights, also helped found the
exclusive Candy Store disco beneath his salon. Shacove did all the
star hair, female and male, and rode motorcycles with his clients
McQueen and Beatty. Andy Vajna was a little bull in this china
shop of stunning stardom, styling the likes of Janet Leigh (and little
daughter Jamie Lee Curtis) and Jill St. John, the latter to the de-
manding specifications of her sugar daddy, Sidney Korshak, the
Teamsters' and the Mafia's Mr. Fixit consigliere in Hollywood.

The only other celebrity hairdresser near Gene Shacove's league was Jay Sebring, who had his salon near Vajna's beauty school on Fairfax. Like Shacove, Sebring was a cool playboy. Sebring's career was cut short by Charles Manson in 1969 when he murdered Sebring and his client and former lover Sharon Tate. On the outside looking in at all the glamorous clipping was a Valley Shacove wannabe named Jon Peters. Big, buff, and seductive, in contrast with the small, unprepossessing Vajna, whose perpetually furtive aura surely came from his refugee roots, Peters looked the part of the Beatty stud. He was also legitimately something of hair royalty. His mother's family owned the venerable Pagano's salon on Wilshire Boulevard.

But Jon Peters, who had gone to reform school, not beauty school, was the Paganos' black sheep. His uncles wouldn't hire him. Instead, he worked in a Ventura Boulevard salon called Bill White's. Peters would sometimes drive his Corvette over the hill to see how the other half blow-dried and eventually opened his own salon around the corner from Shacove's in Beverly Hills. Peters would later, after the deaths of Sebring and Shacove (in 2001), claim that he, and only he, was the true inspiration of Beatty's studly stylist in *Shampoo*. Vajna was there and ridicules Peters's claim to fame. "Warren was Gene's client," Vajna says, resting his case.

Talking big, bigger than life, was the essence of Peters, who ranks up there with Vajna as the most successful hairdresser turned mogul in Hollywood history. Unlike Vajna, who was a totally independent producer, Peters got his start as the most dependent producer in the world, dependent on the whims and the power of his client turned lover, Barbra Streisand. But a hit silences all slurs, and Peters defied all odds when the endlessly lampooned 1976 *Star Is Born* remake was a commercial bonanza that would smash Peters's Streisand chains and start him on the path to a massive moguldom all his own. Nonetheless, like Samson and his locks, Peters never wanted to cut his ties to hairdressing, for he knew that the way to any star's heart, whether for purposes of seduction or production, was through her tresses.

Vajna was less Machiavellian about whose hair he cut. But he was able to turn hair into capital in his unique, if inanimate, way. While doing the hair for the cast of the soap opera *General Hospital,* Vajna became aware of the cheesy state of American wigs, which were all the rage in the late 1960s. He saw the chance to create a better mousetrap and hied himself and a fellow Hungarian stylist from Shacove's named Gabor Koltai to Hong Kong, the wig capital of the world. The wigs were made of hair from India and Indonesia, never China, because America, and the West in general, was suspicious of "Communist" hair from mainland China. Vajna and Koltai brought back three thousand high-quality wigs to L.A. and sold out in a flash. They took another trip and doubled their order, which sold out as well. A new star was thus born. Its name was AGO, for Andy, Gabor, and Oliver, another Shacovian who joined them in what would be a booming business, as AGO became the chief supplier of wigs to Revlon, Pierre Cardin, and all the other prestige beauty and fashion lines.

While his partners stayed in Los Angeles to mine the American market, Vajna stayed in Hong Kong, building a wig factory with over three thousand employers. He lived in a lavish apartment on the Peak overlooking the Crown Colony's spectacular harbor. The hairdresser had become a mogul, but this was only his first incarnation as one. He traveled around the world selling his hair, but at one point he realized that while he was selling tons of wigs, in the chic discos and restaurants where he would go at night, no one was wearing them. He sensed the trend had peaked. Accordingly, he sold his share of AGO and segued into what he believed would be the next hot thing—jeans.

At that point in the early 1970s, most of the jeans in the world were either Levi's or Lee. Vajna decided to fill the void with his designer brands of soft wash denim, Jeans East and Faded Glory.

His timing was impeccable, perhaps too much so. The jeans market exploded so fast that he could not train his Chinese workers fast enough to meet the demand. He simply couldn't keep up with his Moroccan rivals at Guess? or the Israelis at Sasson. So he sold out of his jeans business, just as he had evacuated wigs, and plowed his profits into two grand classic old movie theaters in Hong Kong, the Capitol and the Liberty, and began learning about film from the exhibition side, an angle perceived as a low view that few of the Hollywood powers that were had either interest in or exposure to. The glamour was in film production, not distribution. But Andy Vajna had seen that success, wherever you found it, could buy all the glamour he needed.

Acquiring those two theaters immediately put Vajna right in the heart of the film business, the Hong Kong film business, Hollywood on Repulse Bay. Feral and foxlike and much more European in countenance than all-American, Vajna had the knack for spanning cultures. He began socializing with the moguls of the Hong Kong film subculture, Run Run Shaw, who built the largest film studio in Asia and produced over seven hundred films, and Raymond Chow, former head of Shaw's publicity department, who became the Cecil B. DeMille of martial arts, introducing the world to Bruce Lee, Jackie Chan, and other kung fu wonders.

Chow lined up Vajna to invest in one of the first Bruce Lee fist-fests, but Vajna was less interested in star making than moneymaking. His travels in Asia had alerted him to still another niche he felt he could fill, the better distribution of American films in what he considered an underserved part of the world. So he became an exhibitor-distributor, selling Hollywood studio films in Taiwan, Thailand, Malaysia, Singapore, and Indonesia, though not in Vietnam, as the recently abandoned war there left the country with no more GIs to fill the theaters. Vajna's first release, in 1973, was *Papillon*. He wasn't as far from Beverly High as it seemed.

On his first visit to the Cannes Film Festival in 1973, Vajna, then twenty-eight, met a twenty-one-year-old kid, also in foreign sales, named Mario Kassar. Kassar, a heartthrob wannabe in the Omar Sharif mode, had grown up in Rome, the son of an Italian mother and a Lebanese Christian father who was a film producer at the lower end of an Italian film industry that had fallen on hard times since its *Dolce Vita* heyday of Fellini and Antonioni. Cannes was in its own rut, reflecting the overall depressed state of cinema. The grand prize that year was shared by the American Jerry Schatzberg's *Scarecrow,* with Hackman and Pacino as two tragic drifters, which was a dud at home, and the British Alan Bridges's *The Hireling,* with Robert Shaw and Sarah Miles as a chauffeur and his boss, which similarly failed to make its director a household name.

The festival's torpor, notwithstanding its perennial topless starlets, served to bond the two foreigners, neither one of them invited to the A-parties at the Hotel du Cap or the Moulin des Mougins. What the world needed, these strangers at the party concluded, was no more of these effete art films that were turning the Croisette into a celluloid funeral parlor, but some really kick-ass *action* movies that would bring the empty theaters around the world back to life.

They had big dreams, dreams of being producers, but they started small, building a partnership in what they were already doing, which was being distributors. Vajna kept the Asian territories he knew and whose languages he had learned to speak, while Kassar took Lebanon, Iran, Iraq, and Cyprus, but not Israel, which was off-limits to any Lebanese, Christian or not. Language skills were vital in distribution, which is probably why Americans, who tended to be foreign-tongue-challenged, eschewed the field. Vajna and Kassar called their new company Carolco, named after no one in particular but because they liked the sound.

The studios had their own offices around the world to dispose of their product, so Vajna and Kassar were of necessity bottom-feeders, working with independent producers, who, thanks to a proliferation of tax shelter deals, particularly in Canada, were a growing breed. Two of these Canadians who trusted Vajna and Kassar were the Toronto team of Joel Michaels and Garth Drabinsky, the latter a swashbuckling lawyer who would later be convicted of a billion-dollar fraud and sentenced to seven years in prison. The Canadians were thinking big in the early stages of their career, and the megalomania appealed to the latent showmen in Vajna and Kassar. In 1978 and 1979, the Canadians gave Carolco its first producer credits in return for preselling their films *The Silent Partner,* a thriller with Christopher Plummer, and *The Changeling,* a horror movie with George C. Scott, in the foreign market and thus providing the capital to get those films made.

Next up in 1980 was a seemingly high-prestige film that would put Vajna's and Kassar's names above the title and finally get them some respect in Hollywood, where they were considered sleazy foreign hustlers, if they were considered at all. The movie *Escape to Victory* was also a homecoming for Vajna, for it was a remake of a 1961 Hungarian film about a soccer game between a team of POWs and their Nazi captors. And it was shot in Budapest. Hail the conquering hero. The director was the legendary John Huston, and the stars were Sylvester Stallone as the goalkeeper, Michael Caine as the captain of the team, Max von Sydow as the Nazi major, and the great Pelé himself among a number of global soccer stars the football-fanatic producers rounded up for the epic. Furthermore, it had a score by Bill Conti, who had done the ubiquitous theme from *Rocky.* How could it fail? Easily. The movie was perceived as a very poor man's *Great Escape,* with American filmgoers evincing zero interest in soccer and Europeans unable to accept Rocky Balboa as a footballer.

But it did create a relationship with Stallone, whose post-*Rocky* flops, like *F·I·S·T* and this latest film, already seemed to have worn out his Hollywood welcome. Vajna and Kassar had another kick-ass idea in a project they found in turnaround at Warner Bros. The script, adapted from a pulpish novel called *First Blood,* which *Time* magazine had derided as "carnography"—a fusion of carnage and porn—had to have been one of the most optioned projects in the business, but somehow, after ten years, three studios, eighteen drafts, five directors, and every star in town having come and gone, no one would make it.

*Blood*'s hero, John Rambo, was a deranged and displaced Vietnam War hero, a man without honor in the country he served. It was a variant of the vigilante theme that had worked so profitably in 1973's *Walking Tall,* wherein a vicious but honest cop cleans up a more vicious dishonest town. But Hollywood was very antsy about Vietnam, and it would take two foreigners to have the bravado to assume the risk, especially the risk of Stallone, already a hero without honor in the town that had so recently lionized him. Vajna was the project's true champion. He saw it as another *Rocky* underdog story but, as he put it, "more noble."

The only problem for the team was to raise first the $180,000 Warner's required to bail the script out of turnaround jail and then the $12 million to actually make the film, including Stallone's $3 million salary. They got their seed money from Kassar's godfather, a Lebanese tycoon who owned his own bank in Paris. They then assumed they could get the rest by doing their "thing," which was preselling the whole world, at the 1980 Cannes Film Festival. But a funny thing happened to them on their way to the forum of moguls that was the Hotel du Cap. The package they were offering was not merely Stallone but Kirk Douglas, who was to play Stallone's commanding officer in 'Nam and who was to save the world from Rambo's rage. The world market had no interest in Stallone. Douglas, despite his age, was the real money player on the international scene. But then Douglas insisted that his character kill Rambo, his own Frankenstein monster, at the end. And Vajna said no; you can't kill Rocky.

When Douglas walked from the picture, every country on earth repped at Cannes said No Way, except for Australia, which came up with a paltry bid of $400,000. Vajna took another look at the three-and-a-half-hour assemblage that his second-time Canadian director, Ted Kotcheff, had shot. "I wanted to throw up" was his response, he remembered. Who needed John Frankenheimer? he had once thought. Who needed Sydney Pollack or all the other giants who had once been attached but bailed out? Andy Vajna needed them, and more. He needed D. W. Griffith, and Howard Hawks, and even they might not be able to save this disaster. The ebullient Vajna had never felt more despair, even as a boy in the dictatorship of Communist Hungary. Stallone's agent, Ron Meyer, Ovitz's right hand at CAA, was equally despondent. He offered Vajna $9 million to buy the negative and scrap it, as the price for saving his client's already foundering career. This would be the knockout punch for poor Rocky. But Vajna had $13 million in as it was. He couldn't afford the loss.

Vajna fell back on what he had learned at UCLA Film School. He sat down with the film editor and recut the movie. He realized that less was more here, a lot less. He ended up with an eighteen-minute promo reel, which was all the footage he had any confidence in. Then he showed it to Terry Semel, the co-head of Warner's. Where's the rest? Semel asked him, the three *kindest* words in the English language. With hope in his heart, Vajna added in thirty-two more minutes of watchable footage to show at L.A.'s first American Film Market in Santa Monica. He brought in Stallone to do a dog-and-pony show for the foreign buyers, who tended to be more starstruck than jaded locals. They had come from Bangkok and Bucharest to Hollywood. Give them something to remember. Vajna was adept at fanning the flames of a buzz.

When a German distributor offered Vajna half a million for the film sight unseen, Vajna refused and held out for a million. Read it and weep, that was the idea. The German saw it, and the proof was in the Stallone pudding. You've got your million, he conceded after the screening.

Vajna quickly sold the world, but he still had trouble selling Hollywood. Warner Bros., the most likely customer, continued to balk, getting into a snit over the $3 million Vajna was demanding for their ad campaign. Then the rising colossus of HBO came to the rescue with a huge cable deal, which allowed Vajna to tell Semel to drop dead. He sold the film to Orion for American theatrical rights only, with no cross collateralization from other earning streams like video. Separate but equal, was Vajna's deal motto. Otherwise the accountants would have him tied up for years without ever seeing a profit. Wise he was. *First Blood* opened at $7.5 million its first weekend, spent three weeks atop the charts without a drop, and topped out at $55 million, a smash in those days. But even better were the foreign grosses, nearly three times that of the States. Vajna's hard-won expertise in the foreign market had paid off big-time, and the Carolco formula of separated rights became the industry standard for independent films that enabled the whole genre to explode.

*Rambo: First Blood Part II,* the 1985 sequel to *First Blood* that turned Carolco from a producer into a studio, cost $40 million, all of which was paid for by foreign presales. It grossed over $300 million worldwide. Half of that came from America, a huge percentage in the new arithmetic of movie revenue, aided in great part by the film's biggest fan, Ronald Reagan, who had been re-elected to a second term in a landslide of greed and right-wing patriotism that found a voice in the film. No press agent out of Damon Runyon could have dreamed up a bigger, better stunt than Reagan's declaration, on the eve of the release of American hostages taken in Lebanon, "I saw *Rambo* last night, and next time I'll know what to do." It was surprising that the Hungarian hair guy wasn't invited to the Lincoln Bedroom to "do" Nancy.

If Andy Vajna and Mario Kassar were the most blockbusterish of the new breed of often foreign independent producers who filled the voids left by the studios' general emasculation and risk aversion in the 1980s, then Menahem Golan and Yoram Globus were the most prolific. These two tracksuit-and-gold-chain-wearing cousins came from Tiberias, Israel, on the Sea of Galilee, where Jesus performed his miracle of turning five loaves and two fishes into a feast for five thousand. Though devout Jews, they clearly believed in those kinds of Christian miracles themselves, buying a tiny New York film company and quickly transforming it into an enterprise that would be turning out forty films a year, far more than Fox and the other studios that were terrified to bet the house on anything that didn't have a Spielberg imprimatur or otherwise obvious tentpole potential.

The little company the cousins bought was called Cannon, started in 1967 by two preppy Columbia grad students in New York, Chris Dewey and Dennis Friedland. Friedland had married a Hess oil heiress and could afford to play film. Cannon's only real hit was its vigilante blood-fest *Joe,* with Peter Boyle. The company had made a trashy name for itself by doing sex films, the most prestigious of which was *The Happy Hooker* series, which featured slumming stars like Lynn Redgrave and George Hamilton. Other Cannon titles were *Gas Pump Girls* and *Slumber Party '57.* The two preps were way ahead of their time in living out the widely held Ivy League fantasy of actually being in the movie business instead of just paying admission.

Dewey and Friedland were well connected in Manhattan social circles, and they were even written up in *Time* magazine for their unlikely success with *Joe,* which plugged into Spiro Agnew's rage against the effete liberal snobs that he probably would have derided Dewey and Friedland for being. Half of young Wall Street lived vicariously through the pair's adventures on the fringes of Hollywood. More vicarious yuppie thrills were found through the films of two Yalies, Lloyd Kaufman and Michael Herz. Their company, Troma (as in trauma), in the 1970s began producing, in New York, very low-rent sex comedies like *Squeeze Play!* and moved on to schlock sci-fi like *The Toxic Avenger.* They gave work to such eventual stars as Kevin Costner, Samuel L. Jackson, Billy Bob Thornton, and Marisa Tomei, but more important, they, and the Cannon boys, put the radical idea that preppies could be in Hollywood, too, in the privileged minds of Park Avenue silver spooners like Michael Eisner and Jeffrey Katzenberg.

Eventually, Dewey and Friedland ran out of money and sold Cannon to the Israelis for the pittance of $500,000 in 1979. If Dewey and Friedland were the true preps, Golan and Globus were the antipreps. The Upper East Side gave way to the Lower East Side, the world of our fathers. Golan, the older cousin, fifty when they bought Cannon, had been a director of Israeli films rarely seen outside the Holy Land. But Golan had taken film classes at New York's City College, and had never gotten over it. He wanted desperately to come back to America and be "in the business."

Cousin Globus, a decade younger than Golan, was the business guy. He had L.A. experience, having learned the low-budget ropes in assistant jobs for Roger Corman and Samuel Arkoff, Corman's distributor. The cousins relocated Cannon from Park Avenue to Sunset Boulevard and began making the kinds of subtitled American genre films—teen, soft porn, cheap action, cheaper horror— you might see on a trip to Bulgaria on the marquee of some odd theater in Sofia and wonder how come you never saw it back home. Who made those films? you might ask. And the answer was often Cannon.

Just like Vajna and Kassar, Golan and Globus spoke the foreign language of foreign sales and basically financed all their movies with advances from those distributors in Bulgaria. So what if no

American theaters would show their films; they had already broken even, they'd take their profits in lire or pesetas or yen instead of dollars, and they didn't give a damn about prestige in Hollywood. While they churned out more films than the studios, these films were low-budget, a third of the big boys' films, and non-union, often employing Israeli directors and writers no one else had heard of, much less would hire.

It was ironic, however, that Jewish Hollywood, probably Israel's best friend on earth, gave such a wide birth to these presumable landsmen. Maybe it was because Golan and Globus, with their utter disdain for A-tables at Spago and clothes from Maxfield and golf at Hillcrest, reminded Hollywood's fancy Jews of roots they preferred to forget. Maybe they appeared to be too crass and overtly money-mad and Shylockian. It was all a question of style, a matter of degree, because they were all in the same business of "putting asses in seats," as Jack Warner said in one of his many moments of Golan-Globus crassness. Whatever, Israelis had little luck getting into the Hollywood club.

The only exception to the Israel blockade was Arnon Milchan, who allegedly made his fortune in Middle East arms dealing. In Hollywood, no one asks where the money comes from. They care only where it goes, and Milchan put his in all the right places, starting with financing Barbra Streisand's pet project *Yentl*. It could be said that Streisand was by far the most powerful woman in Hollywood. Anyone who could turn the universally ridiculed *A Star Is Born* remake into a smash deserved the awe of the business. But she had won the Oscar for *Funny Girl,* she had won Grammys, she could direct, she could produce, and she had made it all on talent—no, she was a goddess in a godless town and the perfect wagon for Milchan to hitch his wagon to, flop or not.

Milchan was a lot smoother than Golan and Globus. He had graduated from the London School of Economics and lived in Paris, speaking perfect French. He was so smooth, in fact, that while he was implicated, he was never charged in a scandal involving the shipping of nuclear triggers from a California company to his own in Israel. At the time, it was illegal to export the triggers without a munitions export license, and in the ensuing trial an American, Richard Kelly Smith, was convicted and sent to prison for years. Making movies was a much safer way to be out west, and Milchan eventually got out of the arms trade.

Milchan further secured his place in the firmament by financing Martin Scorsese's likely-to-fail pet project *The King of Comedy,* knowing that with Jerry Lewis, Milchan could at least recoup his investment in France and back home in Israel, where Lewis *was* the king of comedy. And then, through his Israeli production partner, Meier Teper, he became the chief backer of sushi chef to the stars Nobu Matsuhisa's global expansion of his Peruvian Japanese La Cienega Boulevard restaurant formula. Thus, while Golan and Globus were noshing on tongue sandwiches at Canter's, Milchan was supping on *tiradito* and miso cod and soft-shell crab rolls with Nobu. It may have been all a matter of taste, but Hollywood was all about image, and Milchan, who would break the bank with *Pretty Woman* at the end of the 1980s, had all the right moves to beat the curse of the ghetto.

Cannon didn't need respect, but it did need a hit. It got a few early on by taking that never fail vigilante page from *Joe* and recycling an aging but still potent Charles Bronson in 1982's *Death Wish II* and by exploiting Chuck Norris as a poor man's Rambo in *Missing in Action.* Apparently there was a huge audience of poor men out there, and Cannon turned Norris into a major star, though one without any luster in the more exalted Hillcrest Country Club circles.

As independent producers on the world stage, Vajna and Kassar and Golan and Globus looked to one tiny giant as their soul and inspiration. This little big man was Dino De Laurentiis. Dino, as everyone knew him, the son of a Neapolitan pasta maker, had never really bothered to learn English. There was no need to come to English; English came to him, as did supplicant producers of all nations looking to get their films made. Dino had all the scripts submitted to him translated into Italian and then read to him, or more accurately, the very brief coverage was read to him. He was the master of high concept before it ever occurred to the Killer-Dillers at Paramount. The original *Death Wish, The Hurricane, King Kong, Orca: The Killer Whale!, Conan the Barbarian.* With Dino there was zero guesswork as to what the movie was about.

Born in 1919, Dino had forsaken spaghetti for cinema, coming to prewar Mussolini Rome to become an actor. The miniman soon realized he lacked the presence to be a star, so he tried directing. Then he realized he lacked the art to direct, so he settled on producing. He knew he had the drive for that. It took him until the neorealist era to have a hit, 1949's *Bitter Rice.* It was actually a double hit, for he married the star, the lush Silvana Mangano, who towered above the five-foot-four baby mogul.

The 1950s were Rome's commercial heyday as the film capital of the world, and Dino's artistic heyday as well. He teamed up with Carlo Ponti, the husband of Italy's screen queen Sophia Loren, to produce Fellini's *La Strada,* then went solo to mount his first international co-production, *War and Peace,* with Henry Fonda, Audrey Hepburn, and the proverbial cast of thousands. He would also produce Vittorio De Sica's *The Last Judgment* and John Huston's *The Bible: In the Beginning.* Dino's very Italian attractions to themes that were operatic, biblical, and grandiose were set in stone, and he was an easy mark for an epic. Plus, as a Neapolitan, he was also a pushover for anything Mob related. How he raised the money for these epics was another matter, one never fully explicated. There were whispers of Mafia, Masonry, and enough global conspiracies for a Dan Brown novel, but the policy in Rome, as in Hollywood, was don't ask, don't tell.

Dino's first Waterloo—and there were many, including the film

epic *Waterloo* itself—was his attempt to build a new and egoma-
niacal film studio in Rome modeled after the existing Cinecittà.
His would be called Dinocittà. What else? The studio's cost was
over $30 million. Dino made *The Bible: In the Beginning* there as
well as *Barbarella,* proving his diversity in going from the divine to
the profane. But by the 1970s, the *Dolce Vita* heyday was over and
the Red Brigades were kidnapping moguls left and right. The
easy life that was Italy's siren call wasn't easy anymore. In the face
of new xenophobic laws sharply limiting the number of foreign
principals in Italian films, in resentment of Hollywood's apparent
determination to transform Rome into its bargain playpen, the
movie business dried up. Most of the spaghetti westerns, while
produced and directed by Italians, were shot in Spain.

Dinocittà went bust, and Dino left the *città* and went abroad,
first to New York and then to Hollywood, producing some great
films like *Serpico* and *Three Days of the Condor,* but more howlers
like the Dixie-porn *Mandingo,* in which James Mason played a
planter who used a slave baby as a foot cushion, enshrining Dino
forever in the NAACP Hall of Shame. Dino always shot the
moon. He couldn't resist building an American film studio, this
one in Wilmington, North Carolina. Even though he was now
on Tobacco Road, the *Mandingo* backlash kept him away from
any more plantation potboilers.

Dino also opened, in both New York and Hollywood, his Italian answer to Paris's gourmet emporium Fauchon. It was exactly
like today's Eataly, the vastly popular Twenty-third Street food
hall, but three decades ahead of its time. By the same thankless token, in New York it was seen as a déjà vu Dino & DeLuca, a copy
of the hip SoHo grocery that had beaten it to market. In L.A. it
was simply no match for its Beverly Drive neighbor, the über-
Jewish deli Nate 'n Al's. Both stores closed ignominiously, the
*Heaven's Gate* of gourmandia. Dino blew two more fortunes on
*Dune* and *Tai-Pan,* and his American film empire went bankrupt,

acquired in 1989 by a Vajna-less Mario Kassar, who had idolized Dino in his own Roman youth and modeled his career after him. The canary had swallowed the cat.

It often seemed that everyone in foreign sales and independent production was a foreigner. Americans either didn't speak the language or lacked the offshore bazaar ruthlessness and third-world funny money connections that the Europeans seemed more adept at tapping into. In short, Americans, even Hollywood Americans, were too straight for a crooked business. But there were colorful exceptions, like 1980s Hollywood's reigning godfather of foreign distribution, a failed B-actor named Mark Damon who had fled to Italy to make spaghetti westerns in the 1960s and when that fizzled out had nothing to fall back on but the Italian he had had to learn to earn a living abroad.

The uses of Damon's offshore adversity proved to be ironically sweet indeed. He was born Alan Harris in Depression Chicago, and his father, himself né Herskovitz, was a grocer who gambled away his savings and deserted his wife and two sons. Before becoming Mark Damon, young Al Harris was encouraged by his practical Jewish mother to go west to UCLA and become a dentist. However, Al grew up to be a young Adonis, with looks that would be wasted on root canals.

At UCLA, Al was spotted as a babe magnet and as such was rushed by the elite Jewish fraternity ZBT, over which Mike Ovitz would preside fifteen years later. Al became a star in campus drama productions, appearing with a coed named Carol Burnette before she dropped the last letter of her name and became famous. Al also won first prize in a national puzzle contest, all the rage in the 1950s, out of a million entrants, as well as a stipend of $30,000 (which would be like millions today). Inspired by the money, Al went on to enroll in UCLA's M.B.A. course and after that was accepted in a doctoral program in English lit, all the while acting in school plays as well as modeling for fashion ads in the *L.A. Times.*

Al was the big, beautiful man on campus and headed for great
things.

Fate intervened with academe when a talent scout from Fox
offered the scholar-thespian a six-month studio contract in 1955.
For a brief shining moment, the newly self-renamed Mark Damon
was the "it" boy, the Bachelor of Six Months. He had romances
with Natalie Wood and Paul Kohner's daughter, Susan, and his
sixteen-year-old co-star on a Fox TV show, Lili Gentle, who was
the second cousin of Tallulah Bankhead. Even the most distant
pedigree mattered, none less than that of Lili's other suitor, Richard Zanuck, son of Darryl, who basically owned Fox at the time.
Lili would eventually marry Zanuck, while Fox terminated Mark
after his six months expired.

Mark got out of Dodge and moved to New York to hone his
craft at the theater school of acting guru Sanford Meisner, the
Neighborhood Playhouse on East Fifty-fourth Street. His classmates included Gwen Verdon and John Frankenheimer. In 1957, he
returned to Hollywood hoping to be the next James Dean, whose
death in 1955 had created a big market for "troubled young men"
films. Mark soon got one, called *Young and Dangerous,* which could
have been a French farce or Greek tragedy depending on how you
saw the casting situation. The film was at Fox, and who should be
Mark's co-star but Lili Gentle, still hot and heavy for him and also
still unbetrothed to Richard Zanuck. Mark deftly survived the
shoot but not the reviews, which compared him not to James Dean,
but to George Hamilton, who added injury to insult by stealing
Susan Kohner away from Mark.

What followed was a long odyssey through the wasteland of
B- and C-pictures, which was actually wonderful training for
the similar wasteland of foreign sales that Damon would come to
dominate. But despite his M.B.A., it never occurred to this artist
to become a businessman. Dreams die too hard. Damon would

try anything. For his film *The Party Crashers,* he cut a song in Nashville called "I Don't Wanna Go Home" that got him a shot on Dick Clark's *American Bandstand.* From that sublime, Mark went to the ridiculous, or perhaps vice versa, of Roger Corman's *House of Usher.* Vincent Price played Usher, whose cursed daughter Mark's character falls in love with, in one of the most campily doomed of screen romances.

Damon thought he had finally gotten the big break that he deserved when in 1961 his agent received a telegram from Luchino Visconti asking to meet Damon for a role. One of Italy's most revered and certainly its richest and most aristocratic director, the Milanese Visconti was a genuine count and the son of the Duke of Grazzano. He was also a gay Communist, but that was Italy, and as Emerson wrote, a foolish consistency is the hobgoblin of little minds. Visconti was basking in the laurels of his 1960 *Rocco and His Brothers,* starring Alain Delon, and Mark Damon was a near doppelgänger for the French *joli garçon.* Undeterred by the prospect of being not Visconti's cinematic discovery but his object of prey, Damon bought himself a ticket to Rome to meet the dashing master, then in his early fifties. That was Hollywood wherever you found it, and any experienced actor had to know how to navigate its shoals of lust.

Damon was immediately entranced by Rome, which was in its Felliniesque prime, before the disastrous *Cleopatra* would sink the ship two years hence. Visconti was entranced by Damon, as was his very gay circle led by his former lover Franco Zeffirelli and including such luminaries as Pier Paolo Pasolini and Gore Vidal. They all saw Delon in Damon, and they all saw a challenge. The part Visconti was dangling was opposite the French beauty Romy Schneider in Visconti's episode of *Boccaccio '70.* Fellini and De Sica were also doing segments, with Anita Ekberg and Sophia Loren. It was a *Who's Who* of Italian cinema, and it would have elevated

Damon from the Roger Corman junkyard to the pantheon of the big time. But Visconti played sexual hardball, and in Damon's case, it was no play, no pay.

Damon was entranced by Italy, and he really didn't have much to go home to in Hollywood. So he stayed in Rome and began getting work, albeit not at the exalted level he was dreaming of, but instead in Italian movies that would never be seen outside the bottom of a double bill in the mother country, dogs like *The Great Treasure Hunt,* for which Damon had the extra claim to shame of having written the screenplay. Like every other nonstar Hollywood refugee, Damon appeared in a host of spaghetti westerns, called *"maccheroni"* in Europe. While Damon never got into any of the Sergio Leone classics, he did have the distinction of having introduced Leone to a television actor from the *Rawhide* series Damon knew from back home. The name was Eastwood; the rest was history.

When Damon neared forty, which was pasture time for also-rans, he knew he had to get real and fall back on his M.B.A. from UCLA. The business he chose was European film distribution, which he had seen firsthand was a chaotic combat zone of multi-lingual hustlers, like the stolen watch salesmen who preyed on tourists at Pompeii, trying to con American film producers into letting the hustlers handle their films abroad instead of the foreign offices of the Hollywood studios. Why would any sane American producer trust someone outside the studios? Because that someone was the supersmooth Mark Damon, the first credible American to work the continent from the inside. Damon got a job in 1974 with an Italian company and slowly began "confidencing" Americans to let him be their man in Europe. He had all the right stuff, the looks, the languages (he spoke five), the stardom, such as it was, and the gorgeous wife, a Corman bombshell named Margaret Markov, who had starred in two "women in prison" films, *The Hot Box* and *Black Mama, White Mama* with Pam Grier.

His many assets notwithstanding, Damon was still meeting so much resistance from American producers that he knew his only salvation was to become one himself. In 1976, he charmed his distribution company bosses into co-financing, with a pre-*Dallas* Lorimar, flush with TV coin from *The Waltons* and desperate for big-screen respect, an American film based on the Joseph Wambaugh cop novel *The Choirboys,* with an ensemble cast that included James Woods, Randy Quaid, and Lou Gossett Jr. and directed by old hand Robert Aldrich of *Dirty Dozen* fame. It wasn't an A-picture, but it was a cut above Corman. The film was a bomb domestically, but it took off overseas, grossing $40 million. Mark Damon was still not a prophet in his own country, but abroad he was Abraham, Isaac, and Jacob combined.

Emboldened by this success and homesick as well, Damon decided to quit his Italian job in the aftermath of the kidnapping of his boss à la Paul Getty. Damon helped engineer the ransom for over $1 million to a syndicate from Marseilles. The abductors were never apprehended, but Hollywood never looked so good, as the Eternal City was becoming the Infernal City. Damon's plan was to work Europe for distribution deals as he had from Rome, but to do it instead from Hollywood. He started a new company called PSO (Producers Sales Organization) and charmed backing from the Guinness brewery dynasty. He used his European network to get his next big production, finally with some class, Wolfgang Petersen's submarine actioner *Das Boot.*

Damon's next and seemingly biggest score turned out to be his booby prize: handling foreign sales for *The Cotton Club,* made by Robert Evans, like Damon a pretty-boy actor turned producer, but with huge success. *Cotton Club* was Evans's nightmare. It had all the off-screen murder, Mafia, drugs, and abductions that Damon was supposedly fleeing Italy to avoid. But Damon survived Evans to become the undisputed American master of the foreign package, though never able to rival the real foreigners like Vajna and Kassar for their Dinoesque epic hustle.

Maybe you had to be born over there. Maybe being seduced into doing not one but two Mickey Rourke films, at the height of Rourke's 1980s unbankability, *9½ Weeks,* and *Wild Orchid,* indicated that Mark Damon had spent too much time amid the decadent Italians for his ultimate better judgment. The bottom line with all these independent producers, offshore or on-, was that their attention spans were like those of hummingbirds. Don't give them a script; give them a star or don't bother them. Look at all the distractions, from Dino's fifty varieties of olive oil to Damon's bad-boy babysitting. It was enough to make Vajna go to the set to do someone's hair, just to calm his nerves.

# CHAPTER 6
## SCARY RICH GUYS

THE MOST INFLUENTIAL PERSON in 1980s Hollywood had to have been Jeffrey Katzenberg. He wasn't by any means the most powerful, for at Paramount he reported to Michael Eisner, who reported to Barry Diller, who reported to Charles Blühdorn. As Bob Dylan sang, "You gotta serve somebody." But in terms of setting the agenda for Hollywood, for determining what movies got made, nobody had more influence than the wraithlike, bespectacled, horse-toothed young man his mentor Eisner would, under oath, demean as "the little midget." Until that epithet, he was better known as Eisner's "golden retriever," because no bird dog, no attack dog, no foaming pit bull or rottweiler, was hungrier, fiercer, or more tenacious in sniffing out the golden quail that were hit movies.

The key to Katzenberg's influence was the ferocity of his courage of conviction, which is rare in Hollywood. Everyone has opinions, but few stand by them, never in the face of the contrary opinion of someone more powerful. But Katzenberg was beyond certainty, and his dogma made him the top dog. The key to his credibility was that early in his job at Paramount, he became convinced that the relatively middling and long-canceled *Star Trek*

TV series could be the next *Star Wars* tentpole event. Eisner wavered, but Katzenberg did not. He eventually got his way, and his first smash, vindicating the small screen and proving once and for all that cinema, at least commercially, was not the master race.

Mike Ovitz may have been certain in the same way Jeff Katzenberg was certain. But Ovitz was a seller, and Katzenberg was a buyer, and oligopolistic Hollywood will always be a buyer's market. No one in this market was as ambitious, industrious, or ubiquitous as Katzenberg. He'd start at dawn, courting everyone who mattered or who might someday, do three breakfasts a morning, Polo Lounge, Nate 'n Al's, Hugo's, and seemingly never stop eating until the last cognac was served at Morton's, never gaining an ounce. He would have been the envy of any model, who would have surely put aesthetics aside for this star maker, but Katzenberg was a family man with no interest in skinny models. All he cared about were grosses, big, fat grosses.

Katzenberg worked like a Wall Street dog, pedigreed but vicious. He probably should have been at Goldman Sachs, and he, as well as Eisner, had the Park Avenue background for it. But neither had the grades, which led not to oblivion but to an amazing success that any Goldmanite would covet. Katzenberg, whose father was a prosperous stockbroker, went to Fieldston, one of a triumvirate of elite, mostly Jewish private schools (the others were Riverdale and Horace Mann) in the haute Bronx along the Hudson. Unlike so many of his revved-up classmates, Katzenberg was not Ivy bound. He dropped out of New York University after a year and went to work as an advance man for the haute WASP mayor John Lindsay. The job may have given him a different perspective on the Ivy League experience, to see how all that grace worked under the pressure of the powder-keg sixties city that Lindsay was trying to keep from exploding.

Katzenberg's collegiate shortfall put him in good company at Paramount. Eisner, too, was a Park Avenue boy, but a far grander one, both in stature and in roots. His grandfather had made a fortune in the uniform business, outfitting both the army and the Boy Scouts, instilling in the family a sense of John Lindsay–style Establishment that was surely alien to their fellow Jews in the Lower East Side sweatshops who did the actual sewing. Eisner's father went to Princeton and Harvard Law. He didn't need to earn a living and thus had the luxury of doing public service work like heading the state bureau of public housing. Eisner went away to Lawrenceville in New Jersey, the perfect boarding school to prepare him for his father's alma mater next door. But a funny thing must have happened to Eisner on his way to Old Nassau, for he ended up at Dennison in Ohio, a little Baptist college that few Laurentians would have ever considered as an appropriate safety school, not when prep-friendly Chapel Hill and Charlottesville were standing by.

Barry Diller, who had hired Eisner in 1966 when he was making his mark creating television movies of the week at ABC, and then hired Katzenberg as his assistant when he came to run Paramount in 1974, also grew up privileged in Beverly Hills, the son of a real estate developer who built postwar tract housing in the San Fernando Valley near where Michael Ovitz had been raised. Diller went to Beverly Hills High, class of '59. He went on down the road to UCLA but, like Katzenberg at NYU, barely lasted a year. Luckily, at Beverly High, Diller, who didn't have any stars in his family, had befriended Terre Thomas, the scionette of a genuine TV dynasty. Terre's sister was soon-to-be *That Girl* Marlo Thomas (and later Mrs. Phil Donahue), and her brother was future mega–TV producer Tony Thomas (*The Golden Girls*). Terre leaned on her mega–TV star father, Danny Thomas, to get his agents at William Morris to make room for Barry, a showbiz outsider, in one of the coveted slots in the Willam Morris mailroom, which then was the West Point of entertainment. Thomases promises.

The Thomases were also instrumental in introducing Diller to televison honcho Leonard Goldberg, who was then dating Marlo Thomas and would eventually become the partner of Mr. Television, Aaron Spelling. At the time, though, Goldberg was a VP at ABC, and he got Diller a job at the network, which he would come to dominate until Charles Blühdorn made him the offer he could not refuse in 1974. After CBS's "smiling cobra" James Aubrey took the helm of MGM in 1969, Diller was only the second "television guy" to run a Hollywood studio and at thirty-two also the youngest top dog since Irving Thalberg. Still, Diller's bald head, his severe corporate William Morris dress of dark suits, white shirts, and sober ties, and his soft-spoken, big-stick power voice made him seem a decade older and far graver than his tender years.

The man who hired this chain of endlessly overcompensating academic underachievers was himself a City College dropout who went to hustle on the New York Cotton Exchange when he was only nineteen. Unlike his employees Diller, Eisner, and Katzenberg, Blühdorn had no silver spoon in his mouth, only a Nazi jackboot in his rear end. Born in Vienna in 1926, he fled to England with his family a decade later in view of the gathering storm. In 1942, escaping the Blitz, the Blühdorns came to New York.

Blühdorn was secretive about everything, but never more so than about his roots. Everyone in Hollywood assumed, given his family's flight, that he was Jewish, though with his thick, bad-scientist glasses and slicked-back hair, he could have been cast as a Nazi nemesis on *Hogan's Heroes*. Blühdorn was so paranoid that Nazis were lurking everywhere, even in the 1980s, that he would never relieve himself, and possibly reveal the naked truth, at a public urinal without one of his henchmen barring the door until he was finished. There was a joke that for Charlie, ignorance was bris.

Jew or non-Jew, Blühdorn may not have had the patience for books, but he had a great head for numbers and made his first fortune at twenty-one speculating in the postwar commodities market and his second one in auto replacement parts. In 1956, he combined his Michigan bumper company with a Houston parts distributor to create Gulf+Western (Houston and Michigan, which was west to an Austrian) and began to engulf and devour every business in sight until he swallowed his first glamour pill in Paramount in 1966. He was only forty, but while he had a French wife, he was square and unworldly and repressed, a swashbuckler on the stock exchange but not in the boudoir.

Meeting Robert Evans was thus the happiest day in Blühdorn's life, because Evans lived up to every stereotype invented about Hollywood. Handsome, spoiled rich playboy who wants to go Hollywood—that was the young Robert Evans, a failed actor who seduced aging Norma Shearer, à la William Holden and Gloria Swanson in *Sunset Blvd.,* and somehow beat all the clichés to end up a Paramount executive. "It's all about pussy" was Evans's motto. As a scion of the Seventh Avenue women's clothing colossus of Evan-Picone, Evans could provide work for half the models in Manhattan and then provide important men for them to go out with when the work was done. Everyone had to know Bob Evans, Gotham's fix-up king, and no one wanted Evans to work his male matchmaking magic more than Blühdorn, who was, given his unique power as studio head to make any girl a star, easy to love.

Blühdorn spent a fortune in studio funds turning Evans's home behind the Beverly Hills Hotel into his boss' ne plus ultra love nest, turning Evans into a vastly slicker version of the boss-pleasing Jack Lemmon character in *The Apartment,* with the major difference being that there were multiple variations on Shirley MacLaine. How Hollywood's life could imitate Hollywood's art. Blühdorn loved money, but he had all the money in the world.

He bought Paramount to get laid, but by replacing Evans with the obsessive, workaholic, hit-craving Diller, who then hired the obsessive, workaholic, hit-craving Eisner and Katzenberg, Blühdorn turned a plaything into a gold mine.

Blühdorn was a scary guy, who did global deals and kept company with some even scarier guys, like the Italian gangster-bankers Michele Sindona and Roberto Calvi. Sindona, known as "the Shark," died in 1986 in an Italian prison of cyanide poisoning after bankrupting the huge Franklin National Bank. Calvi, known as "God's Banker" because of his Vatican connections, died in 1982 in the City of London, site of many of his massive deals, hanged from Blackfriars Bridge over the Thames, after bankrupting the huge Banco Ambrosiano. Both Italians were close to Dino De Laurentiis and surely figured in the labyrinthine offshore financing of his films, which were released by Blühdorn's Paramount. Blühdorn himself died in 1983 at fifty-six under equally mysterious circumstances, but without having destroyed any bank, at least that the public was aware of.

It was reported that Blühdorn had expired of a sudden heart attack on his private G+W jet coming back from the Dominican Republic, where he had huge sugar and resort interests. However, it later became known that Blühdorn had been secretly suffering from leukemia and getting chemotherapy since 1978. He supposedly had passed away in the Dominican Republic and had given orders that his body be flown back to New York, sort of like the dead Charlton Heston in *El Cid* being propped up on his horse to lead a final charge against the Moors. Because no one fears a dying mogul, and power is a function of that fear, Blühdorn was as covert about his illness, even in death, as he was his ethnicity. Confounding to the end, he had his funeral held in a Catholic church in Connecticut. Henry Kissinger was the mourner of honor. With Blühdorn at the helm, Paramount certainly was the ideal studio to have made *The Godfather*. It was cinema *à clef*.

Speaking of scary, I met Jeffrey Katzenberg through the Zucker brothers, the shorthand for the team of David Zucker, Jerry Zucker, and Jim Abrahams who jointly created, produced, and directed *Airplane!*, one of the biggest low-budget moneymakers of all time. Hailed as comic geniuses and, more important, respected as business geniuses, they had an overall production deal at Paramount, which had released *Airplane!* and gotten rich from it. Katzenberg was their point man at the studio. Like all comic geniuses, the Zuckers were desperate to be taken seriously as straight men, and that was where I came in, to write a script for them about the New Orleans district attorney Jim Garrison's quixotic quest to solve the Kennedy assassination. And no, there wasn't anything at all funny about it.

I had met the Zuckers through a fellow writer who had grown up with them in Milwaukee. He had gone on to Harvard and was poor; they had gone to Madison and were rich. But they were true to Wisconsin. In fact, I once asked them if they ever worked with then comic Al Franken, who was from Minneapolis, which I figured was in their neck of the woods. They were appalled at the question. People from Minneapolis, I learned the hard way, were perceived by them as somewhat inauthentic city slickers. The likes of Franken did not share the uniquely Wisconsinoid sense of humor that the Zuckers had honed in a little theater of the absurd that they had set up in college and which had led to their first film, *Kentucky Fried Movie,* directed by John Landis, who then went on to his own low-budget glory with *Animal House.*

The prime mover on the Garrison project was Jim Abrahams, who had worked as a security guard and was fascinated by law enforcement and conspiracy theories. These passions would also result in the Zuckers' *Naked Gun* series of police spoofs. But now the Zuckers were dead serious, ready for their close-up, ready for their Oscar. Garrison's obsessive quest to solve the greatest mystery of the century was a great film subject, and they had bought the life rights of Garrison, now a judge in New Orleans. I felt very lucky that they hired me to go down to the Big Easy and write the script amid the pleasures of oyster po-boys and crayfish étouf-fée. Why me? I was southern and spoke the language, I was a lawyer and could speak that language, and I had written a book about the wicked ways of the southern aristocracy that the comedi-ans had, mirabile dictu, read and liked. Then again, maybe reading was a Milwaukee thing.

The Zuckers had invited me to join them for a screening at Paramount when we ran into Katzenberg. We had just passed the famous arched Bronson gate, the one Eric von Stroheim drove the Isotta-Fraschini roadster through to see DeMille in *Sunset Blvd.* What glory, I marveled at the place. As we were parking, the Zuckers spotted Katzenberg getting out of his trademark Mustang convertible, the opposite of the Isotta. He was wearing a wind-breaker. There was no trace of Park Avenue. Everything about him shouted out, Hey, I'm just an ordinary guy. He wanted to blend into the mass market he was courting. The Zuckers said hello, then started to introduce me.

"Hey, Jeff, do you know Bill Stadiem?" David Zucker asked.

"I know *precisely* who he is," Katzenberg snapped back.

He didn't shake my hand. Instead he just flashed that death's-head smile of his and dashed away. The Zuckers shrugged, embarrassed and speechless. Even they were at a loss for a one-liner. Surely Jeff couldn't be serious. He was dead serious. And don't call me Shir-ley, I thought to myself in Zuckerese.

I found out exactly where I stood at Paramount a few months later when I went to pitch an idea with a producer to one of Kat-zenberg's acolytes, a junior Killer-Diller named Ricardo Mestres.

Although the name may have sounded like an affirmative action outreach hire to access the Latino market, Mestres himself was as WASPy and rooted in the *Social Register* as Mayor Lindsay. I had never met Mestres before, but I knew about him, for I had worked under his father when I was a junior legal associate at Sullivan & Cromwell. The two had the same name; to distinguish them (behind their backs), the father was known as Big Ricky and the son was Little Ricky, in a nod to the *I Love Lucy* show.

Little Ricky had gone to Exeter and Harvard and in another era would have followed his distinguished father into the law. But we were in the movie era, and it was considered way cool to be a studio executive. Katzenberg was known to love to flex his power by hiring the Ivy Leaguers that he may have secretly regretted not becoming, and no one was more Ivy than Little Ricky, whose grandfather, also Ricardo Mestres, or Ricky One, had been vice president of Princeton, where he had captained the baseball team as an undergrad in the Roaring Twenties. Thwarted Princetonian Michael Eisner had to have been impressed with that résumé item.

We cordially exchanged acquaintances, and I inquired about his parents, whom I had known at firm events at Piping Rock and other enclaves of the rich and low-profile. I was also friends with a woman who had taught Little Ricky (I of course called him Ricardo, if not "sir") at St. Bernard's, Manhattan's toniest K–9 private school, and she had asked to send her regards. I thought we had a connection, but he seemed incredulous that I had actually left his father's firm. That was the chance of a lifetime, he said, puzzled. Without wanting to denigrate the boredom of that majesty, I gingerly queried why Ricardo himself hadn't pursued it. "I didn't have to," he said, with the heavy implication that he was already part of the aristocracy. And I was not and had blown my big chance at the big time.

I pitched the idea, whatever it was. Amazingly, Ricardo seemed to like it. He expressed enthusiasm about its commercial appeal, but then he pulled me up short by asking, "Who's going to write it?" The producer and I looked at each other, taken aback. He answered that I was. Ricardo looked annoyed. "Do you want to write this or do you want to get it made?" Well, both, I replied. He rolled his eyes. The implication was that the two possibilities were mutually exclusive. In urging me to bow out and accept a producer credit when the film was made (and not a penny until then, either), he went down a list of "hot" Paramount writers who had worked on "go" projects that never "went" and who subsequently were never heard of again. It was the old Wall Street strategy of buy on the rumor, sell on the news.

Again, it was the old "If we don't already know you, we don't want to know you." Heat was all that mattered. I had none, even by reflected thermal transfer, at Paramount, even though my patrons the Zuckers were very happy with my first draft of the Garrison script. The problem was that the Zuckers' *Police Squad!* series had been canceled by ABC after only six episodes. Their temperature was just way down, their godlike status eroded, and the Garrison movie was viewed by the Paramount high-concept boys as anything but, an eccentric vanity project rather than what Katzenberg et al. were waiting for, which was another *Airplane!* I had read recently that the studios wouldn't even hire Philip Roth to adapt one of his own books, so I couldn't feel too bad. But I stubbornly held to my guns, and Ricardo was as nonplussed by that decision as he was by the one to leave his father's noble firm. "You had it made," he chided me as we left, and I had strong doubts that I would be eating lunch in the Paramount commissary anytime soon.

One lesson I learned from this was that in Hollywood, old school ties could strangle you to death. Accordingly, although the fledgling producer son of the new owner of Twentieth Century

Fox was right behind me at Harvard Business School, I didn't dare mention it when I met him through his interest in optioning one of my books. Ah, these studio heads. What characters they were. If Charles Blühdorn was a piece of work, Marvin Davis, the Fox man, was a labor of Hercules. Davis was a Denver-based oil wildcatter who had made so much money during the Arab oil crisis of the 1970s that he was flush enough to buy the film studio run for decades by that celluloid wildcatter Darryl F. Zanuck. It was the prize for the man who had everything.

If the phrase *oil wildcatter* conjures up wildly romantic notions of Jett Rink, the oily rags to Texas riches character James Dean portrayed so unforgettably in *Giant,* think again. Marvin Davis was the son of a Seventh Avenue *garmento,* a privileged Jewish prep like Jeff Katzenberg who went to Horace Mann and NYU. But Davis cultivated a legend, which was aided by his enormity, in every sense. The man was gargantuan, six feet four and 350 pounds, and ravenous, sitting in meetings and eating mayonnaise from a large jar with his bare fingers, ordering the entire menu for all of his Spago dinners, his bodyguard team arriving before him with a thronelike chair that would accommodate his Falstaffian proportions. Here was a man too big to fail.

Marvin Davis's father, Jack Davis, was a British sailor who washed ashore in New York in his teens. He had lied his way into the Royal Navy after fleeing home when his mother insisted he train to become a rabbi. Instead he ended up in the rag trade and built a large low-cost fashion house called Jay Day Dresses. Marvin Davis grew up in Upper West Side affluence. At Horace Mann the sleek, tall, blond Davis was known as "Marv the Suave." On one of the family's winter vacations at Miami's Roney Plaza, which was to garment czars in the 1930s what the Hotel du Cap would become to film czars, Jack Davis met a cardsharp-hustler from Indiana named Ray Ryan, one of whose hustles was oil wells in his hometown of Evansville, which happened to be sitting atop a rich field. Davis took a shot with Ryan, and he hit two wells in a row. It seemed much easier than schlepping samples on Seventh Avenue, and Jack refocused his energy on energy, partnering with Ryan and bringing in a lot of his *garmento* friends as investors.

Jack Davis began drilling all around the country and eventually relocated to the oil-rich cow town of Denver, where he lived the life of a Rocky Mountain squire, the toast of the Brown Palace Hotel. Meanwhile, Marv the Suave thought it would be an adventure to join the oil rush. He apprenticed to Ryan in Evansville and later around the country. Evansville, for all its potential wealth, could not contain men like Ryan and young Davis, who learned as much about high life as about oil from his new mentor.

Ryan himself, who would eventually split from the Davises, used his card and oil winnings to become one of the leading developers of Palm Springs in the 1950s, palling around with desert rats Sinatra and Martin and Crosby and selling an estate to Clark Gable. He was best man at singer Patti Page's 1956 wedding and the chief backer of William Holden's Mount Kenya Safari Club. Marvin Davis could only have been wowed by Ryan's celebrity connections. Always the high roller who ran in the highest Mafia gambling circles, Ryan was killed in an unsolved but suspected gangland slaying in 1977 when he turned on the ignition of his brand-new Lincoln Continental Mark V and the car exploded, almost exactly like the failed attempt on the Robert De Niro Vegas boss character in Scorsese's *Casino*.

Having grown up in such fast company, Davis would inevitably find Denver too slow. He was married to a nice Long Island Jewish girl he had met in New York after college, had a family, and was the biggest fish in the Mile High pond. But it was not enough for a man of his appetites. When his father passed away in 1979, the wildcatter was ready to go tomcatting. He had been spending winters in Palm Springs and had caught the Hollywood bug. His first star friends in the desert were Lucille Ball and her husband, Gary Morton, a former Borscht Belt comic who laughed all the way to the bank as the head of Lucy's own gusher, Desilu Productions.

Davis, who had already bought a theater in Denver and had his kids making popcorn at the concession stand, now thought, Why not just buy a studio. Furthermore, the boom days of oil were over. Prices were declining, and Davis was being sued for hundreds of millions by insurance giant Aetna for allegedly duping them to join him in oil explorations that came nowhere close to his promises. A master salesman, Davis was able to dump nearly a thousand wells for $700 million to Canadian distiller Hiram Walker, which subsequently also cried foul. But Davis was Teflon. He had taken the money and run to Fox. He bought the studio in 1981 for around $750 million, almost all of which was borrowed money.

Not that Marvin Davis would have ever dreamed of using his own money, no matter how much he had. To buy Fox, Davis lined up two partners, two very cagey partners with whom he had done some big oil deals. These were the world's two sharpest oil traders, Marc Rich and Pincus Green, two names that would later go down in the caginess hall of infamy. Rich and Green, both raised as Orthodox Jews, had made billions trading with Islamic dictators during the Arab oil crisis. They were the particular darlings of the despotic America hater Iranian Ayatollah Khomeini, for despite being as opposite as humans could be, they made each other rich beyond anyone's dreams of avarice.

Although Marc Rich had also gone to a New York prep school (the down-market Rhodes, alma mater of Robert De Niro and James Caan) and was only a few years behind Marvin Davis at NYU, the future Fox partners arrived there by totally divergent routes, Rich's being the rockiest of roads. Born Marcell Reich in Antwerp, Belgium, Marc Rich seemed always in flight. His father

had fled the czar's pogroms in Galicia to Frankfurt, from which
he then fled Hitler's persecutions to Belgium, then to Marseilles,
Casablanca, and, of all places, Kansas City, where Marcell, now
Marc, went, pre-Rhodes, to school and summer camp with hu-
morist Calvin Trillin, who was impressed with Rich's fluency
in multiple foreign languages. Those language skills also served
Rich's father, who was a trader in global commodities, selling
burlap bags to Bolivian tin miners and Bengali jute to American
burlap makers. The U.S. Army needed lots of burlap during the
Korean War, and that demand made the Riches rich enough to
flee once again, trading the wild frontier of Kansas City for the
adjacent urbanity of Forest Hills, Queens.

Marc Rich was even more bored at NYU than Jeff Katzenberg
would be. There was no way to keep the boy down at Washington Square once he tasted the action on the floor of Philipp
Brothers, Wall Street's and the world's biggest commodities traders. Rich's father was successful enough to have contacts with the
venerable old-guard German Jewish firm, but no contacts could
exempt any new hire from starting in the mailroom, just as Barry
Diller had at William Morris. At the firm, later to be known as
Phibro, Rich bonded with Pincus "Pinky" Green, an uneducated
math genius whose family had fled to Brooklyn in the midst of
the carnage of the Russian Revolution. Pinky Green, whose father lost all his savings from his grocery business during the Depression, had dropped out of high school to work as a Seventh
Avenue garment stockboy, so he knew how to talk *schmattes* when
he eventually met Marv the Suave. But Philipp spotted Pinky's
talent with numbers and logistics and let him into the mailroom,
from whence he soared to the top of the firm's European operations in Zug, Switzerland, outside of Zurich.

Pinky Green remained a scholarly, rabbinical backroom wizard;
Rich was the pair's worldly front man and Marvin Davis–style
bon vivant. The first market Marc Rich would corner was mer-

cury, a key component in not only thermometers but bomb detonators. The cold war of the 1950s, with its demand to stockpile bombs, made mercury Marc a star at Philipp, which dispatched Rich to Bolivia, then to South Africa, and then made him their man in Havana right after Castro took power in order to protect their investment in a pyrite mine that Castro had nationalized. Rich and Castro hit it off famously, and Rich developed his taste for Cohibas.

Despite America's trade embargo, the Belgian-passported Rich was able to evade restrictions by doing the deals through the firm's Madrid office, which Rich came to head in 1964. If this sounds like something out of *Goldfinger,* it was. In the 1960s, the firm was taken over by metals king Charles Engelhard, Ian Fleming's dear friend and inspiration for Auric Goldfinger. Engelhard, loving the joke, nicknamed the chief stewardess on his private jet Pussy Galore. He doted on his stars Rich and Green and resembled Marvin Davis in his appetites, supposedly dying at fifty-four from an overdose of Coca-Cola, of which he apparently drank crates a day.

It wasn't all wheeling and dealing. In Madrid, the aquiline, Savile Row–dapper Rich met a sexy Boston University hippie dropout named Denise Eisenberg from Rust Belt Worcester, Massachusetts, and married her in 1966. Denise's father was a Holocaust survivor who became a shoe manufacturer in America. Their émigré roots, and their aspirations to conquer the world their families had fled, gave the lovebirds a lot in common. Denise had musical talent and wanted to be the next Joan Baez. In her dreams, perhaps, but Marc Rich saw in Fox the perfect opportunity for billionaire showbiz dreams to come true.

It was the Arabs who set Rich and Green free from Philipp, made them tycoons, and threw them into the bear hug of Marvin Davis. The people running Fox in 1981 who made the sale to Davis, Rich, and Green were as different from their buyers as any

sellers could be. No one in Hollywood was less Hollywood than
Fox's chairman, Dennis Stanfill, living proof that you didn't have
to be Jewish to love owning the movies. Dennis Carothers Stanfill was born in Centerville, Tennessee, in 1927 and graduated from
Annapolis and Oxford, where he had gone on a Rhodes Scholarship. He followed the conventional power path to Wall Street and
Lehman Brothers, where he was recruited by the all-powerful
Chandler family, who owned the *Los Angeles Times,* to move west
and run the finances of their Times Mirror Company. He and his
family lived in San Marino, near the Huntington Library and
spiritually far removed from Hollywood.

But Hollywood has a way of getting its tentacles around the
most reluctant of victims. In 1969, Fox chairman Darryl Zanuck
anointed his son, Richard, to run the studio. Zanuck next, pour-
ing on all the charm, stole Stanfill from the Chandlers to support
twenty-four-year-old Richard on the business side of things. Oe-
dipal resentments soon surfaced, and in two years Darryl had
kicked the chip off the block. But very quickly after Darryl
axed Richard, the banker-heavy Fox board axed Darryl and
replaced him with Stanfill, one of their own. For a navy man and
a banker, Stanfill did amazingly well in pictures. He presided
over a Fox that produced *Star Wars* and *Alien.* But there was always the question of credit where credit was not due, and most of
Hollywood gave that credit not to Stanfill but to one of their
own, Stanfill's studio chief, Alan Ladd Jr., who just happened to
be the best childhood friend of the ousted Richard Zanuck.

In 1979, Laddie took that credit and ran to start his own production company, based at Warner Bros., and Stanfill replaced
him with another of *his* own, the former Allen & Company investment banker Alan Hirschfield. The idea that Hollywood was
a world of its own, the world of our fathers, with studios run
by self-made rag traders was rebutted by the presence of Joseph

Kennedy in showbiz in the twenties and had become an anach-
ronism with the death of the first generation of moguls. Big
Establishment businessmen were always in Hollywood; the
business-focused eighties just made them even more dominant.
Nowhere is the clash between Old Hollywood and New, between the Hollywood of the gut and the Hollywood of the head,
better illustrated than in the persona of Alan Hirschfield.

Even though Alan Hirschfield was an Oklahoma "country
Jewboy" à la Kinky Friedman, he always knew he was destined
for Wall Street. He was born with friends in high places. His father, Norman, and Charles Allen were both runners on Wall
Street in the golden years before the Crash of '29. Both had pros-
pered, Charles Allen founding the media's favorite financier,
Allen & Company, and Norman Hirschfield setting off for the
heartland to make his fortune in natural gas and other ventures
that flowed from that wealth.

Alan Hirschfield, born in 1935, stayed home for college, where
he was a big man on campus at the University of Oklahoma. He
got his first taste of show business directing the *Sooner Scandals*
variety show. He went east to Harvard Business School, then took
his inevitable place at Allen & Company only slightly under
Charles Allen's nephew and the firm's heir apparent, Herbert Allen. The two young men were like family. When Herbert Allen
graduated from Williams in 1962, he married a Smithie from
Oklahoma City whose father was the Hirschfields' family doctor
and whose sister was an old flame of Alan's. At the Oklahoma City
nuptial festivities, the Hirschfields hosted a round of lavish events
for the visiting Wall Streeters. Oklahoma Jewry proved to be a
fertile recruiting ground for future Wall Street leaders. Henry
Kravis would soon come out of Tulsa to Columbia Business School
to take his place at the high table of private equity kings.

Early on in his career at Allen & Company, Alan Hirschfield

was put on the entertainment desk. Allen & Company were the chief financial advisers to Jack Warner, and one of Hirschfield's first tasks at the firm was to handle the sale of Frank Sinatra's share of Warner Records back to the parent company. He became friends with Sinatra in the course of the deal, and he also become closely acquainted with the Allens' favorite Hollywood client, Ray Stark. Known as "the Rabbit" because of both his sexual voracity and his buck teeth, Stark was a Rutgers flunk-out and a former Forest Lawn funeral florist turned agent of such stars as William Holden and Ava Gardner. The Rabbit struck conjugal gold by marrying Frances Brice, daughter of vaudeville legend Fanny Brice. He then became Mr. Funny Girl; he seemed to own Barbra Streisand, and that gave him immense power. Hirschfield tried to broker a merger between Stark's production company Seven Arts and Filmways, the vehicle of producer Martin Ransohoff, whose TV smashes *The Beverly Hillbillies, Petticoat Junction,* and *Green Acres* had enabled him to begin producing more ambitious nonbarnyard feature fare like Evelyn Waugh's *The Loved One.*

Hirschfield proved not to be much of a matchmaker. Stark and Ransohoff couldn't stand each other. Stark was old school, Ransohoff the precursor of a new breed of educated, analytic businessman-producers. Born in New Orleans, the son of a prominent coffee broker, Ransohoff went to Colgate and then into advertising on Madison Avenue before making the first page of *The Wall Street Journal* as the youngest man ever to take an entertainment company public.

While Ransohoff was taking Filmways public, Stark was doing his best to keep private some of his darker associations at Seven Arts. The darkest of a dark lot was a behemoth Canadian stock promoter of Marvin Davis proportions named Louis "Uncle Lou" Chesler, who gave a special meaning to the expression "big in Hollywood." Chesler, who for a while was actually Stark's boss and board chairman of Seven Arts, was considered by the FBI to be a close associate of Jewish Godfather Meyer Lansky and got Seven Arts involved in the deeply murky world of casino development in the Bahamas in the 1950s. However, with the help of Charles Allen and the other great movie banker Serge Semenenko of the First National Bank of Boston, Stark managed to sanitize Seven Arts by easing Chesler off the board and getting the company's shares listed on the American Stock Exchange. Ray Stark had thus had his escutcheon effectively laundered, and he now sat at the high table of Hollywood statesmen. Martin Ransohoff, who was of the "above reproach" business school, still wanted no part of Stark; Hirschfield's attempted big setup fell through.

One failed deal did not a failure make. Alan Hirschfield's Hollywood studio odyssey, propelled by the Allens, was only just beginning. In 1967 they sent him to Warner Brothers, when they engineered the sale of Jack Warner's stock and merged Warner Bros. with Seven Arts, effectively making Ray Stark the new Jack Warner. But Stark was happy now just being Stark, so he left the company and set up his independent shingle at Columbia, leaving Hirschfield to go back to New York and the Allen mother ship.

These were the go-go years of takeover mania, with Transamerica Corporation buying United Artists and ex–bush pilot Kirk Kerkorian buying MGM and ex–funeral director Steve Ross's upstart Kinney National Services buying Warner Bros., with the Allens handling the deal for the sellers. In that period, Columbia had been taken over by Geritol tycoon Matthew "Matty" Rosenhaus, but by 1973 no amount of Geritol could energize that studio's tired blood. Its stock plunging, the company faced bankruptcy. This gave the Allens a chance to be even more powerful. Guided by Ray Stark, the top dog on the lot, they took a controlling interest and sent Alan Hirschfield out west again to be Columbia's chief executive.

But Hirschfield was basically a square Oklahoma B-school guy, with no natural instincts for show business. So he hired two of the biggest operators in the business, David Begelman, felon-to-be, to run the movies, and Clive Davis, felon-that-was, to run the music. Davis had been fired from CBS Records for allegedly charging his son's lavish bar mitzvah as a business expense and was also indicted for tax evasion, for which he got a suspended prison sentence. But Begelman, who was Stark's pick, and Davis, both were major players who got big results. Who was Hirschfield to look behind the balance sheets?

If only he had. When Begelman was exposed for forging the checks of Cliff Robertson and others, Hirschfield's basic instinct was to fire him. But this was Hollywood, where the only real crime was a box office flop. David Begelman had brought Columbia back from the dead with hits like *Shampoo* and *Close Encounters,* so Stark convinced the Allens to forgive and to forget and to fire Alan Hirschfield as Hollywood's party pooper. That, of course, made Hirschfield the perfect man for Fox's party pooper in chief, Dennis Stanfill, who quickly hired Hirschfield in 1979 to run the studio under him.

About a year after assuming his tenure, Hirschfield discovered another party to poop on. The partyer was Fox's head of television, Harris Katleman, like Hirschfield a midwestern Jew who made good in the entertainment world. Born in Omaha, Katleman had come to UCLA for college, then, as a distant cousin of Mark Goodson, got a job with the game show king in New York. He was so successful selling shows like *The Price Is Right* and *To Tell the Truth* that MGM hired him to come back west to run their TV division. From there he was stolen away by Columbia TV and eventually by Hirschfield himself to Fox TV. How Hollywood loved to shuffle the same deck. If they already knew you, they kept wanting to know you, no matter what they knew about you. Familiarity bred success.

And success bred arrogance. Eagle eye Stanfill had been checking Katleman's expense reports and claimed that en route to a TV conference in Monaco, Katleman had stopped in Paris and had some personal joie de vivre, allegedly about $2,500 worth, at Fox's expense. Stanfill wanted to turn this into Begelgate II. But Hirschfield, chastened from his experience in trying to censure Begelman, did an about-face and took the Hollywood position of "What's wrong with a few meals at Tour d'Argent and a little shopping at Hermès? It takes a bit of indulgence to make great art."

Hirschfield's newly tolerant position put him sharply at odds with by-the-book navy man Stanfill; when Marvin Davis took control of the studio, the high liver of course sided with Hirschfield, especially because Katleman's numbers were so good. If they had been bad, the alleged defalcation would have been a good excuse to fire him, but his division was thriving, far more so than the film division. So out Stanfill went. And Hirschfield, who perhaps had finally gotten religion Hollywood style, succeeded him as Fox chairman and CEO, of course under Marvin Davis, which was a heavy weight to be under.

Groaning most painfully under the Davis avoirdupois was Hirschfield's production chief Sherry Lansing. Lansing's appointment had been hailed by the press as a great leap forward for womankind in the unkind boys' club that Hollywood had historically been. However, Lansing found that her supposed power was far more ceremonial than actual. Lansing, born Sherry Lee Duhl, had come from Chicago, studied at Northwestern, and taught arithmetic in the Watts ghetto. At the same time, she was a Max Factor cover girl and won bit parts in two films, *Loving* with George Segal and *Rio Lobo* with John Wayne. Like the boys in Hollywood, Lansing had bounced around the studios but never out, from MGM to Columbia and now to the presidency of production at Fox. Bouncing with her was her mentor, Dan

Melnick, a close ally of Hirschfield's in the Columbia debacle with Begelman. Hirschfield had rewarded Melnick's loyalty by giving Melnick's IndieProd Company an unprecedentedly lucrative ten-year deal at Fox. No wonder Harris Katleman's fun in Paris was seen as less than a trifle by comparison.

There is a Hollywood legend that when Davis first met Sherry Lansing, he dispatched her to bring him some coffee. Or was it mayonnaise? The joke, on her, was that he thought his new toy's production chief was called Jerry Lansing, so he was expecting a guy. Even when he was disabused of his sexist presumptions, he still called Ms. Lansing "Dollface." Davis quickly got into the Hollywood game, renting a bungalow at the Beverly Hills Hotel for a million a year, until he eventually bought the Knoll from singer Kenny Rogers for $20 million. Until Aaron Spelling built his Holmby Hills monstrosity, the Knoll was the biggest house in L.A. And Davis was the biggest man.

Showing off his bigness, he put his famous pals like Henry Kissinger and Gerald Ford on the Fox board. He would have lunch in the Fox commissary with favorite stars like Mel Brooks and began treating the studio like his oil company, putting insiders like Kissinger and George Lucas in on his "can't miss" oil wells, which, alas, more often went dry. So did the movies that Davis assumed would become blockbusters: Kenny Rogers's *Six Pack,* the Dolly Parton–Sly Stallone *Rhinestone,* the John Travolta–Olivia Newton-John *Two of a Kind,* all big-time disasters. At the Knoll, Davis had a museum-quality collection of French paintings. Walking his guests through the mansion, he had a favorite joke. Want to see the most expensive picture I ever bought? he'd ask his guests. And instead of a Cézanne or a Degas, he'd show them, on another wall, a poster for the $19 million *Rhinestone.* Monet was no match for Sly.

An even bigger publicity disaster befell Fox when Davis's partners, Marc Rich and Pinky Green, came under the scrutiny of the hyperzealous then federal prosecutor Rudolph Giuliani. In 1983, Giuliani indicted both men for illegal trading with Iran, circumventing the U.S. boycott during the hostage crisis, and massive income tax evasion. It was the biggest tax evasion charge in history. The indictment came down while Rich and Green were in Switzerland. Neither would return to the United States to face the music. The low-profile pair quickly rose to prominence on the FBI's Ten Most Wanted Fugitives list. The government froze their American assets, including their huge share of Fox.

The Rich-Green affair was deeply embarrassing to Fox, especially board members like Kissinger and Ford. But Marvin Davis, who did not know the meaning of shame, saw it as only one more oil well to drill. He made an offer to the Justice Department, which was holding the stock, for the very distressed price of $116 million. Justice wasn't a stockbroker. It merely wanted to unload its holdings and have something to show, for it was certain it would never see Rich and Green again (and it wouldn't, even after the pardon that was the second-most shameful act of the Clinton presidency). So Justice took the offer, and within two years Davis would flip the shares to Rupert Murdoch for $162 million. There were no regrets.

Dennis Stanfill may have left Fox, but he didn't go quietly. He sued Fox and Davis for $22 million for breaching his contract and for sanctioning what he considered to be Katleman's fraudulent behavior. His lawsuit in turn triggered a Los Angeles District Attorney's Office probe into white-collar crime at the studios. The probe got headlines, but it went nowhere. No status quo anywhere, even Wall Street's, is as immutable as Hollywood's. Yes, the task force's report noted, there were indeed expense account "discrepancies." But they weren't "material" enough to warrant prosecution. What would have been material enough was not defined.

Perhaps later in the decade, when Jon Peters was accused of using a studio jet to deliver a planeload of flowers to New York when he was courting supermodel Vendela, maybe, just maybe, law enforcement might have found that de trop. But by then there were no Stanfill-like curmudgeons in the game to blow the whistle.

# CHAPTER 7
## STRANGE BEDFELLOWS

ONE OF THE SADDEST COMMENTARIES on the state and status of women in Hollywood in the 1980s was the exalted state and high status of a procuress named Alex Adams, otherwise known as Madam Alex, madam to the stars. No unlisted phone number in Los Angeles was more coveted, and not just by stars and moguls and other players in the "industry," as the film business was known, but also by the players in real, "heavy" industry, the kind that made things like planes and oil, as well as by the financiers who bankrolled all these industries, not to mention the politicians who greased the wheels that turned the machines of money. Madam Alex's estate on Stone Canyon Road, just up from the Hotel Bel-Air, was an exclusive Elysium that was one of the few venues in L.A. where these diverse tycoons could actually cross-fertilize, as it were, a middle-aged, New World take on the playing fields of Eton. Laying fields was more to the point.

Madam Alex had a revolving roster of about five hundred MAW (model actress whatever) lovelies to dispatch to these lords of capital. She called these charges her "creatures." The term ostensibly referred to their extraordinary beauty, in a town and a world where beauty was the coin of the realm. But this period was the heyday of plastic surgery, and many of these creatures were less of the *Vogue* variety than that of Dr. Frankenstein. The Hugh Hefner silicone Playmate was the local standard of beauty. Neither Audrey nor Katharine Hepburn need have applied, as they would not have been appreciated, though Alex always kept a few offbeat types on her rolls for iconoclastic clients. A number of her girls went on to become movie stars, "discovered" by the star makers to whom Alex had introduced them. Others married millionaires, some billionaires. Most, however, vanished into obscurity, leaving on those proverbial midnight trains to Georgia.

No one could blame Madam Alex for the glaring paucity of decent roles for women in eighties films, but her presence at the pinnacle of women in film spoke volumes about the predominating bad-boy sexist culture of this money decade, which would be capped by *Pretty Woman* as its poster film, with Julia Roberts as an idealized hooker and Richard Gere as an idealized tycoon. Story of our lives, the players would say. Ironically, Julia Roberts herself would barely have stood out on Madam Alex's roster of flesh and fantasy.

The few women in theoretical positions of movie power didn't really have very much. Sherry Lansing was the moguls' geisha, Dawn Steel their gun moll. Neither could give a green light. On the other hand, the red light of Madam Alex was the beacon that glowed brightest for the male "deciders," whose basic view of the opposite sex was a glittering trinket that could be purchased for the top dollar that was the measure of the male Angeleno. That emblematic "women's film" of the era, *Thelma & Louise,* was less an anthem of empowerment than a suicidal cry for help.

If a hooker was the eighties' poster girl, the poster boy for the period was the Master of the Universe, the Marvel Comics caricature that Tom Wolfe turned into his lead character in *Bonfire of the Vanities.* Michael Lewis, in nonfiction, anointed the same creature the "big swinging dick." These were Wall Street guys, big-money guys, but their DNA was straight out of Hollywood. Or, more accurately, 1980s Los Angeles, which had become the ultimate melting pot of swaggering, swinging, untrammeled all-powerful wealth that perfectly complemented the mythology of the blockbuster action heroes of this *Die Hard* decade, heroes who turned the film business into big business as well as into the world's most glamorous virtual casino.

In the film industry itself, the real-life action heroes were the stop-at-nothing producers who put those stars up on the screen, while the studio heads these producers had to supplicate were nothing short of gods. But there was more to the industry than the industry. The swagger and big swinging dickishness (cockiness, indeed) that came to be personified by the likes of Eddie Murphy and Tom Cruise and Bruce Willis and then adopted by the Wolfeian Wall Streeters, had been internalized by the Hollywood dream makers from the high financiers in their own palm latitudes. In the new age of Reagan, the traditional separation between big business and show business, akin to church and state, no longer applied.

For most of the twentieth century, Los Angeles was all about Jew versus non-Jew. The film industry may have had its lots in Burbank, but its soul, if that weren't an oxymoron, was in Beverly Hills. Money and banking, and oil and aerospace, and all other businessy things that made Southern California rich were on the Pasadena–San Marino–Hancock Park axis. The gentile elite of California were, if anything, far more intolerant of Jews than the New York Establishment. After all, some of the great banking houses on Wall Street were Jewish: Lehman Brothers, Goldman Sachs. Jews learned, and mastered, the WASP game of mobility through an Ivy League education and eventually beat the WASPs at it. Assimilated Jewish social climbers like August Belmont had managed to get themselves into the "400" and into Mrs. Astor's ballroom.

Not so the Jews of Hollywood, of whom the western tycoons like the Sinclair and Doheny oil kings of the Teapot Dome scandal, or the all-powerful Chandlers, who owned the *Los Angeles Times,* wanted no truck, or Cadillac. The elite Jews of Manhattan had their own Harmonie Club, if they couldn't get into the Knickerbocker or the Union. The Jews of Hollywood had only golf at Hillcrest, with no purely social club that would compensate for their exclusion from the California Club downtown. Elite education was far less of a passport to aristocracy than it was in the East, where the "mobility schools" of the Ivy League were located. For Hollywood Jewish dynasties, the Warners, the Mayers, the Goldwyns, living well at the Ritz or the George V was the best revenge, and the only one.

The rise of Ronald Reagan changed all that. Money, in effect, became America's creed, and the old caste and class system crumbled in the wake of leveraged, junk-bonded wealth the country had never seen before, not even in the Roaring Twenties. The stock exchange became the country's established church, where all were free to worship. Reagan's diverse, ecumenical kitchen cabinet said it all: There were Jews and gentiles, upper crusts and arrivistes, all united by massive success and to some extent by a fascination with show business and celebrity. Movies somehow became the country's new religion, where the cineplex overwhelmed the church and the gods of celluloid overwhelmed the god of heaven. The old-time religion was simply not good enough anymore.

Just as America in the eighties became obsessed with the film business, the rulers of the film business themselves were far less obsessed with the films they were making than with the money these films would make for them—and, in turn, all the fantasy sex that blockbusters could win or buy. Movies had always been about money, and they had always been about "pussy," but in the eighties, it was a clear case of now more than ever. A young producer once asked the decade's blockbuster king Don Simpson what was the most important lesson he might impart to this aspiring Selznick. The advice, it turned out, had nothing to do with budget, stars, directors, release dates, concepts, or anything connected with making films. It was about making love, not cinema.

If your movie has sex scenes, never shoot them until the last two days of production, Simpson told the acolyte, confounding him massively. What did that have to do with the price of tickets? the young man asked, puzzled. Because, Simpson explained as if the fellow were retarded, that way you had the maximum window of opportunity to tell wannabe starlets that you might be able to cast them and avail yourself of all the exploitative pleasures that such casting might yield. For Simpson, as well as so many of his fellow moguls, the religion of movies was basically all about the pussy. Not that Simpson depended solely on the casting couch for his amours. With an insatiable appetite for sex, he was one of the most addicted customers of Madam Alex, who could have established her own personal Twelve Step program.

The high priestess of this Dionysus-goes-Hollywood cult was one of the most unlikely high priestesses in the history of worshipping false gods. Her original name was Alexandra Kuntze, born in Manila in 1933 to a prosperous German butcher who was considered the meat king of the Philippines and, as such, the antecedent of a line of purveyors of quality flesh. Not that Alex, as she was known, had any dream her fortune would be made in those dark precincts. Her mother, a charter member of the Spanish colonial aristocracy, sent her to a posh and proper Catholic finishing school called Holy Ghost.

When World War II broke out, Alex's father could have used his German roots to forge an Axis connection to the occupying Japanese. But he refused. A staunch patriot, he ended up in a concentration camp. After the war, Alex's mother, terrified that her daughter would lose her virginity to a triumphant American GI, sent her to live with an uncle in Japan. Frau Kuntze apparently overlooked the fact that the American GIs were occupying Japan as well. Within a year, young Alex, who had cottoned to the American soldiery, was safely back in Manila at the conventlike Maryknoll College. At this point Alex was extremely multilingual, English, Spanish, Japanese, German, Tagalog, and Chinese, a fluency that would later put her in wonderful stead with the melting pot of big global money, whose idolatrous minds became the devil's workshop in eighties Los Angeles.

Her parents divorced after the dislocations of war, and Alex and her brother were taken to San Francisco by their mother in 1951 to start a new life in America. On the *President Wilson* coming over, Alex, then eighteen, met her first Hollywood mogul, Howard Strickling, Louis B. Mayer's fabled publicity genius at MGM, the man who had "made" Garbo, Leigh, Hepburn, and so many other stars. The flirty Strickling told the cute eighteen-year-old the definition of a wolf: a man who will protect a fair lady from everyone—except himself.

Alex loved the new world, but she felt smothered by her old-world mother. Somewhat akin to her French counterpart Madame Claude, whose first job was selling bibles door-to-door, Alex also went to work for the Catholic Church, taking a position as housekeeper to the priest of the Oakland parish. Having been pampered her whole life, Alex loved the idea of pampering a man, even if there was no future in it. It was at the parish residence that she honed her great skills in flower arranging and cooking. By 1953, Alex, ready for something secular, moved by herself to Los Angeles and took a job as a receptionist in a sub–Arthur Murray Hollywood dance studio. Soon she met a bright young physicist in the aerospace industry headquartered in L.A. They married, had two kids, lived in a big Spanish colonial house in Los Feliz down the street from Cecil B. DeMille, and drove a boaty Cadillac with huge tail fins.

Alex's Eisenhower-era idyll lasted eight years, ending soon after John Kennedy was elected. The physicist was anything but combustible, preferring to sit at home at night watching Lawrence Welk and Ed Sullivan rather than seeing the real thing in the nightclubs of the Sunset Strip. After her divorce, Alex, who loved to work, took a job running the flower shop at the Ambassador Hotel, best known for its nightclub, the Cocoanut Grove. At the hotel, Alex met her second husband, an Austrian importer-exporter. They settled down in another big mansion, this one in Hancock Park, near the hotel, where Alex continued flowering.

In 1971, Alex's flowering evolved, or devolved, into deflowering. One of her clients, a very ritzy English dog breeder, called her to ask if she might be interested in buying her business. What do I know about dogs? Alex demurred. Actually, it wasn't the dog business she was selling, the woman said. It was her madam business. Alex was floored, without necessarily being insulted. In her homeland of the Philippines, prostitution was an accepted way of life. But why me? Alex asked. The woman, who wanted to devote herself exclusively to pets, and not of the *Penthouse* variety, said she had been impressed with Alex's charm, people skills, and singular telephone manner. She also had learned that Alex's husband was ill; there were, she said, virtues in being able to sell vice from home.

This woman, who turned tricks as well as arranged them, wanted $5,000 for her "book" of twenty-five clients (no one famous) and five working girls (no one fabulous). The going rate was then $100 an hour. Alex would need to arrange only fifty dates to break even. Alex had just received a $5,000 insurance check for cracks in her house from the 1971 6.6 Sylmar earthquake. She signed the check over to the seller and suddenly was in a whole new business.

Alas, those fifty tricks did not come easy. The reason, it turned out, for the former owner's motivation to sell was that most of the men were getting old, too old to cut the mustard anymore, as the

1950s country classic, famously covered by Marlene Dietrich, went. Nor were her damsels Dietrichs, but rather salesgirls and bank tellers out to earn a little extra pin money. To succeed, or at least to break even, Alex needed new blood. She found it from a client at the flower shop, a construction millionaire who ran with the Hillcrest Country Club set that constituted the Hollywood elite. The contractor gave Alex a list of players but forbade her to use his name. Just cold-call them, he suggested.

To heat up those cold calls, Alex knew she needed more distaff talent than she currently possessed. Thus she began recruiting at her beauty parlor, Pagano's on Wilshire Boulevard. In the small world of Hollywood, Pagano's belonged to the family of the mother of Jon Peters, who would cut his own lothario teeth at the salon, the teeth that would bite Barbra Streisand. Jon Peters, who would rival Don Simpson in the eighties blockbuster sweepstakes, would, like Simpson, become a dear friend and confidant of Alex. When Streisand was preparing to play a fancy prostitute accused of manslaughter in *Nuts,* Peters took the diva straight to the source, to learn the tricks of the trick trade from Alex and her charges. Alas, all the authenticity was for naught. *Nuts* bombed. But the Streisand tutorial showed how accepted Alex was in the Tinseltown firmament. Having tea with Alex and her cats was just as much an obligatory stop on the insider's power tour as going to a screening at Robert Evans's.

At the beginning, before she became an institution, Alex, who had a sweet, ingratiating manner, kept an eye on which young women were wearing wedding rings and which weren't and invited the latter to her impeccably furnished home to reassure them that she wasn't some white slaver or a sinister madam like the one Dietrich embodied in *Touch of Evil*. Once her targets were reassured, she would tell them how much money they could make for sleeping with important men they would be thrilled to meet under any circumstances.

A lot of these girls were hippies, girls who ate at the Aware Inn and hung out at the Whisky a Go Go and whose fantasies ran more to Jim Morrison than Robert Evans, or the agents and executives in suits whom the contractor had Alex cold-call. Alex, the Manila Pygmalion, would give these girls makeovers and turn them into Sharon Tate look-alikes. In her first year in business, 1972, Alex was a hit.

The 1970s were boom years for Alex's new business. First, the 1973 OPEC oil embargo made the Arabs the richest people on the planet. The most sybaritic of them began buying mansions in Los Angeles and living like burnoosed versions of the Beverly Hillbillies, or what they thought were movie stars. That lifestyle included hiring top-dollar call girls. The Arabs were the opposite of price-sensitive. The more they paid, the better they assumed the purchase was, and Alex was delighted to cater to these assumptions. After the rich Arabs came the rich Persians, in droves after the fall of the shah in 1979. Beverly Hills was their fantasy as well, as L.A. became known as Tehrangeles, and the pinnacle of that fantasy was the California blonde.

The third new high-rolling constituency in L.A. in the seventies were the Milkenites, the junk bond specialists from Michael Milken's Drexel Burnham. Milken, a Valley Boy who went to Wharton but was always homesick, moved his high-yield operation from Wall Street to Beverly Hills in 1978. Although Milken himself, with his bad toupee and rumpled suits, seemed to be an exercise in supersquare sublimation, his acolytes had money to burn, and nothing could light them up like Madam Alex. If the Milkenites, more than anyone of the era, made big money sexy, what sexier way to spend that big money than on sex itself?

And spend they did. Milken's mythic presence on Wilshire Boulevard as the oracle of leverage made Beverly Hills a new mecca of high finance for swashbuckling corporate raiders from all over the world, who came to do huge deals with Drexel. These high financiers, the "big swinging dicks," could find no better place to swing them than chez Alex, or Casa Pussy, as her Bel-Air manse was known. A visit to Alex was as integral a part of the money tour of L.A. as Milken's annual Predators' Ball. The Milken money mania was highly contagious, infecting in particular the movie people, who were also growing exponentially rich with their creation of the blockbuster, which was to Hollywood what the junk bond was to Wall Street. They, too, had more money to burn, and Alex provided them with delectable tinder.

The Casa Pussy appellation had a double entendre, referring not only to Alex's sleek two-legged "creatures," as she called her makeovers, but also to the dozens of four-legged felines that had become her obsession and to whom she accorded pride of place, even over the sheikhs and tycoons. Alex's second husband died soon after she started the business, although not from the shock of it all. He never knew. Everything Alex did was basically over the phone, except for meeting her charges at Pagano's, where they would slip her envelopes with her 40 percent cut. By the end of the 1970s, Alex had an active roster of over five hundred girls and a seven-figure bank account, not to mention extensive real estate holdings and a golden portfolio of stock tips from the Masters of the Universe.

Once widowed, Alex moved to a big beach house in Malibu and began entertaining. Almost as if to prevent herself from falling prey to the charms of her clients, she began putting on weight and dressing in very unsexy muumuu housecoats. It was all highly at odds with her elegant antiques, her fine art, her gourmet meals. But that was what eccentricity was all about, and her clients loved her for it. Alex became as sexless as her creatures were sexual. Instead of men, she surrounded herself with cats, countless cats. Still, she was witty and engaging and could talk endlessly to the rich and famous about what interested them more than anything else: themselves.

Alex thus became a unique, only-in-Hollywood character, something akin to what speakeasy queen Texas Guinan was in the Roaring Twenties. The Waco-born Mary Louise Cecilia Guinan had been the first movie cowgirl, known as "Queen of the West." She used her celluloid fame to bankroll New York's top Prohibition speakeasy, the 300 Club on West Fifty-fourth Street. What the 300 had that the 21 Club down the block did not was Guinan's troupe of forty half-naked fan dancers, with George Gershwin doing piano duties for a clientele that ranged from Vanderbilt to Valentino. Her trademark greeting to her rich and horny café society customers, whom she called "butter and egg men," was "Hello, suckers!" Madam Alex, in her muumuus, was running a similar show for the fat-cat "suckers" of her wild and crazy times.

Eventually, traffic and mud slides made Malibu too far and chancy a drive for men with tight schedules, and Alex moved to Stone Canyon Road, which couldn't have been more in media res. The only challenge to Alex's hegemony was the arrival of Madame Claude from Paris in 1980 to cash in on what was at the moment the hottest sexual market on earth. Everyone thought that Claude, with her genuine *nouveau pauvre* countesses and moonlighting Ford models, would blow Alex out of the business. Then again, everyone also thought that the arrival of branches of both the Stage and Carnegie Delis from New York would blow out Nate 'n Al's. Everyone underestimated, or misunderstood, what men in L.A. wanted. They wanted L.A., not Paris. They wanted Malibu beach girls, Playboy Mansion bunnies, Sunset Strip hippie goddesses. They didn't want aristocrats or haughty runway models. Class was never a major selling point in the brave nouveau world of Los Angeles. The battle of the supermadams ended up as no contest at all.

Knowing Madam Alex became a luxury status symbol, like an A-table at Spago, an account at Bijan (the world's most expensive clothier), a membership at Hillcrest, a Bentley. Usually, if you had one, you had them all. Except Alex was one connection no one flaunted. There were wives to consider, and alimony. And there was still the all-American macho "I don't have to pay for it" posture that most of Alex's foreign clients found quaint. Actually, Alex was less like the got-it-flaunt-it Spago than the real celebrity restaurants of L.A., secret speakeasy hideaways like the Steak Pit on Melrose Avenue, founded before Melrose became a West Coast version of London's King's Road. The Steak Pit had no sign, no listed number, and a door that was always locked. The owner was a former chef from Chasen's, and he served what he felt like, and not always steak. But it was the one place in town where you had high odds of spotting Cary Grant, if only you could get another regular like James Stewart or Joseph Cotten to take you in.

Another closed shop was the also unlisted, unmarked Irish pub known as Scollay's that was as dank and paneled as something in Galway but faked you out by being in a moderne dive motel called the Beverly Terrace. Owned by another former Chasenite, Scollay's served breakfast only, but it dispensed more alcohol in the morning than Chasen's did at night. Johnny Carson and Ed McMahon got drunk there almost every day. That was the closed world that Madam Alex was a part of, and a visit to one of these restaurants was often the prelude to an encounter with one of her creatures. Mere mortals needed not apply.

When I first came to Hollywood, Madam Alex occupied the same unreachable fantasy Valhalla as Cary Grant. Even though I knew Madame Claude through our book project, I entertained no hope whatsoever of meeting Madam Alex, who was as inaccessible as Howard Hughes. I knew Casa Pussy was on Stone Canyon, but I could never find out precisely where. The mystery was part of the exclusivity. The odds of getting invited to the White House seemed higher than getting into Casa Pussy.

It took me until the nineties to meet Madam Alex, once more over a book, and find out what I missed in the eighties. By then she had theoretically retired to a perfect antique-and-cat-filled designer cottage in Boys Town in West Hollywood. Of course, old madams never die, or even fade away. Now Madam Alex had become the brains behind the operation of her former acolyte, the Jewish princess turned madam Heidi Fleiss. Now names began to drop. They hadn't before, because outing someone as a client of prostitutes, itself only a misdemeanor, was still an accusation of a crime and, as such, subject to libel suits from powerful men whose attack dog lawyers no reporter would dare to cross.

But the superskinny, revved-up Heidi, a Holly Golightly on speed, was brazen. She bought Michael Douglas's mansion in Benedict Canyon across from the death house of Sharon Tate. She gave parties for Mick Jagger, where Jack Nicholson was the guest of honor. Nobody was accusing these stars of actually paying for sex, but if you judged someone by the company they kept . . . Alex herself was always cagey about the names. She was fully aware that only the dead could not sue. The sibyl of sex, she held court, surrounded by felines and former creatures, now glamorous Hollywood wives who came in Rollses for tea, the untellable tales of whose courtships were the stuff of miniseries.

No sex took place at Casa Pussy. This was no *maison de tolérance*. It was just an endless pool party, tea party, or cocktail party where the richest men could connect with the prettiest women. All the amour took place off premises, at the luxury hotels or the mansions, all under the radar, with the girls dropping by Casa Pussy day and night bearing their fat envelopes of tax-free cash that constituted Alex's finder's fees. It wasn't that different from William Morris or CAA, just off the books.

Legally, Alex's creatures were pretty much above the law, probably because physically they were below it. Alex was literally in bed with the LAPD, at its highest echelons. For all the indiscretions of the stars, the authorities of Los Angeles went a long, long way to preserve the mystique of its most important industry.

Outing VIPs had not yet become a global blood sport, so what went on, or was arranged, at Casa Pussy stayed at Casa Pussy. Madam Alex made a lot of women a lot of money, though this so-called financial empowerment was toxic to the image of women, as created by her Hollywood clientele. These men felt no need to *take* women seriously, not so long as they *paid* them seriously. Hugh Hefner had nothing on Alex when it came to objectifying women and pedestaling these objects. An old-fashioned woman from an old-fashioned society, Madam Alex was a major force in perpetuating the Hollywood culture of sexism.

Given Madam Alex's overlapping constituencies, it is interesting to try to determine who influenced whom. It wasn't as if the producers and the raiders and the Arabs were all at the same sex orgies at Casa Pussy and what emerged from all the ultraconfident ectoplasm was one prototypical swaggering übermensch. In fact, Alex rarely mixed her markets, and for the most part, all but the most exhibitionist of her famous clients were far too paranoid to be seen in the presence of anyone else. Yet cross-fertilization did occur, whether it was at Alex's or Morton's or just at separate banquettes in the Polo Lounge. Jon Peters, for one, developed a major man-crush on Michael Milken. Peters, who had made one small fortune in hair salons before making another large one in films, never ceased to view himself as a businessman, or that uniquely eighties hyphenate, the businessman-producer. He identified with Milken, who grew up close to where Peters did and had beaten similarly long odds to get to the top of the game.

Milken, however, saw himself not as Valley Boy but as Encino Man. Peters was dealing with millions, Milken trillions. Milken was anything but starstruck. He didn't have a crush on Peters or even on Barbra Streisand. Movies, until the conglomerates moved in later in the decade, weren't yet the big business they would become. Milken was dead serious, and deadly boring to the glitter crowd of Hollywood. But to Jon Peters, he was as alluring as

Clark Gable and Cary Grant put together. Peters, who thought he could seduce anyone, tried to get to Milken and work his magic. Alas, Milken avoided him completely and passed him down to his equivalent of a development boy, a young Clevelander and Whartonite named Terren Peizer, who was more impressed by showbiz than his spoilsport master.

Peters was a compulsive seducer. If he couldn't seduce Milken, he would seduce Peizer. And so he tried, doing the Hollywood dazzle routine: dining at Morton's, clubbing at Helena's, jetting to Aspen, dropping more names than Hedda and Louella combined. All Peters got from all his efforts was an introduction to a fringe businessman–producer named Burt Sugarman. Like Peters a local boy and self-made businessman, Sugarman had been a professional drag racer and a car dealer to the stars. Just as Peters had met Lesley Ann Warren and then Streisand through his blow-dryer, Sugarman, who looked like a slick game show host, met his women over the hoods of Maseratis and Excaliburs. He nearly married Ann-Margret, who broke off the engagement. He did marry *I Spy* TV bombshell Carol Wayne, and then *Entertainment Tonight* original anchor Mary Hart, whose legs were insured by Lloyd's of London for $1 million.

Sugarman had gotten into show business by teaming up with Pierre Cossette, who was Ann-Margret's manager and a Grammy Awards show producer. Sugarman and Cossette had a success with the late night rock show *The Midnight Special,* but it wasn't enough to keep Sugarman in Excaliburs. So he got into cement, not in the Mafia sense but by buying a factory that made the stuff in South Carolina. Nothing could have been less glamorous. Desperate to become a takeover artist somehow, Sugarman got in the door at Milken's Drexel and preceded Milken in drawing the scrutiny of the SEC. No charges were ever filed, however, and Sugarman was able to leverage himself into a controlling position at Chuck Barris Productions, which had created *The Gong Show* and *The Dating Game,* the springboard from which he was able to join forces with Jon Peters and his new partner, Peter Guber, whose production company would merge with Barris in 1987 and become Guber-Peters Entertainment, which in 1989 they would sell to Sony for hundreds of millions, in a Milkenesque tour de force of leverage.

In the 1980s mogul universe, wherever you were, someone else's grass was always greener. Wall Street guys wanted to go Holly-wood; Hollywood guys wanted to go Wall Street. If you look at Hollywood's "big swinging dicks," there was clearly a big business lust in the group. But who exactly were they? Don Simpson, who had no business interests of his own other than making his tril-lions in blockbusters, promulgated his list of "club members," the men who ruled Hollywood, in his notorious 1985 *Esquire* profile. "Simpson's List" was a compilation of the Groucho Marx school, one that no one wanted to be on. But here it was: Simpson's Para-mount execs Eisner and Katzenberg; David Geffen; Simpson's ICM agents Jeff Berg and Jim Wiatt; director Michael Mann; ac-tion producer Larry Gordon; Loews theater and hotel heir Steve Tisch; and executive Craig Baumgarten. Where was Jon Peters? Where was Mike Ovitz? Where was Steven Spielberg? Where was Lew Wasserman, who was still alive and kicking? And *who* was Craig Baumgarten?

Craig Baumgarten was a name on another list, one nearly as ab-breviated as a list of Swiss naval heroes: Jewish porn stars. Before becoming a Hollywood studio executive, the hirsute, sinisterly handsome Baumgarten had produced and starred in, along with such porn legends as Harry Reems and Jamie Gillis (also Jewish), a very X-rated film entitled *Sometimes Sweet Susan.* But instead of making Baumgarten persona non grata in the aboveground movie industry, it gave him a mystique as a superstud. Besides, Hollywood was way short on really handsome studio executives. Baumgarten was filling a void, in more ways than one.

Pre-porn, Baumgarten had had still another incarnation as an aide to New York's preppy WASP aristo-mayor John V. Lindsay, for whom he worked alongside Jeff Katzenberg. He and Katzenberg also shared a brownstone together and developed a close friendship, which resulted in Baumgarten's getting a Paramount executive job with Katzenberg. After all, the man did have hands-on filmmaking experience. They made an odd couple, the stud and the "squirt," which was Katzenberg's Lindsay-era nickname.

Jon Peters may have claimed to have inspired Warren Beatty's in *Shampoo,* but Baumgarten didn't have to boast. It was all on the screen and available at your local porn shop. In a business where size did matter, he became known in Hollywood as Craig "10 1/2" Baumgarten. Adding to Baumgarten's myth was his marriage to Melissa Prophet, a former Miss California and Miss World runner-up who was the right-hand "entertainment director" for Adnan Khashoggi and a co-producer with Robert Evans on his ill-fated *Cotton Club.* Prophet was also the subject of a layout in *Playboy,* the first one featuring a Hollywood producer. Baumgarten may not have been a Master of the Universe, but when it came to Hollywood's big swinging dicks, he could not be denied, even if Columbia Pictures fired him when Simpson's List came out.

The Gordon Gekko character from Oliver Stone's *Wall Street,* the eighties ultimate Hollywood meets Wall Street movie, shows how the worlds of power influenced each other. There the Michael Douglas character was widely recognized to be channeling Ivan Boesky, who along with Milken was one of the twin towers of crooked high finance and an important figure in Wall Street's continental drift to the West Coast. In real life, Boesky may have been channeling Douglas. The master arbitrageur, the god of good greed, was originally a Detroit native with an undistinguished résumé badly in need of a Hollywood makeover.

The son of a topless bar owner, Boesky could boast of only one prestige item on his curriculum vitae: two years at Cranbrook, Detroit's most august private school. He soon left for public schools and did end up with a law degree, albeit from a diploma mill called the Detroit College of Law that didn't even require a college degree for admission. The best thing Boesky got from Cranbrook, aside from inflated bragging rights that he was an alumnus, was a glamorous best friend named Hushang Wakili, a Persian exchange student whom he went to visit in Tehran and who would open countless gilded portals for him in Tehrangeles.

Although Boesky looked like a cross between Ichabod Crane and the Grim Reaper, he somehow won the heart of one of Detroit's prime heiresses, Seema Silberstein, whose father, Ben, was a property tycoon in the same league as Eli Broad, another Detroit Jew who would become the real estate overlord of Los Angeles. It was Seema's millions that bankrolled the arbitrage business of her husband, who lacked the Ivy credentials to get in the snooty doors of Wall Street. Ben Silberstein himself owned one of L.A.'s greatest trophies, the Beverly Hills Hotel, which Boesky acquired in an estate wrangle when his father-in-law died in 1979. He made it his headquarters for all his countless wheelings and dealings with Milken, whose Drexel was a two-minute Bentley ride down Rodeo Drive.

Once Seema's property money had gotten Boesky started on the Street, Milken's junk money put Boesky in the Gordon Gekko stratosphere, the stuff movies are made of. The stuff porn movies were made of took place in the after hours of Milken's annual week-long Predators' Ball blowout, where every corporate raider on earth converged on Beverly Hills. With Boesky playing host, his Beverly Hills Hotel's largest cabana, Bungalow Eight, became party central during this "money week," with Madam Alex providing her creatures as the prime catnip for the global greenmailers.

The players of Hollywood were fascinated with the money and

power of both Milken and Boesky, but neither man had star quality. It took Michael Douglas to make Boesky memorable. With
Milken, no one even tried. More suited to Hollywood's imagina-
tion were the great and charismatic British raiders, the lords of
money, Sir Gordon White, Sir James Hanson, and Sir James
Goldsmith. This Brit Pack loved coming to Beverly Hills, not
just for Milken's junk bonds, but for all the fun they would have,
with Madam Alex as their den mother.

White, Baron White of Hull to you, was straight out of central
casting and actually inspired the Terence Stamp character Sir
Larry Wildman in *Wall Street*. A RAF pilot in Burma during
World War II, the tall, aquiline, regal White was indeed a wild
man obsessed with Hollywood, probably because the only thing
he ever failed at was his first job, after the war, as a theatrical
agent. He dated the likes of Grace Kelly, Rita Hayworth, and
Jean Simmons, but he couldn't sign any of them. So he chucked
showbiz and went into the greeting card business with his fellow
Yorkshireman James Hanson, who was equally starstruck, having
been engaged to Audrey Hepburn until she dumped him for the
career that took off after *Roman Holiday*.

The tacky-joke cards they imported from the States proved to
be a liberating howl for the uptight British market, and they
turned Hanson White into the Hallmark of England. They went
on to acquire such famous brands as Smith Corona, Eveready,
Farberware, and Jacuzzi, as well as knighthoods. Given their un-
requited love for show business, it is surprising they never took
over a studio. Had it been up to Gordon White, they probably
would have. But while White provided the flash in the partnership, James Hanson provided the cash, and he was ultimately the
more grounded of the two.

The Hanson fortune was made in moving vans. White had befriended James's younger playboy-horseman brother, Bill, in the
army in Asia; when Bill died of stomach cancer in his twenties,

James inherited the friendship. Gordon began taking James gambling in all of London's top clubs, where they discovered a mutual appetite for beautiful women and, more productively, for risk. Accordingly, they sold the Hanson haulage business and used the millions to take over undervalued companies.

Snapping back from his jilt by Audrey Hepburn, Hanson married a New York model, whom he wooed by hiring her to run the Hanson White greeting card Manhattan office. White married a series of beauties, his first a Swedish Venezuelan cover girl named Elizabeth Kalen; the second an Anglo-American Bond girl, Virginia North, who was in *On Her Majesty's Secret Service* as well as in the British Bulldog Drummond series; and the third a rangy San Diego model named Victoria Tucker, whom he met, at age twenty-two, when he was in his sixties, through producer Robert Evans. Hanson kept a winter compound in Palm Springs, White a palace in Beverly Park, the gated Shangri-la on Mulholland Drive, where his neighbors included Eddie Murphy, Sylvester Stallone, Rod Stewart, and Michael Eisner. The two starstruck lords' best Hollywood friend was George Hamilton. They could go to Buckingham Palace whenever they wanted, but what they really wanted was Mr. Chow.

Lord White's daughter Sita, from his Venezuelan marriage, who was also lured by the call of the Hollywood wild, lived in a Beverly Hills mansion and would die very mysteriously in a Santa Monica yoga class in 2004. The torment of what should have been a charmed existence was her love child with jet-setting heartthrob Pakistani cricketer Imran Khan, who refused for years to accept paternity of the girl, Tyrian. Adding to the insult was Khan's marriage to Jemima Goldsmith, Sita's social rival and the daughter of her father's billionaire raider rival Sir James Goldsmith. Sir James was as much of a movie (or actually a miniseries) character as Sir Gordon, the former an ultrasmooth Jewish aristocrat, someone out of *Darling,* the latter an ultrahungry Midlands striver, someone out of *Room at the Top*. Those two iconic sixties British films were both dissections of ruthless upward mobility, although in Sir James's case, he was the top that the climbers were striving for.

Goldsmith came from a long line of Jewish bankers, the Gold-schmidts of Frankfurt. They weren't quite in the league of their fellow Frankfurters the Rothschilds, but they did well. (The ghetto came full circle to Mayfair when Goldsmith's son married a Roth-schild in 2003.) Goldsmith's father, Major Frank Goldsmith, who saw action in the Levantine theater during World War I, became a hotelier in France after the war, developing a chain that included such superprestige properties as the Hôtel de Paris in Monaco, the Carlton in Cannes, and the Prince de Galles in Paris. This last was where James was born, to a French Catholic mother, the daughter of a Vichy farmer, *très loin* from the Prince de Galles, but beautiful and half the age of Frank. Jimmy, as he was known, was born when his father was fifty-four, which was like having Methuseleh for a parent in the short-lived days of 1933.

Goldsmith was sent to Eton, but he hated it and left after two years. Used to the glamorous nomadic life attendant to being heir to a chain of hotels, Goldsmith preferred the gambling tables of Monaco to the playing fields of his starchy school. He loved being around the movie stars, from Moreau to Bardot, not to mention the visiting Americans, at the Cannes Film Festival, which began in 1946 and was informally headquartered at his father's Carlton. He was as handsome as any star, six feet three with dazzling blue eyes that hypnotized, when he was barely twenty, one of the world's richest heiresses, Isabel Patiño, whose father was the tin king of Bolivia. The tin king made it public he wasn't comfort-able having a Jew for a son-in-law, to which the irrepressible and never politically correct Goldsmith replied that he was equally uncomfortable having an (American) Indian for a father-in-law.

Parental misgivings notwithstanding, the pair eloped, and their romance made the front pages of the world. The runaway marriage ended in tragedy a few months later, with Isabel dying in childbirth. Goldsmith rebounded and showed he was no snob by marrying next the daughter of a Paris Metro janitor. Then he proved how snobby he could be by keeping as his cross-Channel mistress Annabel Birley, the daughter of the Marquess of Londonderry. In the 1960s, he had helped finance London's most exclusive private disco, Annabel's, named after Birley's wife, whom Goldsmith eventually appropriated as his mistress. He made it legal in 1978. Never without a mistress in either London or Paris, Goldsmith next took a French aristo as his mate and openly fathered another family. The usual rules never applied to him.

Given his insatiable appetite for conquest, of companies as well as women, Goldsmith (who as he aged made being bald as sexy as Sean Connery did) was a great patron of Madam Alex in Los Angeles. Goldsmith's best Lotusland friend was Selim Zilkha, the scion of the preeminent Jewish family in Iraq's good old days. The Zilkhas had escaped with their fortune to England and multiplied it into the billions in banking and in creating Mothercare, the British maternity-goods colossus. Zilkha had immigrated once more, to one of the noblest estates in Bel-Air, where he was host with the most to the international financial set who came to L.A. in ever-increasing numbers to get the easy money Michael Milken, nobody's aristocrat but everybody's friend, was seemingly giving away.

At one point, in 1977, following the Begelman scandal, Goldsmith was seriously considering buying Columbia Pictures, for a song. But the song never got played, thwarted by the blood feud between Herbert Allen and Alan Hirschfield. Goldsmith would have to enjoy Hollywood vicariously, as did his fellow British raiders. It is hard to imagine how the likes of Sir James Goldsmith could have had much of an influence on the likes of Don Simpson and Jon Peters. Don Simpson liked to mythologize himself as a roustabout on the Alaska pipeline. He boasted in his *Esquire* profile, "I love trash. I *am* trash." Jon Peters like to mythologize himself as a reform school runaway. He once confessed to Barbara Walters on national television, "I am a hustler." It is more likely that the British lords were fascinated, awed, by the success of these unportfolioed cheeky bounders in rising through the mucky quicksand of the entertainment business and actually getting blockbusters *made*. Taking over companies was the art of sleight of hand and funny money, but making movies was pure *magic*.

The one high financier, and alleged charter member of the Madam Alex club, who made the biggest impact on its Hollywood contingent was the arms and power broker Adnan Khashoggi. Khashoggi had mansions everywhere, Paris, Beirut, Marbella, Gstaad; a triplex with a swimming pool in the Olympic Tower in New York; one of the world's biggest yachts, the *Nabila;* a DC-8 flying orgy. But his heart was in Beverly Hills, where he was a secret but honorary member of Reagan's kitchen cabinet, a major source of (illegal) Republican funds that got Nixon elected and the architect of the Iran-Contra deal that freed the American hostages in Tehran just in time to put Reagan in the White House. Khashoggi was tiny, bald, and mustachioed, a debonair Mr. Fixit in the mode of Sydney Greenstreet in *Casablanca*. His fixings were so epic that to most who met him, he seemed like a genie who had been uncorked from a bottle, a genie who could make any dream come true.

The son of the personal doctor of King Abdul Aziz of Saudi Arabia, Khashoggi was born connected, and in Mecca, in 1935. He was sent to Victoria College in Alexandria, Egypt, then the Eton of the Middle East. His schoolmates included the future movie star Omar Sharif, the future Arabist scholar Edward Said, and the future King Hussein of Jordan. Khashoggi's initial ambition was to become a petroleum engineer, and to that end, he came to America to attend the Colorado School of Mines. But he soon dropped out and, California dreaming, went west to the podunk

Chico State College, in a nowheresville a few hours from San
Francisco, a haven for rich Middle Easterners who didn't want to
study. Even at Chico State, Khashoggi lasted only three semes-
ters. He began trading on his Arab royal contacts to make himself
a sales agent for foreign trucks and cars. He sold himself to
Chrysler and to Rolls-Royce, and he took off, soon trading up
from cars to arms, winning exclusive sales agency contracts with
Northrup, Raytheon, and Lockheed, which brought him to Los
Angeles, his personal mecca.

A Hollywood intimate of George Hamilton (the out-of-town
moneymen loved Hamilton, who was the last of the old-school
matinee idol types; he fit the stereotype; he *was* the stereotype)
and Elizabeth Taylor, Khashoggi was a particularly dear chum of
Alfred Bloomingdale (to whom Madam Alex had introduced
Vicki Morgan, a truly fatal attraction) and Walter Annenberg.
Even these masters of the high life knew Khashoggi lived better
than they. Khashoggi, whose sister had married Mohamed al-
Fayed, who owned Harrods in London and the Hôtel Ritz in
Paris, was the uncle of Dodi Fayed, tragic lover of Princess Di.

Dodi Fayed had the Hollywood dream, too. He was the money
behind *Chariots of Fire* and a credited producer on that and other
studio films. His uncle Adnan was way beyond producing. To
him, a studio would have seemed like tiddlywinks compared with
the game of nations; that's why the Hollywood moguls thought he
was so cool. If you don't need them, they *love* you. But even Adnan Khashoggi couldn't make his daughter Nabila the movie star
she dreamed of being. He could make a president, but he couldn't
make a star. That's why the Masters of the Universe thought Don
Simpson and Jon Peters were even cooler than they, the Masters,
were.

# CHAPTER 8
## JON AND DON

THE TWO MOST EMBLEMATIC and colorful producers of the eighties would have made the worst role models for this most emblematic of that decade's dream jobs. That's because there would be absolutely no way in the world for anyone else to replicate the preposterous career paths of Jon Peters and Don Simpson. Other producers, yes. Peters's partner, Peter Guber, for example, was a middle-class Newton, Massachusetts, Jew, son of a junk dealer, who credentialed himself with a J.D.-LL.M. and worked his way up the studio executive ranks until he had amassed enough contacts and favors to go out on his own.

Or Simpson's partner, Jerry Bruckheimer, another middle-class Jew, from Detroit, who got a degree from the University of Arizona and then learned the nuts and bolts of filmmaking by producing commercials that won him the task of doing Simpson's unglamorous nuts and bolts. Or Joel Silver, still another middle-class Jew, from South Orange, New Jersey, who armed himself with a degree from NYU's Tisch School of the Arts that enabled him to become an acolyte of action film guru Larry Gordon and then steal Gordon's thunder with the *Die Hard* series. Or Gordon himself, a middle-class Jew from Belzoni, Mississippi, who got a Tulane degree and thereafter a job in television with Aaron Spelling, who had a soft spot for fellow southern Jewboys. Those producers offered the ultimate in role modeling: Be born to some comfort, get those higher degrees, get a good job, and then, only then, start killing.

Jon Peters began killing straight out of the womb. Despite his blond, voluptuous Lana Turner–esque mother being something of Hollywood beauty royalty, given her family's fancy Pagano's salon, Helen Pagano had a penchant for bad boys and married the baddest one she could find. Jack Peters was a handsome, brawling Cherokee war vet who ran a diner in Hollywood. Big Jack taught little Jon, born in 1945, to fight, to shoot, to use a knife, and to ride a pony, the last activity getting Jon "discovered" in Griffith Park by a casting agent for Cecil B. DeMille, who put Jon in *The Ten Commandments* playing an Israelite on the run from the pharoah. Young Jon took instantly to playing a Jew, a role he would assume to enormous profit later in his life.

Jack Peters died of a coronary when Jon was nine. Helen married another brawler who began brawling with her. Jon couldn't stand seeing his mother being brutalized. The little tough guy thus tried to stand up for his mother, even if she would not. The stepfather then beat the hell out of Jon, but Jon continued to fight back. The household became a boxing ring, with no holds barred. Something had to give, and that something was Jon. One afternoon, Helen sweetly took Jon out for ice cream; the police were waiting to take him off to reform school. Helen had picked her new husband over her son. It was a terrible betrayal, but, like everything in Jon's life, it prepared him for the betrayals that went with the territory in Hollywood. It was also a lesson in love. Whatever she did to him, Jon continued to adore his mother. Separated from her for three long years, Jon committed himself to winning her back. Again, that sort of kamikaze commitment would make an older Jon Peters one of Hollywood's most successful ladies' men of all time.

Jon was the littlest hoodlum on the chain gang he was sent on by the state reformatory to build roads and other public works. It was child labor, but that's what officially "bad" boys had to do. Jon learned a lot in reform school, but he never learned how to read. Never. Again, that would have been a fatal flaw in any other career trajectory. But in Hollywood, where the higher one rose, the less one read, Jon, by not reading, had no choice but to start at the top. And that he would do. By thirteen, Jon came back home, less than a student but more than a man. The fights began again, with his mother in the middle. In one of the slug-fests, the middlewoman got a broken leg. Helen once again sided with her husband over her son. This time she exiled Jon not to reform school, but to Manhattan in the care of two gay hairdressers she knew from the beauty circuit.

The beauty boys turned out to be child molesters, and Jon, who was a contemporary Oliver Twist in being able to fend for himself, escaped from the predators and slept in the streets. Eventually, he fell back on more beauty contacts and got a job as a pubic hair colorist and coiffeur, or "muff dyer" to the trade, in a West Fifty-seventh Street salon that catered to strippers. Jon would later boast that quite literally, no man in Hollywood knew "pussy" better than he. Sleeping in a storeroom above his salon, Jon, at fourteen, met another beautician, Marie Zampitella, who was sixteen, at a Manhattan trade show. He followed her back home to South Philadelphia, pretended he was twenty, and talked her into getting engaged to him, charming her tough Italian family in the process. He stayed in Philadelphia, moving up from the nether regions to the Main Line, where he got a job cutting society hair at Nan Duskin, the Bonwit's of Brotherly Love.

But the Valley Boy missed his mother, and he missed Los Angeles. So he took his new love out west and tied the knot at the

courthouse across from the "Superman" skyscraper in downtown
L.A., little knowing that he would one day produce a blockbuster
feature of the TV series. Declaring that his daughter-in-law was a
teen hooker, Jon's stepfather refused to let the newlyweds live in
his house. So Jon rented a dirt-cheap apartment in the Valley,
where the couple took jobs at a teens-only nightclub called the
Peppermint Stick, a riff on Times Square's Peppermint Lounge.
Jon was the doorman and got the club written up in *Time* magazine for rejecting starlet Tuesday Weld as overage. During the
day, Jon was going to beauty school and doing hair, often black
hair. His first "name" clients were the mothers of dance-craze
progenitors Chubby Checker ("The Twist") and Dee Dee Sharp
("Mashed Potato Time").

Jon's first white star was Lesley Ann Warren, who had starred
on Broadway in *Drat! The Cat!* with Elliott Gould, who was then
married to Barbra Streisand. How the connections would accrue.
Warren, née Warrenoff, was a ballerina turned youngest member
of the Actors Studio. No one could been a more perfect Jewish
princess, especially when she starred in *Cinderella* on network television in 1965. Through a family tie, Jon was called in to do Warren's hair. He soon became not only her stylist but also her
"enforcer," when she complained that her then beau had gotten
rough with her.

His blades and his fists winning Warren's heart, Jon quickly
divorced Marie, gifting her with a Corvette as a good-bye present,
and proposed to Warren. Sammy Davis Jr. tried to warn Warren
about marrying "beneath" her. But it was sort of akin to the way
May Britt had been warned against marrying Sammy. Young
love (they were both twenty when they met) would not be de-
railed, and in 1967 Jon and Lesley Ann were wed by a rabbi at the
Sands in Las Vegas, precisely where Frank Sinatra and Mia Farrow had tied their own ill-fated knot a year before.

While Warren continued to pursue her career, Jon stuck to

hair. He stayed in the Valley, albeit now living in a mansion in Sherman Oaks and working in his own salon on Ventura Boulevard. He got some new celebrity clients, gossip queen Rona Barrett, *I Dream of Jeannie* star Barbara Eden. His biggest break, however, was "doing" Sonja Henie, the Norwegian skating champion and movie star who in all her young, Aryan perfection had been pursued madly, if unsuccessfully, by Adolf Hitler. Jon did far better than the Führer. He took Henie, then in her fifties, riding on his motorcycle, just like the scene in *Shampoo,* and made her feel younger than Warren Beatty made Lee Grant feel in the film.

In still another instance of the Mixmaster of life and art, while Jon was networking Henie, one day he came home and found his star wife in flagrante with Warren Beatty himself, perhaps doing long-in-advance homework for the 1975 film. Jon, as was his wont, put the fear of God in Beatty by threatening him with reform school justice, not a typical Bev Hills alienation of affections suit. Beatty left Lesley Ann far alone, and he and Jon never spoke until after *Shampoo,* when Jon seized all the credit he could for being the inspiration Beatty would steadfastly deny.

In return for Jon's elixir of youth, Henie backed Jon in buying out his Pagano uncles from their fancy Wilshire salon. Jon deeply resented his relatives for forsaking him in reform school and beyond. Evicting them gave him the last laugh, though he kept his beloved (if elusive) mother on as cashier. Pagano's became the Jon Peters Salon, and, finally, Jon was a player in Beverly Hills. He began dressing like a designer biker, à la *Easy Rider,* and doing "big" hair, not Dallas-style bouffants but the hair of "big" actresses, with whom flings were often part of the Jon Peters experience. He "did" Jackie Bisset, Leigh Taylor-Young, Linda Evans, the future Bo Derek. And then, in 1973, the Biggest Hair in Hollywood, Barbra.

His multifaceted reputation preceding him, Jon was summoned by Barbra to be her hairdresser on the bomb-to-be *For Pete's Sake,* which was shooting in Manhattan. What a triumphant return to the Big Apple for the erstwhile muff dyer. The movie was a loser, but the romance was a smash. Jon and Barbra couldn't have been more opposite than Redford and Barbra in *The Way We Were,* and the chemistry was even more explosive. The schadenfreude crowd in Hollywood immediately reduced the pairing to a rich ugly duckling and a gigolo. But Streisand had enjoyed romances with her lady-killer co-stars Redford and Ryan O'Neal, and her ability to attract an A-list man was no less than Woody Allen's to attract A-list women like Diane Keaton and Mia Farrow. Stardom has its own aesthetic. Furthermore, Jon didn't need her money. He had his own millions and his own aura as a ladies' man. What he didn't have, even through his lesser star of a wife, was entrée to the top of the film business, with which he, like almost all Angelinos in its vast shadow, whatever their day jobs, had become intrigued.

Now he had his passport. Right away Barbra introduced Jon to her original Svengali, übermogul Ray Stark, producer of *Funny Girl* on stage and screen. By now, like most Trilbys, Barbra hated her Svengali. When she confided to Jon that Stark had taken advantage of her when she was young and struggling, another amazing coincidence presented itself. Lesley Ann Warren had told Jon of the exact same experience with the man who was known as "the Rabbit" for both his overbite and his insatiable libido. When Jon first met Stark, he thus automatically went into his default position, which was to kick ass for his women. He picked up the minimonster and spun him around as if he were a Howdy Doody puppet, then put him gently down on the couch. Jon pretended to be a playful orangutan. But Jon knew that Stark knew, and his guilty conscience, combined with a fear of physical reprisal, would prevent Stark from ending Jon's career before it ever began (something Stark would have normally done with such an interloper, and would do, famously, with later interlopers like David Puttnam).

Once Jon had gotten his name up on the boards in 1976 as producer of the critically savaged fiscal bonanza (ah, that sound track) rock remake of *A Star Is Born* (he wanted to be both co-star and director as well, but Barbra drew the line), Jon went to the Stark-controlled Columbia Pictures to get a production deal that didn't leave him beholden to Barbra's deal at Warner's. Wanting to avoid Jon but afraid to say no himself, Stark passed Jon down to studio head David Begelman (pre-embezzlement). But before Begelman could say no, Jon pulled out a trump card of hairdresser gossip: A call girl client of Jon's had told him that Begelman, a client of hers, liked to refer to his member as "Winkie."

"So how's Winkie?" was Jon's opening salvo.

Begelman instantly inked a three-picture deal with Jon, the first of which was another hit, *The Eyes of Laura Mars.*

It was on the lot at Columbia where Jon met the next great love of his life, Peter Guber, former executive there who was running the film division of Casablanca Records (Donna Summer) with mogul Neil Bogart and had had two music-fueled hits, *Thank God It's Friday* and *Midnight Express.* The proto-yuppie Guber was the Jewish American prince that Jon had long dreamed of being. If Jews had a *Burke's Peerage,* Guber would have been in it by his marriage to Lynda, the Isaac Gellis meat-packing heiress. In addition to her kosher pedigree, Lynda Guber was totally connected. It was she who put Peter together with Bogart, whose first wife had been her best childhood friend and who, post-Bogart, would marry Peter's brother. Hollywood was, if anything, all in the family. Guber not only had the background, he had the credibility that big hits like *The Deep* gave him.

On the other hand, Guber was something of a nerd, a square, anything but a ladies' man. He was tall and slim and dressed well, but he still looked just like an uptight lawyer. He had an oversize nose, but his biggest liability where the rules of attraction were concerned was his voice. It was high-pitched, shrill, and nasal, and he spoke a mile a minute in a grating "Paaahk the caaah in Haaahvaaahd Yaaahd" Boston accent. Guber's voice was made for deals, not dates. If Jon's fantasy was to be Guber, Guber's was to be Jon.

Like many record czars, Neil Bogart was a coked-out madman. When he died very young, Guber needed another madman in his life. Jon was it. They became the most unlikely partners in Hollywood since Laurel and Hardy. Between the two of them, they seemed to have the town covered. They had everything— except a hit. Their first two ventures together, *An American Werewolf in London* and *Endless Love,* were commercial disasters. The three-strikes law loomed over Hollywood, as it did over California. It was 1982. They needed proof that they could make magic, or at least money. Enter Don Simpson and *Flashdance.*

When it came to women (and in Hollywood it somehow always came to women), the main difference between the two superproducers was that Jon Peters was a stud and Don Simpson was a dud. Jon was a cool urban cowboy, something out of a New Age Bev Hills spaghetti western. Don, on the other hand, was an uncool country doughboy, a big pot of overcooked spaghetti. Dressed head to toe in black, the fiercely competitive Don, who was short, squat, and overmuscled from too many trainers, conjured up images of Johnny Cash, with a fillip of warpath Geronimo. He *tried* to be cool, with too-tight designer jeans and too-taut designer plastic surgery and too-flashy designer Porsches and Ferraris; but the failure of his enormous efforts made him seem that much more pathetic. Now, to be fair to Don Simpson, he was by no means the first, nor the worst, "flop with chicks" in the mogul corps. It can be said that most producers became producers at least as much to make women as to make films. Call it the revenge of the nerds, but the nerds had been having their day for as long as there were movies, from Thalberg to Selznick to Mike Todd to Sam Spiegel.

Jon Peters was the very rare producer who used women to get films made. Simpson, on the other hand, used his films to get women—or, more accurately, to buy women. How many women did he need? All of them. Producers are control freaks, and Don Simpson, having been stung by chance as a failure, wanted to leave nothing to it as a success. He wanted to control, to buy more women than Nero, than Caligula, than Hefner, than Khashoggi. Hence his blockbuster imperative. The grosses from something like *Tender Mercies* were not going to get him laid to his heart's insatiable content. He needed *Top Gun,* but the Simpson hit mystique started with *Flashdance.*

Well, actually, it started in Alaska. If one was to believe him, Don Simpson was the Sarah Palin of Hollywood, a Bible-toting, moose-hunting, snowmobile-driving mountain man who did time for four felonies while still in high school. He sounded a lot like Jon Peters. Except it wasn't true. The truth was boring, prosaic, as were Don's true roots. Born in Seattle in 1943 to a mechanic father and a housewife mother with plain, and plains, midwestern roots, Don moved to Anchorage with his parents when he was two. Unlike the real juvenile delinquent that Jon was, Don was a good, grindy student in high school who, despite his chubby frame, was elected "Best Dressed" in his senior class.

Don may have described his parents as Southern Baptist Holy Rollers who drilled the boy in original sin, but the story was far more original than the sin itself. His parents' main devotion was to the advancement of their children. They scrimped and saved to send Don to the University of Oregon. Don would go Jon one better by creating a legend for himself not as a mere juvenile delinquent, but as an *intellectual* juvenile delinquent, one who read Descartes and Spinoza, Balzac and Dostoyevsky, between convenience store stickups. He told everyone he was Phi Beta Kappa at Oregon.

Don's classmates back in Anchorage and Eugene, when pressed

by the press, recalled neither the crimes and misdemeanors nor
*Crime and Punishment.* He was in a fraternity, not Phi Beta but
only a social one, and a lesser social one at that, at a campus that
in the 1960s was considered, along with Berkeley and Madison,
one of the nation's premier "drug schools." His contemporaries
remembered Don as a comic book addict who memorized the
school texts to get good grades, then got his true reading pleasure
from *Uncle Scrooge* and *Superman,* which proved to be the best syl-
labus for Hollywood, anyway.

Nevertheless, Don had a college degree, even if one tinged by
cannabis, and with it, he went the yuppie route, to San Francisco,
where he worked in an advertising agency and then in film marketing for the Northern California office of Warner Brothers.
These were white-collar jobs Jon Peters could never have gotten.
Jon wasn't a yuppie; he was street. With his education and his
"Best Dressed" threads, Don, conversely, was eminently employ-
able, so much so that Warner Brothers in 1972 brought him down
to home base in Burbank. Don had officially gone Hollywood.
The problem was that for all his external probity, Don was a
hoodlum wannabe. Warner's saw this and soon fired him, and
Don went adrift for a long three years, dabbling at becoming first
an actor, then a screenwriter, and spending his days hanging out
at Schwab's drugstore, where Lana Turner was discovered at the
counter and where a million copycat dreams were born and died.

Hanging out, doing drugs, living the seventies' high life without
earning a living, Don met a lot of future players, Craig Baumgarten in his porn days, Julia and Michael Phillips before *The Sting,*
Paul Schrader before *Taxi Driver,* Steve Tisch, who was always
rich, but long before *Risky Business.* The most important connection Don would make was Jerry Bruckheimer, whom Don met
through Jerry's future ex-wife, Bonnie, who worked with Don
at Warner's. Jerry, like Don, came out of advertising, but he had
no aspirations to be hip or cool. Like Peter Guber at Syracuse and

Mike Ovitz at UCLA, the frail, wispy Bruckheimer was a ZBT at the University of Arizona, but he spent most of his nonstudy time in the campus stamp-collecting club. Nonetheless, he segued from the ad business into films and amassed actual producing credits, including a remake of the noir classic *Farewell, My Lovely*. Jerry's films were flops, but they were still credits, which was more than Don, drowning in a sea of debits, looked as if he were ever going to have. When Jerry got divorced from Bonnie, he and Don moved in together in a house in funky Laurel Canyon, then L.A.'s hippie and drug central as memorialized by Joni Mitchell in "Ladies of the Canyon."

Eventually Don's ship came in, providing him with enough names to drop to finally get a job at Paramount, under eminent production designer (*Chinatown, Shampoo*) turned production head Richard Sylbert, an émigré from the Elaine's hard-drinking, hard-bluffing set in New York who had a natural affinity for fabulists like Don. Sylbert had been courting heir Tisch for the creative executive job, but Tisch, who didn't want a job, remembered the neediest and pushed Don on Sylbert. Bruckheimer had to lend the formerly best-dressed Don a sport jacket to wear to the interview, where Don's Palinesque discourse on fly-fishing in Alaska seemed wonderfully romantic to the urbane Sylbert, much more so than the riffs on Robert Bresson or Carl Dreyer he was getting from other applicants. Sylbert sent Don to meet his new boss, Barry Diller, who had taken the reins of the studio from Robert Evans. Diller liked Don, too, and gave him the job.

Don lasted at Paramount for five years, a key cog in what would become the Paramount high-concept wheel. His biggest triumph as an executive, having risen to president of production in a tangle of confusing, ego-stroking titles (Eisner was president of the company, Diller chairman), was *An Officer and a Gentleman*, an earthbound precursor of what Don would later wreak in *Top Gun*. But *Officer*'s big grosses were still not enough for big bosses

Diller and Eisner to keep Don on after one drug embarrassment after another (wrecked Porsches, public temper tantrums, secretary abuse), the last straw being when Don literally fell asleep face forward into his soup at a packed lunch at the studio commissary. Eisner personally put Don out to pasture with the standard kiss-off independent producer deal. To show how much but actually how little they cared for him, Eisner gave Don as a going-away present the project that would be known as *Flashdance*. Everyone familiar with it laughed it away as a booby prize.

*Flashdance* actually had previously been a Jon Peters project and as such should have been a classic case study of the clash of two emerging titans. However, it is more a case study in avoidance, wherein Hollywood's two baddest boys gave each other the widest of berths and then, after the assumed loser became a monster hit, waged a public relations battle to claim credit for the retrospective genius of their courage in making this unlikely winner. In a business where a failure is an orphan and a success has many fathers, no film has had more proud parents than *Flashdance*. Furthermore, most of these soi-disant creative wizards used the film as a springboard to build amazingly powerful careers. This silly, incoherent Cinderella story, which was more an extended MTV video than a motion picture, may have spawned more big shots than any other film of the decade, which in itself is perhaps the saddest comment of all on the decade's artistic efforts. The art here was in the deal, and there were a great many dealers in the mix. It is an illuminating story of how bad movies get made and become hits.

Janet Maslin's withering *New York Times* review of *Flashdance* was typical of a nasty lot, making fun of the preposterous premise of the Pittsburgh welder who wants to become a ballerina, played by Jennifer Beals, a young Yale alumna who had the similarly unlikely distinction of being the only woman to grace the covers

of *Ebony* and *B'nai B'rith* magazine. Among the film's most notable qualities, Maslin declared with withering disdain, was "the
heroine's remarkably soulful-looking dog." In *The New Yorker*,
high priestess Pauline Kael was even meaner. " 'Flashdance' is like
a sleazo putting the make on you," she wrote, damning it as
"soft-core porn with an inspirational message . . . selling the kind
of romantic story that was laughed off the screen thirty years
ago." She even took a swipe below the belt at the macho men
who made the swill, implying there was more to their flaunted
masculinity than met the eye: "The producers have put together
a prime collection of rumps: girls' rumps, but small and muscular
and round, like boys." Maybe, she was implying, Jon and Don
and the whole rotten cocksure bunch were all really gay.

For all the film's inanities, when the project began over five
years before (a mere instant in glacial Hollywood time), it had a
quasi-literary provenance. The author of the original screenplay
was a young Canadian named Tom Hedley, whose influential
editorial tenure at *Esquire* in its glory days in the late sixties and
early seventies was a precursor to that of his fellow countryman
Graydon Carter at *Vanity Fair*. Hedley, like his inspiration Clay
Felker at *New York* magazine, was one of the midwives of the Tom
Wolfe/Gay Talese–led "New Journalism," whose hallmark was its
novelistic reportage. Rather than become Graydon Carter, Hedley
had gone back to Canada to transcend ink-stained wretched editorial salaries by making some real money as a screenwriter.

That was possible north of the border; inspired by the success of
the Toronto Film Festival, the cold-Cannes begun in 1976, Canada had created all sorts of tax shelter incentives to make movies
there. It worked for Hedley, who in 1980 had three of his screenplays made into features. They all had lesser stars, people like
Tony Perkins, Michael Sarrazin, James Coburn, Tatum O'Neal,
and they were all flops. But tax deals were supposed to be flops,

and Hollywood was always impressed with credits, by the sheer chutzpah of getting a film made. Tom Hedley was ready for his close-up.

Thinking big, the tall, handsome Hedley relocated to Malibu, began dating big blondes, and bought a Cadillac that had belonged to Elvis Presley. All the clichés inevitably brought him to the attention of his big blonde–loving neighbor, Jon Peters, who had put the blondes on hold after moving in with Barbra Streisand at her vast Tiffany lamp–filled Malibu compound. Jon, flush from *Caddyshack* and newly partnered with Guber at the German-Dutch deep-pocketed PolyGram production company, gave Hedley a development deal to write a script for Barbra. It went nowhere, but anyone who had a deal with Barbra was a man the rest of the town wanted to meet.

The Guber-Peters d-girl at PolyGram, Lynda Obst, a former editor herself at *The New York Times Magazine,* sparked to Hedley instantly. The cocky, opinionated Scarsdale girl who had come west to attend Pomona and whose brother Rick Rosen was becoming a major television agent, Obst was considered "Queen of the D's." The joke that "d-girls can't say yes, and they can't say no" didn't apply to the no-flirt Obst. She had been married to onetime super–book agent David Obst, who had sold *All the President's Men* for Woodward and Bernstein. Now all she did was work. Obst couldn't give a green light, but she gave great meeting, a lot of death by encouragement, to be sure, but good story ideas as well.

Even if Obst loved an idea, it couldn't move forward unless the ultimate nonreader, Jon Peters, sparked to it. Hedley soon came up with one that was right down Jon's darkest alley. It was the story of strippers at a defunct Toronto bar called Gimlets that Hedley had frequented in his lowly editor days. At Gimlets the dancers, with names like Muscles Marinara and Gina the Sex Machina, weren't mere strippers, but rather artistes who turned their acts into elaborate *tableaux vivants*. Hedley's movie would tell the story of one of these artistes who worked at the phone company by day and at something resembling Gimlets by night. Jon, of course, was intrigued, because the idea provided him with a cover for endless "research" at strip clubs not only in L.A. but all over the world.

The movie might have drowned in that research but Peter Guber, who was embarrassed by it and didn't see any potential, happily unloaded it on Paramount for a cool $225,000, which would cover Hedley's writing fees and Jon's research. At Paramount, the idea was embraced by Obst's studio counterpart, Dawn Steel, who saw the film not in Jon's terms of male voyeurism, but in feminist terms of "empowerment." Steel somehow identified with the tale and wanted to make it a parable of her own unlikely rise from selling Gucci toilet paper to the lofty heights of studio executive-dom. Unlike the cerebral Lynda Obst, Dawn Steel was much more "street," one of the guys. Raised middle-class on the wrong side of the tracks in rich Great Neck, Steel was blessed with the original name of Spielberg. But how could her father, a textile jobber and Walter Mitty weightlifter, who loved to think of himself as the Man of Steel, have ever dreamed what doors the name Spielberg would have opened for his daughter or that she would ever be in show business?

After dropping out of NYU, Steel got a job selling products like penile mittens, or "cock socks," for Bob Guccione at *Penthouse*. No wonder she learned how to be one of the guys. In 1975, she left *Penthouse* to start her own company, Entrepreneuse Enterprises (note the feminism under all that porn), whose inaugural blockbuster gimmick product, in the age of the Pet Rock, was designer toilet paper. Steel's sales instincts were better than her legal research. The toilet paper took off, but then Gucci took off after her, suing her for trademark infringement. It was time to get out of New York.

At *Penthouse,* Steel had met Craig Baumgarten, who had traded in his own cock socks and X-rated films for an executive job at Paramount. Baumgarten urged Steel to come west, promising he would try to get her a marketing job at the studio. She had just had another taste of Hollywood, a brief fling with an unknown actor named Richard Gere, who was just about to get his break in *Looking for Mr. Goodbar.* The romance didn't work, but Steel had caught Hollywood fever. Michael Eisner took Baumgarten's recommendation, and soon Dawn Steel was selling a slightly tonier product, *Mork & Mindy* suspenders. Eventually, she did so well merchandising *Star Trek* paraphernalia that Eisner gave her a chance to cross over to the creative side and become a production executive.

*Flashdance* would be Steel's baptism of fire. The watchword under the Paramount of Diller and Eisner was "passion." Only make films you were passionate about. Accordingly, the main line of the theme song of *Flashdance,* the Irene Cara number one hit that synergized the film into becoming the number one movie, was "Take your passion, and make it happen." And that was precisely what Dawn Steel set out to do. She first took her passion to Tom Hedley. Their affair did not stop Steel from replacing Hedley on his own project with the hot upcoming screenwriter Joe Eszterhas, like Hedley a journalist, from *Rolling Stone,* who had just written the Stallone flop *F·I·S·T.* But a Stallone flop in those days still had cachet as a Stallone movie, and the very fact that Eszterhas could be trusted with a superstar's image gave him both credibility and cachet. Eszterhas's biggest contribution was to change the lead character from a dull phone company drone to a welder. The Hungarian American from Cleveland brought the project true grit and blue-collar cred. He was a Simpson kind of guy, an Alaska pipeline roustabout guy, more so than the more effete snobby city slicker Hedley.

At this stage of the project, Simpson had yet to fall in the soup and lose his job as production president. It was Steel's task to sell

*Flashdance* to him, and Simpson still wasn't interested. Only after Simpson was fired and *Flashdance* was given to him as a farewell offering did he start paying attention to it. Pushing Don along was Jerry Bruckheimer, whom he sold on partnering with him in his new company. Jerry had had a succès d'estime, if not at the box office, with Steel's ex Richard Gere in *American Gigolo,* where Jerry had worked with Giorgio Moroder, the Austro-Italian composer from the Tyrol whose music proved so instrumental to the success of *Flashdance.* Peter Guber had worked with Moroder as well on *Midnight Express,* but Bruckheimer seemed to "get" the importance of a hip MTV music video style for modern movies more than Guber did.

Even with Moroder involved, twenty-seven directors turned down Steel and Simpson's offers to direct the movie. Steel's next epiphany was to turn what was still a sexist pig strip-fest into a chick flick. To do so, she hired an unproduced writer pal, Katherine Reback, to rewrite Eszterhas. Reback made the final change of the heroine to an aspiring ballerina. Both Steel and Reback got off on all the shoes the movie would have, from welder's boots to toe slippers. Such was feminist empowerment. That pipe dream of an absurd only-in-movies fantasy was allegedly what made the script finally "work," attracting the English commercials director and fog machine specialist Adrian Lyne and getting the project a green light from Eisner and Diller.

Once *Flashdance* went into production, Don Simpson decreed that Jon Peters be banned from the set. Not that Don was there himself. The movie was shot mostly in Pittsburgh, which wasn't the kind of location either Don or Jon would have been tempted by. Although the two men barely knew each other, Don had no interest in remedying that situation. Both men counted Madam Alex as a friend, but Alex knew better than to try to match them up. Don was a new client, who would become, with success, a superclient. Jon, whose mantra "I don't have to pay for it" may have been a case of the gent protesting too much, was an Alex pal from his hairdresser days.

Don resented Jon's success with movie stars, and he hated the fact that Jon had risen to his level on Barbra's coattails. Don only wished he could have done that. Don had told the world that his greatest idol was Warren Beatty. If he could be anyone, it would be Warren Beatty. Jon told the world that Warren Beatty wanted to be Jon, so reductio ad absurdum, Don wanted to be Jon. But for all the pussy envy, Don had a streak of the Puritan in him that hated the idea that Jon had gotten something for nothing. He didn't *work* for his success. Luck counted, but for everything? Don saw Jon as a gigolo, which Don knew he never could be, and an illiterate gigolo at that. Jon was known to assemble a group of actors to read scripts to him. It wasn't just his short attention span; he really never was in school long enough to learn to read and write.

Besides, who read scripts anyway, other than lowly d–girls who wrote coverage? Who? Don Simpson, that was who. Don loved reading scripts, loved hiring and firing writers, loved firing off fifty-page script memos, which may have been cocaine rants but often still contained the germ of a good idea. Don felt he knew the audience. But Jon *was* the audience, a school-skipping, girl–obsessed adolescent who was looking for heavy action and raw emotion. Teenage boys, not *Cahiers du Cinéma* Ivy Leaguers, were the golden demographic for the blockbuster era, and Jon was that teenager at heart. But just as Don was intimidated by Jon's success with women, Jon was intimidated by Don's yuppie trajectory, his college degree, his running the studio gauntlet, those fifty-page memos. They were both kids from nowhere, but Don had come in through the front door and beaten all the odds to get where he was, while Jon had come in through the stage door and skipped the odds entirely. The two unlikely moguls were probably the two most insecure men in Hollywood.

In a business of credit hogs, Don proved to be an even bigger *chazer* than Jon. Don was also, if possible, more of a press whore than Jon. Jon was too ambivalent about his own background to flaunt his Dickensian trajectory. Don, on the other hand, who was pretty straight middle-class, fabricated Jon's actual juvenile delinquent persona but fused it with an intellectual overlay and then went out of his way to say outrageous things like "I love trash. I *am* trash," which the press ate up. He was a maniac brainiac. No producer had ever made for better copy, and this was years before Don's Madam Alex addiction had hit the headlines. Furthermore, while Jon was bogged down plotting his next move with Guber, Don decisively followed up *Flashdance* with a much more monstrous hit, 1984's *Beverly Hills Cop*. Ironically, Don's Alex handle was "Beverly Hills Cock."

*Cop,* originally conceived for Mickey Rourke and later for Sylvester Stallone, before Eddie Murphy became bankable, generated its own credit battle, albeit an internecine one at Paramount. Michael Eisner, for one, claimed he had gotten the idea when getting a traffic ticket in the 90210. He had just moved out from the East and was driving a battered station wagon with New York plates. Eisner felt so looked down upon by the soigné Beverly Hills cop that he immediately went out and bought himself a Mercedes to keep up appearances with his new neighbors. He felt like a fish out of water, which was Paramount's trademark comic character. Eisner then transmuted himself into a cop from the sticks, up against stuck-up Bev Hills cops, and the idea began to germinate. Bullshit, Don Simpson blustered to the press. Eisner was lying, Simpson declared, which did not endear the producer to the mogul. But Don wasn't in the endearment game. Per Don, *Cop*'s gnarled roots went back to a late 1970s pitch meeting Simpson and Eisner took with a Croatian-born, Harvard-bred writer named Danilo "Don" Bach, who ended up nearly a decade later with a story credit from the Writers Guild.

Over the years, as a Paramount executive and later as an independent producer, Don claimed to have used eleven different writers and close to forty drafts of something whose success had nothing to do with writing and everything to do with the face of the eighties, Eddie Murphy. Paramount had basically made the template of *Cop* two years before by pairing Murphy with Nick Nolte in the action-comedy *48 HRS.*, produced by Larry Gordon and his acolyte Joel Silver, who would become the master of these violent buddy pictures with his *Lethal Weapon* series. Like Silver's other future franchise, *Die Hard, Cop* simply dispensed with the buddy and created a one-man show for Murphy. When Simpson was overseeing the development of *48 HRS.,* he originally dismissed the casting of a "TV guy" and pushed to team up Nolte with Gregory Hines.

That was the old studio prejudice, that movie audiences would not go out and pay to see what they could get for free at home. But Diller and Eisner had cut their teeth in television, and they understood the power of the small screen far better than the traditional moguls, who had been inculcated with the snobbery of the studio system. Others at Paramount, including Jeffrey Katzenberg, had no idea what they had, until Murphy's "nigger with a badge" line won the hearts of America.

But when Don was fired, *48 HRS.* hadn't come out, and it was looking like a dud. Thus it didn't seem like that much of a sacrifice for Diller and Eisner to throw the long stalled *Cop* project into Don's severance package. One more booby prize, like *Flashdance,* turned into the fiscal equivalent of the Nobel Prize. Don had beaten the odds. Hollywood had bet that he would fail, one more indie-prod RIP. Instead he had turned dross into gold. He was the new Midas; he was a phenomenon. His megalomania was based not on his cocaine but on the hard reality of his box office, hundreds upon hundreds of millions. It wasn't a delusion of grandeur; it was grandeur itself. Unfortunately, that kind of success and the enablement that came with it was just the thing to turn a garden-variety Hollywood cocaine addict into the drug Godzilla Tony Montana in the remake of *Scarface*.

While Don Simpson was beginning his reign of grosses, Jon Peters was doing the limbo rock. PolyGram, the company that had bankrolled him and Guber, decided to close up shop, orphaning the two would-be moguls, who had just diversified their portfolio and gotten directly into the business of money by buying a "gay" bank in West Hollywood called Bel Air Savings and Loan. But they needed a studio lot to call home. They had planned on Universal, but the old-school new head man there, Frank Price, knew what wastrels the boys were, so that was a no-go. What saved the day was Jon's ability to play the Barbra card. Jon had actually been playing it for years, snowing the Warner's head of distribution, Terry Semel, when *A Star Is Born* was made there. He invited Semel to the Malibu "ranch," with the dogs and the horses, teaching the city Jew, a Brooklyn-born onetime accountant, how to be a kick-ass country boy, sort of the way Jon "countrified" Barbra herself.

Also, Semel, who co-ran the studio with another Brooklyn-born accountant type, Bob Daly, reported to Steve Ross, the head of the whole company. Ross was a huge Streisand fan and friend. Always lurking in his agile mind was the possible megacoup of stealing Barbra from Columbia Records for his Warner music label. Between records and films, Barbra was still the biggest female star on earth, and Jon was the ultimate gatekeeper. Furthermore, Ross's success story was outrageous in the Jon mold. Ross had begun his career as a mortician and made his first fortune in janitorial services and parking lots. He knew how to read, but he didn't let it get in his way. He had an undertaker's courtliness and solicitude, always proffering the grand gesture, the corporate jet, the villa in Acapulco, the ranch in Aspen, the best restaurants, hotels, tickets, all on him. If Jon wanted to be someone, it certainly wasn't Don Simpson. He wanted to be Steve Ross, the *grand sei-gneur* from Brooklyn.

Guber-Peters came to the Warner lot and set up lush mirrored offices that reminded many visitors of Jon's hair salon. To hear Jon's side of the story, his first triumph at Warner's was to "discover" Madonna for the first Guber-Peters film there, *Vision Quest,* a New Agey title (Jon loved anything New Age or spiritual) for what was basically a male *Flashdance* set in the world of wrestling. Maybe Pauline Kael was on to something with her innuendo about those tight masculine buns. But nobody came out to see Mathew Modine, whose gluteus proved to be minimus. The only thing that worked in the movie was Madonna's song "Crazy for You," which became a huge hit, but unlike Irene Cara's "What a Feeling" did nothing to propel the film into national consciousness.

What the song did do was precipitate a major incident on the Warner's lot. Warner Bros. Records, headed by Mo Ostin, a disc king who went back to Sinatra days, was planning a major launch of Madonna's first album, *Like a Virgin*. Ostin saw the movie as a stiff and didn't want it to tarnish the debut of what he believed would be a superstar. Accordingly, Ostin requested that Bob Daly take "Crazy for You" and another Madonna song off the *Vision Quest* sound track. When Jon got the news, he went crazy, as only Jon could go crazy.

Why should Madonna be Mo Ostin's superstar? She was Jon's superstar, his discovery. He had even taken the cross-wearing waif to meet Barbra, who might have been jealous but wasn't and bestowed her benediction. Actually tearing the door off Bob Daly's serene office suite, Jon went psycho on the studio head far more menacingly than he had on Ray Stark for what he had done to Barbra, or Warren Beatty for seducing Lesley Ann. Instead of throwing Jon off the lot, Daly succumbed to the threat of irrational violence. Daly was just added to the list of powerhouses whom Jon cowed into submission.

The list also included Barry Diller, who had made fun of Jon's 1982 Brooke Shields disaster *Endless Love* at a party at the Malibu house of Dolly Parton's manager, Sandy Gallin. The only segment of America that embraced the film was the gay one, who loved Brooke almost as much as they loved Barbra. The crowd at Gallin's was largely gay, and when Jon reputedly "bitch-slapped" Diller, standing up for Brooke's honor, the guests cheered Jon on. Jon claims to have kissed Diller's cheek to make up for the humiliation. All these incidents were proof that Hollywood would rather switch than fight, and they only added to Jon's legend as an "enforcer" who could not be denied, at risk of bodily harm. Don, on the other hand, never raised a hand to anyone. That was another major difference between Don and Jon. Jon might beat you to death; Don might talk you to death.

Given Jon's explosive temper, no one dared tease him about his string of flops at Warner's. *Vision Quest* was followed by major misfires like the teen revenge movie *The Legend of Billie Jean;* a remake of the board game *Clue; Youngblood,* which was *Vision Quest* in hockey; *Head Office,* an unfunny corporate comedy; and *The Clan of the Cave Bear,* which mauled a bestseller. The only notable credit was *The Color Purple,* which was a book that Guber had bought. Furthermore, Spielberg, like Don Simpson, famously issued a decree barring Jon from the shoot. That did not stop Jon from taking credit for "discovering" Oprah Winfrey for the film or for her Oscar nomination and the ten others the film received. No one won.

Despite the bombs, and despite the occasional temper meltdown, Jon, unlike the undiplomatic bulldozer Don, was brilliantly Machiavellian in playing the game of studio politics. If he could get along with the mercurial Streisand, he could get along with anyone. And anyone who had seduced as many women as Jon had, with his combination of little bad boy lost and the Brando-Dean–Beatty persona, could charm the most savage beasts in the Hollywood jungle. He also had a real knack for hiring the moguls of tomorrow as his development boys and girls, people like Laura Ziskin, who would go on to head Fox 2000, Amy Pascal, who would head Columbia, and Mark Canton, who would head Warner's.

Canton was particularly useful to Jon during his early stumbles at Warner. The Queens-born son of an advance man for Sam Spiegel, Canton, who grew up around the likes of Hitchcock and David Lean, Alec Guinness and William Holden and Audrey Hepburn, early on acquired his father's publicist tact, hype, and tolerance, qualities that, after frat-boying it at UCLA, propelled him up the studio ladder, though his taste in films leaned far less to David Lean than to John Landis. An avowed populist, Canton, with Jon running interference, was able to displace his predecessor Mark Rosenberg, a relatively highbrow former University of Wisconsin SDS student radical who had made his name with serious projects like *The Killing Fields*.

Aiding Jon in his machinations was his hairdresser's mastery of studio gossip. Remember how he used the tidbit about David Begelman's pal "Winkie" to get himself a studio deal? It was a small world indeed, bursting with delicious soap opera intrigue, and Jon's knowledge of every detail was power that gave him a great deal of leverage.

Another area of mastery was Jon's (and partner Guber's) expertise at draining the studio pork barrel. Their most outrageous early extravagance (before *Batman* and *Rain Man* gave them license to spend) was their boat (in Guber's name), the *Oz*, which would have made a James Bond villain right at home on the high seas. After all, as producer of *The Deep*, wasn't Guber of all people entitled to sail in style? The raison d'être, and tax deductibility, for this leviathan was a television series called *Oceanquest* (viz *Vision Quest*) that Guber had sold to Brandon Tartikoff, the new head of NBC, a very eastern Lawrenceville-Yale Jewish preppy who was an emblem of the new breed of Ivy Leaguers skipping Wall Street and finding their way into show business, particularly television.

The show was anything but Ivy League, more like *20,000 Leagues Under the Sea* with a bimbo instead of Nemo. Said bimbo was Shawn Weatherly, an ex–Miss Universe, swimsuit-clad diving cruise hostess on the *Oz,* circumnavigating the globe in search of sunken treasure and exotic fauna. The idea was that Weatherly would become the Mary Hart of the high seas. She didn't, though she did later make it on *Baywatch*. The show died, canceled after four of the most expensive episodes in the annals of the small screen, but it enabled Jon and Peter to cruise in style and it established the dynamic duo as Steve Ross–worthy showmen capable of the beau geste.

Aside from his lack of a real hit, the worst thing that happened to Jon in the mid-eighties was the loss of Barbra. The songwriting team of Marilyn and Alan Bergman ("The Way We Were"), Barbra's closest friends from the way she was back in Brooklyn, and Cis Corman, her best girlfriend, had for years led a Greek chorus of disapproval over Jon. After over a decade, the message seemed to be registering, mainly because now that Jon had Peter, he didn't need Barbra anymore to validate him. He claimed he begged her to marry him over and over, but she couldn't take that long, strange trip to the altar with him.

How sincere his proposals were is subject to question, as he was busy, in secret, making propositions, particularly to Goldie Hawn, the only other Jewish movie star who could begin to match the power and clout of Barbra. The problem was that Goldie might come close, but she couldn't equal Barbra, and hell would have had no fury like a Barbra publicly scorned for someone like Goldie. Fearing for the rest of his life to ever invoke the wrath of

Streisand, Jon put Goldie aside and let himself be smitten by a nonrival to Barbra, a young Dutch model named Christine Forsythe whom he met strolling on Rodeo Drive in 1986.

Again, Jon had his cake and ate it, too. He remained BFF (best friends forever) with Barbra and readied himself for his next career assault, which would win him Oscars and make him a studio head, the craziest trajectory in the history of film. For Don Simpson, Jon's woman troubles must have seemed like problems from another planet. The only woman he needed was Madam Alex. He paid women to *go,* not to come. And who needed women when he had Eddie Murphy and Tom Cruise, the biggest aphrodisiacs, certainly for a producer, Hollywood had ever concocted?

**TOP** Dig You Must. Ronald Reagan and his guru, MCA chairman Lew Wasserman. (BE Images)

**BOTTOM** I Can Get It Wholesale. Betsy and Alfred Bloomingdale, the Reagans' best friends. (BE Images)

**RIGHT** T for Two. Nancy Reagan and Mister T, her idea of Black Power. (Ronald Reagan Library)

**BELOW** The High Table. Chef Wolfgang Puck and restaurateur Patrick Terrail, caterers to the stars, in the Rolls-only parking lot of Ma Maison.

**TOP** Call Me Madam. Madame Claude, another caterer to the stars. (Corbis)

**BOTTOM** The Yale Man. David Begelman, who never met a lie he couldn't tell. (BE Images)

**TOP LEFT** Elysian Fields. Freddie Fields, Begelman's agency partner, with mentee Sherry Lansing, the cynosure of female studio executives. (BE Images)

**BOTTOM LEFT** The Little Fox. Richard Zanuck, son of Darryl, both of whom ran Twentieth Century Fox, and his wife Lili, hoisting their *Driving Miss Daisy* Oscars. (BE Images)

**OPPOSITE** Son of Shane. Alan Ladd Jr., who ran Fox and MGM. (Corbis)

Fear Factor. Power broker Mike
Ovitz of CAA, the most hated
man in Hollywood, with his prom
queen wife Judy. (BE Images)

A Boy Named Sue.
Superagent Sue Mengers,
who was considered one
of the Big Guys, with one
of them, her dear pal Jack
Nicholson. (BE Images)

Don't Call Me Swifty.
Old Guard agent Irving Lazar,
who despised the nickname
Humphrey Bogart gave him,
with Diana Ross. (BE Images)

**TOP** Rambo Warriors. Andrew Vajna, who turned lowbrow foreign sales into a global action empire, with his point man Sylvester Stallone. (BE Images)

**BOTTOM** The Go Go Boys. Israeli shlockmeisters Menahem Golan and Yorum Globus.

**TOP** Little Big Man.
Italian impresario Dino
De Laurentiis with wife
Martha. (BE Images)

**BOTTOM** The Two Mouseketeers.
Michael Eisner and Jeffrey
Katzenberg, who resurrected
Disney. (BE Images)

**OPPOSITE TOP** Too Big to Fail. Marvin Davis (right), the Denver wildcatter who bought Fox, with board member Henry Kissinger. (BE Images)

**OPPOSITE BOTTOM** Funny Boy. Producer Ray Stark, who rode his marriage to Fannie Brice's daughter to the pinnacle of Hollywood. (BE Images)

**ABOVE** Penthouse Pet. Dawn Steel, who rose from marketing Gucci toilet paper and penile mittens for Bob Guccione to running Columbia Pictures, with fellow power femmes Jodie Foster and Madonna. (BE Images)

**LEFT TOP** Pop Guns. Jerry Bruckheimer and Don Simpson, the hottest of all studio producers, with their boy-toy twin Ferraris. (Getty Images)

**LEFT BOTTOM** The Weather Overground. Longhaired *Rain Man* producers and SONY-Columbia co–studio heads Peter Guber and Jon Peters. (Corbis)

**ABOVE** Arms and the Man. Saudi munitions dealer Adnan Khashoggi, Hollywood's ultimate *mal vivant*. (BE Images)

**ABOVE** Stiff Upper. Sir James Goldsmith, the Anglo-Jewish aristocrat corporate raider who came to Hollywood to play like a Player. (BE Images)

**LEFT** Star of David. Brit *Chariots of Fire* producer David Puttnam (right), whose installation as head of Columbia Pictures to raise its tone was a fiasco that brought down the house, with Brit *Chariots* director Hugh Hudson. (BE Images)

**ABOVE** Clown Princes. The odd couple of the decade, Eddie Murphy and his Harvard lawyer–manager Bob Wachs. (Courtesy of Bob Wachs)

**LEFT** Predators' Ball. Sony record czar Walter Yetnikoff, with subjects Cher and Gene Simmons. (BE Images)

**ABOVE** Upward Mobility. Giancarlo Parretti, who went from a Hong Kong fish cannery to the chairmanship of MGM, and then on the lam. (Corbis)

**LEFT** Color Me Barbra. Streisand and Peters, the power couple of the era. (BE Images)

## CHAPTER 9
### BRITISH COLUMBIA

IF YOU WERE TO JUDGE a film studio by the quality of its lot, then Columbia Pictures, the company behind such epics as *The Bridge on the River Kwai* and *Lawrence of Arabia,* would in the eighties barely qualify as a film studio at all. Paramount had its iconic Bronson gate, which inspired Charles Buchinsky to change his last name, and its classic Roaring Twenties Jazz Age star offices. Universal had its ominous black tower, its *Psycho* house, and Steven Spielberg's mutated Taco Bell–like Amblin compound. Fox, despite having sold off much of its acreage to create Century City, still had the *Hello, Dolly!* set of old New York and a cool celebrity-filled garden commissary. MGM, although on its last legs, still reeked of art deco splendor. Disney, before Michael Eisner hired Michael Graves to architecturally immortalize the Seven Dwarfs, was like a military barracks, a sad study in animators' Quonset huts. And Warner's intimidated with its wall of giant sound studios and its luxurious mission bungalows. Columbia, in a prefab two-story seventies blockhouse, was an afterthought in the back of the Warner's lot, known formally as the Burbank Studios but known to everyone else as just Warner's.

How the mighty had fallen. Created by Harry Cohn, the coarsest and most vulgar of filmdom's founding fathers, Columbia was as traumatized by Cohn's death of a heart attack in 1958 as the rest of Hollywood was relieved. Cohn was said to have had the biggest funeral in movie history, bigger than Valentino's, because his countless enemies and rivals wanted to be sure he was dead. By 1972, the desperate studio, in order to survive, sold its Gower Street lot and moved in at Warner's over the hill in Burbank. An even bigger blow to the studio than the demise of Cohn was the 1977 David Begelman scandal, which even his hits like *Close Encounters* and *Taxi Driver* could not counterbalance.

Still, the Columbia brand, however tarnished (its torch lady logo had been plagiarized by the unschooled, ex–streetcar conductor and song plugger Cohn from the alma mater statue of Columbia University), was still a major emblem of big-time Hollywood. In June 1982, Coca-Cola, that global symbol of syrupy all-American goodness, decided the brand was worth $750 million. The figure was $25 million more than Marvin Davis, Marc Rich, and Pincus Green had paid the year before for Fox. The Coke acquisition, though, was significant in that this wasn't some play by a wildcatter and two soon-to-be offshore felons, but the first move by a true blue-chip eastern Establishment company into the Wild West world of show business. Yes, Paramount was owned by Gulf+Western, but that place was fast and loose and always under the scrutiny of the SEC. Charles Blühdorn was a long way from the above-reproach bourbon-and-branch aristocrats who ran Coca-Cola down in Atlanta.

Coke, perhaps along with Marilyn Monroe, may have been America's most symbolic product. It was only fitting, then, that Coke would feel there was international synergy to be had by acquiring a film company. Leading the move into Hollywood was Coke's new international chairman, a pre-Castro Cuban flight aristocrat named Roberto Goizueta, who had prepped at Cheshire Academy in Connecticut en route to Yale. He liked to tell people he learned his English less from his Ivy League tutors than from watching American classics by Preston Sturges and Frank Capra, which, incidentally, were Columbia films. Goizueta, whose dark-suited bankerly cautious mien was tempered by a slightly naughty Latin gleam in his twinkly eyes, was fifty-one at the time of the Coke takeover, but he had a yuppie's obsession with Hollywood, plus the wherewithal to make his fantasy come true.

Furthermore, despite the continuing stranglehold on the studio by Ray Stark, now in his seventies but strong as ever, the controlling banker Herbert Allen had significantly cleaned up Columbia's sleazy act by installing his fellow Williams alumnus Fay Vincent as Columbia's new head man. Vincent basically had zero interest in Hollywood, hence the temptation factor that was the ruin of many a Begelman was absent. Vincent, a Washington, D.C., corporate power lawyer who had gone to Yale Law School (unlike Begelman, who had pretended to), had worked at the SEC when it was investigating the Begelman affair. That put him one step further above approach, not that he needed to be.

A devout Jesuit and football hero at Williams, as his father had been at Yale, Vincent cut his sports career short when he broke his back falling off the roof of his dorm. He wasn't drunk; his roommates had pulled the collegiate prank of locking him in his room, and he wanted to demonstrate his escape artistry. Vincent remained partially crippled for life. When he tried to join the Jesuits after Williams, the order turned him down because he wasn't ambulatory enough, in their minds, to do God's work. So he did Herbert Allen's instead, and he did it so well that Coke ended up paying $75 a share for stock that the Allens had bought for $4. The Allens made a $40 million profit on the deal. God's work indeed.

When Goizueta took a good look at what Coke had bought, he quickly fathomed that he was dealing with a major case of Hollywood déjà vu, a reshuffling of a very tired deck, with Ray Stark doing the dealing. Because Vincent—who was balding and

bespectacled, walked with a cane, and was totally antithetical to
the flashy Hollywood stereotype—knew little and cared less about
the Burbank power game, he had deferred to Herbert Allen's
mentor, Stark. The Rabbit was a disciple of the "if we don't already know you, we don't want to know you" school in choosing
leaders to make the movies while Vincent stuck to the numbers.
Goizueta inherited Stark protégé Frank Price as Columbia's production chief under Vincent. On the surface, the dowdy, unflashy
Price seemed as un-Hollywood, and un-Jewish, as Vincent.

Born in Decatur, Illinois, and raised in Flint, Michigan, Price
had joined the navy, then worked as a police reporter on the *Flint
Journal* before attending Michigan State. But somehow in the
1950s he ended up in Hollywood, where he became a lifer, beginning as a script reader at Columbia, then working his way up
the slippery and treacherous Lew Wasserman ladder at Universal
Television. Inspired by his days on the police beat, Price was the
executive behind such gumshoe staples as *Kojak, Columbo, Baretta,*
and *The Rockford Files,* making Universal the top television producer in the business.

By the eighties, success on the small screen spelled qualifica-
tion for the large, and Stark thus had cover in bringing over his
dear friend Price to helm Columbia. Price justified Stark with
two huge Dustin Hoffman hits, *Kramer vs. Kramer* and *Tootsie,* but
soon crashed and burned with Stark's megaflop *Annie,* which did
as much to kill the market for Broadway remakes as Stark's
*Funny Girl* had done to create it. In Hollywood, such failure
seemed to alchemize into success. Price wasn't banished from the
business at all. Instead he went back, with full honors, to head
the feature division at Universal, where he would crash and burn
with *Howard the Duck,* a George Lucas–produced sci-fi comedy
about an alien duck who finds love on earth with a lounge singer
named Cherry Bomb (played by the now forgotten Lea Thomp-
son), then saves his new planet. The movie proved that George

Lucas was not infallible. The *Variety* headline said it all: DUCK COOKS PRICE'S GOOSE. But Price proved to be no dead duck. When Guber and Peters pulled the ultimate sleight of hand in taking over Columbia in 1989, whom did they appoint to run the studio? Frank Price. Unlike old soldiers, old studio heads never died.

Vincent replaced Price with another Ray Stark man, Guy McElwaine, whom Stark paid his ultimate compliment in calling him "a Jew in goy clothing." His faith notwithstanding, McElwaine was even more of a Hollywood lifer than Frank Price. Born in L.A. in 1933 and bred in Culver City in the shadow of MGM, where his father toiled as a studio publicist, McElwaine was a baseball whiz and won a sports scholarship to USC. He actually played Minor League baseball for the Hollywood Stars, the farm team of the Pittsburgh Pirates. Alas, a torn rotator cuff took him off the field and into the studios. He started in the Paramount mailroom, then segued back to do publicity at MGM, where he was discovered by Colonel Tom Parker doing *Jailhouse Rock* there.

McElwaine went on the road with Elvis, eventually got fired, and then went on the road with Frank Sinatra, which led to his starting his own PR firm, representing a wide range of talent from Natalie Wood and Warren Beatty to the Righteous Brothers and the Mamas and the Papas, not to mention Judy Garland. His stellar handholding for the difficult Judy, who was Ray Stark's original choice for *Funny Girl,* brought him not only to Stark's attention but to that of Judy's CMA superagents Freddie Fields and David Begelman, who took the blond, jockish McElwaine out of publicity and into management. He looked much less like an agent than an actor client, and his being different served him well. McElwaine's biggest coup was signing Steven Spielberg, and when CMA became ICM, he became the head of its film division.

In 1980, when McElwaine was passed over to head ICM in favor of the younger Jeff Berg, he was given the consolation prize of heading Rastar, Stark's prolific production company, which in turn led to his becoming Frank Price's chief lieutenant at Columbia. When *Annie* priced Price out, McElwaine took Price's top job. Once ensconced, and newly and rightly cautious about Broadway remakes, McElwaine was somehow emboldened to bite the hand that had fed him. He had the audacity to turn down Stark's planned films of two Neil Simon plays, *Brighton Beach Memoirs* and *Biloxi Blues*. Stark promptly took both projects to Frank Price, who green-lit them at Universal, while McElwaine was green-lighting the disaster *Sheena, Queen of the Jungle*. Although McElwaine could take pride in his *Karate Kid* franchise, in the eyes of Coke *Kid* was less of a credit than *Sheena* was a debit. In 1986, Goizueta assigned Vincent the brief of finding Coke a new man, and if it were possible, his own man, as opposed to Ray Stark's man.

At first, it seemed that Vincent's brief was also to bring Goizueta a fellow Yale man. His first two candidates were both Yalies and both named Brandon. One was Brandon Stoddard, the head of ABC Entertainment. The other, even stronger prospect was Brandon Tartikoff, the head of NBC Entertainment. Tartikoff, whose main claim to fame at that point was having put the high-concept *Miami Vice* on the air, had also attended Lawrenceville, the same tony prep school that had given Hollywood Michael Eisner. In Tartikoff, Columbia could have a Jew and a preppy, too. But Vincent was so straight a shooter that he couldn't conceal his zeal for Tartikoff from Vincent's close bigwig friend and Tartikoff's boss, Jack Welch, whose GE had just bought NBC in 1985, in another major incursion of eastern power into western glitz. Not wanting to lose Tartikoff, Welch signed the Yalie to a long-term contract to keep him out of Vincent's aboveboard clutches. Vincent realized he would have to look elsewhere, probably beyond the Ivy League.

If Fay Vincent couldn't get a polished Yale man, what about a

Brit? If he wanted polish, why not go straight to the source, the mother country? The new target was David Puttnam, the forty-five-year-old putative "savior" of the once august British film industry, the man who had defied all odds by dominating the Oscars of 1981 with his artily nostalgic dark horse *Chariots of Fire,* about two British Olympic runners, one Jewish, one not, and then followed that up with his high-minded antiwar film *The Killing Fields.* There was no *Howard the Duck,* no *Sheena,* on this man's résumé. He was even Jewish, via his mother, for those who cared. And there were a lot of people in Hollywood who did care. All in all, Puttnam was a class act. Plus he was a foreign act, which was no liability at all to the internationalist Goizueta. Coke made the majority of its profits abroad. It was a global brand. Movies, too, were making more and more of their money abroad as well. Why not put a globalist at the helm of Columbia? The trick was how to get him.

The biggest problem here was that David Puttnam had gone on the record (as a publicity hound, he loved to go on the record) as basically hating Hollywood, at least the big-bucks crony Hollywood of Ray Stark and, now, of Mike Ovitz. He had tried Hollywood once, before *Chariots,* running Casablanca Filmworks for Peter Guber, before Guber fell for Jon Peters. Puttnam had a big hit, *Midnight Express,* about an American hash dealer sentenced to life in Turkish prison, but he still hated it. He was ashamed that *Midnight Express* was the worst thing for Turkey's image since the Armenian genocide, ashamed that the film, despite Oliver Stone's screenwriting Oscar, was totally exploitative, S&M prison porn syncopated to a Giorgio Moroder technobeat. The *Express* experience, pure Hollywood commerce, made Puttnam feel so soiled that he fled back to England. The squeaky clean, uplifting *Chariots* had to be seen as his atonement piece. And he kept atoning, with *Local Hero,* with *Killing Fields,* with his upcoming *The Mission,* more high-mindedness about Jesuits versus slavers in colonial South

America. Why, in the name of Coke, would he even consider re-
turning to the Sodom he had so guiltily left behind him, never
looking back?

Fay Vincent did a lot of homework on David Puttnam's background and realized that inside the savior was a showman who
may have been closer to Hollywood than he cared to admit.
Puttnam, born in 1941, was a war baby who had grown up bourgeois and ambitious in heavily Jewish and heavily blitzed north
London. His father was a successful Fleet Street photographer
and a war correspondent who postwar moonlighted as a wedding photographer.

In the fifties David grew up on American films, even though
those years were something of a golden age of British cinema,
particularly the "angry young man" films like *Room at the Top* and
*The Entertainer.* Still, Americana, embodied by Marilyn Monroe
and James Dean, and even Rock Hudson and Doris Day, was pure
catnip to deprived English lads. Puttnam even admitted to having
had a crush on Debbie Reynolds, who inevitably got dumped for
Brigitte Bardot, when . . . *And God Created Woman* gave Puttnam a new appreciation for "world cinema."

All Puttnam's teen moviegoing did not an Oxbridge man make.
In fact, following a hallowed Hollywood tradition, he didn't even
finish high school. Instead, he went to work as a messenger boy in
an ad agency. But he quickly worked his way up to become an account executive, one of the hottest admen in the "swinging London" of the early 1960s, a city whose Beatles, Stones, and miniskirts
made everything English the coolest things in the world in those
glory days. Puttnam looked the part. With his Beatles–copycat
long hair and King's Road meets Carnaby Street gear, he could
have been on the cover of the *Sgt. Pepper* album. Just as British film
of the period was thriving, with movies like *Darling, Alfie, Blow-
Up,* and the Bond series, British advertising was having its own

heyday, with Puttnam working with such star photographers as David Bailey and Lord Snowden and making indelible connections with the slick, brash, up from nowhere, largely Cockney commercials directors who would become Hollywood's biggest-buck auteurs in the decades to come—Tony and Ridley Scott, Alan Parker, Adrian Lyne, and Hugh Hudson (a smooth Etonian in an otherwise rough sea).

One of Puttnam's ad mates was Charles Saatchi, who with his brother Maurice eventually developed the biggest agency in the world, one that he would have been happy to make Puttnam a part of. But Puttnam, who had become a photographers' agent to cash in on the cachet of Brit lensmen, had met an American who had put the dream of becoming a moviemaker so deeply into his psyche that he could focus on nothing else. The American was Sanford "Sandy" Lieberson. A dashing, sporty, and unusually sophisticated Los Angelino, Lieberson had fled to Europe after UCLA in the late 1950s to work as a film publicist in *Dolce Vita* Rome. When the Hollywood crowd abandoned Rome in the 1960s for the newly greener pastures of London, Lieberson was in the vanguard, running the new ICM office in Soho. He soon was lured into production, his first effort being a package of all his clients in *Performance*, Mick Jagger, James Fox, co-directors Nicolas Roeg and Donald Cammell. It was a classic, but nobody outside of the in crowd actually saw it.

David Puttnam, who had married his childhood sweetheart but was anything but a homebody, was a key member of that in crowd. He was smitten with Lieberson, who introduced him to the sizable American film community in London, where stars like Julie Christie, Sean Connery, and Michael Caine were erupting and production was dirt cheap. Puttnam got to know important Yank players like Alan Ladd Jr.; Mike Francovich, who ran Columbia's international division; hustler extraordinaire Elliott Kastner; and the ex-con icon Sam Spiegel, who had produced the very movies, like *On the Waterfront, Kwai,* and *Lawrence,* that had forged Puttnam's tony tastes.

Eventually, Lieberson made Puttnam his partner in his production company, Goodtimes Enterprises. Their first effort was the 1971 *Melody,* a low-budget love story between two ten-year-olds whose main lure was a Bee Gees sound track. The principal financial backer for *Melody,* corralled by money wrangler Lieberson, was Edgar Bronfman Sr. of the Canadian liquor empire Seagram's. The investment was a kind of gift from his father to Edgar Jr., only fifteen at the time but a huge Bee Gees fan and even as a teen a wannabe producer. Such are the gifts only billionaires can bestow. In 1995, Seagram's, with Edgar Jr. at the helm, would buy MCA-Universal from the Japanese Matsushita.

*Melody* did not become a preteen *Saturday Night Fever,* except in Japan, where it was a smash. Goodtimes had an even worse time with its next effort, *The Pied Piper,* starring Donovan and two hundred rats who followed him around during the bubonic plague. The movie was a precursor of Puttnam's high-minded ambitions, but not even Ray Stark could have made a hit based on the Black Death. Not that he would have tried. Undeterred in their ambitions, Puttnam and Lieberson set out to do a film version of Albert Speer's *Inside the Third Reich,* which never could come together. In its place was another music movie, *That'll Be the Day,* starring Ringo Starr and a much lesser Brit rocker, David Essex. The film, focusing on the dark side of fame, did so well in England (though nowhere else) that Goodtimes made a sequel, *Stardust,* sadly minus Ringo.

The bad times at Goodtimes found their Waterloo when Lieberson and Puttnam decided to produce a series of six biopics about famous musicians, from Mahler to Gershwin, all to be directed by the over-the-top Ken Russell. Russell quit after the disastrous *Lisztomania,* starring the Who's Roger Daltrey, whom Russell had directed in his smash *Tommy,* which Goodtimes regrettably had no share in. Lieberson and Puttnam's final effort was the Jodie Foster teen gangster flick *Bugsy Malone,* directed by Puttnam's commercials mate Alan Parker, who would also soon direct *Midnight Express.* Despite lots of press attention for the gimmicky premise, the film made very little money. Puttnam's work was as far from Hollywood studio fare as film could be. It was, without necessarily being hostile to commerce, totally antistudio. It was also antiprofit, intentionally or not. The time had come for David Puttnam to start thinking about getting a paying job, and that was what led him into the tentacles of Peter Guber, hot from *The Deep.*

Guber was the total studio man, and his pairing with Puttnam was akin to Lucifer teaming up with Jesus to do a loaves and fishes concert. Few people in the entertainment business seemed more Mephisophelean than Guber and his Casablanca partner, Neil Bogart, who gave the world the demonic rock group Kiss. Despite the directorial presence of his friend Alan Parker, Puttnam blamed the horror of it all on Hollywood's base basic instinct. He was so traumatized that he even sought the counsel of a Jesuit priest, who inspired him to transcend Hollywood, which he did, to the Vangelis tune of *Chariots.* David Puttnam had been had, and he'd been soiled, and he returned to England surely singing the Who's anthem, "Won't Get Fooled Again." But now in 1985, with a slew of Oscars and other honors under his belt for doing it "his" way, he was back in Hollywood, singin' in the rain, singin' for a multimillion-dollar supper. Won't get fooled again? His new anthem may have been "First I Look at the Purse."

Coca-Cola was desperate; 1986 had been a dismal year at the box office for Columbia, pockmarked with such bombs as Blake Edwards's aptly named *A Fine Mess* and Richard Pryor's act of autobiographical self-abuse, *Jo Jo Dancer, Your Life Is Calling.* Columbia was turning out to be a bigger disaster for Atlanta than

General Sherman. On Puttnam's job interview in Atlanta, he and
Goizueta totally bonded, two foreigners who were inspired by
old-time Hollywood movies.

The summit meeting was a love-in, with Puttnam and Goizueta
on the exact same page about restoring the studio system of yore to
make inspirational, unforgettable films to raise the spirits of the
whole world, the Coke world, not just to raise the incomes of stars,
producers, and agents. Puttnam didn't seem to have problems about
Coke rotting the world's teeth or causing the world's obesity. The
only fat that mattered at the interview were the fat cats of Hollywood, whose crime wasn't so much their fatness as their bad taste
in films, a taste that was dictated by greed, not by art.

Goizueta having found his soul mate, Coke acceded to Puttnam's request for a very short three-year term, coupled with a very
long golden parachute of $3 million. Although Coke had made
Puttnam an offer he simply couldn't refuse, he was deeply ambivalent about sleeping with the enemy and, as if to assuage his own
guilt, used his new perch atop Columbia as a bully pulpit to de-
nounce the current studio system and long for the old studio system, which he vowed to resurrect. Even before Columbia, Puttnam
was known to have one of the biggest mouths in show business.
The man loved lecturing so much that, simultaneous with the
Coke courtship, he had been in negotiations with Harvard to teach
a course on the business of cinema. In the end, he took Coke over
Harvard. In the process of working out his own guilt over his
Coke windfall, Puttnam would alienate virtually every power that
was in Hollywood.

Puttnam's first target was the upcoming comedy that Coca-
Cola was counting on to turn Columbia's fortunes around. It had
two of the biggest stars in the world and one of the cleverest directors. We know now that the $50 million *Ishtar* was up there
with *Howard the Duck* in the 1980s Hall of Shame, but when Puttnam came on board, *Ishtar* was Coke's Great White Hope, and

nobody except David Puttnam was audacious enough to rain on Coke's parade. Puttnam had no choice but to rain on it, then recuse himself from working on the film and its release, because both Dustin Hoffman and Warren Beatty had already been alienated by him and didn't want the Brit outsider meddling with their masterpiece.

Puttnam had had his contretemps with Hoffman soon after *Midnight Express* when he returned to England to purge the *Express* experience by producing, in 1979, a very English, very arty, very uncommercial quasi-mystery story called *Agatha,* about the brief disappearance of Agatha Christie in 1926. This wasn't the Lindbergh kidnapping, or Leopold and Loeb, but a fictional trifle, concocted by the wife of famed critic Kenneth Tynan, about the romance between a fleeing mystery queen, played by Vanessa Redgrave, and an American journalist, played by Hoffman, who tracks her down. It wasn't a whodunit at all; it was a why-did-they-make-it.

Dustin Hoffman, that's why, or at least why the little art movie became a big, bloated Warner's release, the last thing Puttnam wanted for his "rehab" project. With a huge star name came the attendant huge star ego. In return for bringing the financing to the project, Hoffman also brought his own writer for rewrites. He fought with Redgrave, and he fought even more with Puttnam, so much so that Puttnam walked off the project, but not before trashing Hoffman, and his ego, in the *L.A. Times,* a slight Hoffman would never forget. Hoffman's riposte was to cite his own film, *Who Is Harry Kellerman and Why Is He Saying Those Terrible Things About Me?* Hoffman, playing the innocent, claimed he had met Puttnam only three times. But that was three times more than he ever wanted to see him again. The feeling was mutual, but it didn't make for an auspicious debut for Puttnam at Columbia.

Puttnam had made an enemy of Warren Beatty when his *Chariots* beat Beatty's *Reds* for the Oscar for Best Picture of 1981.

*Chariots* was a picture that Puttnam might not have even made were it not for his ex-partner, Sandy Lieberson, leaning on his old London friend Alan Ladd Jr. to put up the money for United States rights. An even less likely helping hand came from Dodi Fayed, who was dabbling with his father's fortune in the film business. Lieberson had an internal Geiger counter for locating global billionaires susceptible to the lure of cinema. Just as he had found Edgar Bronfman, who wanted to spoil his son rotten by giving him a movie, he now found Mohamed al-Fayed, who wanted to similarly make his Dodi the boy who had everything. The Muslim Fayed received an "executive producer" credit (to Puttnam's sole "producer") for putting an essential $3 million of his father's money into a film about a Jewish runner. It was also a film his father had so little confidence in that he had tried to unload his investment into Twentieth Century Fox until Laddie came to the rescue.

Lieberson and Puttnam had first crossed paths with Dodi Fayed at Tramp, the louche Jermyn Street private nightclub founded by former Brighton bookie Johnny Gold, which was frequented by all the stars, star photographers, and star models in Puttnam's ad-man set. The shy but wildly generous Fayed was doing his best to replicate the lifestyle of his uncle Adnan Khashoggi, not only in London but in Los Angeles as well. Before he got to Lady Diana, Fayed had dated David Bailey's ex Marie Helvin, one of the prime faces of the sixties, as well as Prince Andrew's ex Koo Stark, one of the most notorious bad girls of the seventies. In Hollywood, Fayed dated Tom Cruise ex Mimi Rogers, as well as Valerie Perrine, Brooke Shields, Winona Ryder, and Tanya Roberts of *Sheena, Queen of the Jungle,* which may have given Fayed and the Columbia-bound David Puttnam something else to talk about.

Once *Chariots* got released and became an Oscar contender (and the Fayeds more than tripled their investment), Puttnam took to his soapbox and characterized it as the little Brit underdog to Beatty's ironically and capitalistically deep-pocketed paean to an American Communist. The non-u(niversity) Puttnam had always resented the exclusionary elitism of the British caste system, which he now saw repeated, minus the education, in Hollywood. It wasn't fair to him that those at the top, like Beatty and Ray Stark, could spend and spend on unnecessary extravagances with total impunity and immunity from criticism.

Puttnam's propaganda actually worked, and Beatty, notwithstanding his Best Director statuette, forever resented getting upstaged and out-Oscared on his lifetime pet project. When Puttnam descended on Columbia, Beatty, even more than Hoffman, was convinced that Puttnam would again spoil his party, and he may have leaned on Fay Vincent to keep his new hire away from his sacred *Ishtar.* As it turned out, Puttnam never even screened *Ishtar* for himself, but its stars still managed to blame him and his anti-big bias, and not their own big selves, for its wretched failure.

Aside from *Ishtar,* David Puttnam simply couldn't stop talking and putting his foot in his mouth. He quickly pissed off CAA's Mike Ovitz, one of his prime targets, who deserved a lot of the blame (or credit, if you were an Ovitz client) for driving up the cost of films a staggering 400 percent from 1977 to 1985. Ovitz's client Dan Aykroyd was scheduled to star in *Vibes,* a daffy Columbia comedy about psychics. Puttnam fixated on co-starring opposite Aykroyd the daffy songstress Cyndi Lauper. Lauper had never acted before, and Aykroyd felt he deserved a bigger name with his on the marquee. Ovitz insisted to Puttnam that he drop Lauper. Instead, Puttnam dropped Aykroyd, replacing him with Jeff Goldblum. It was a major "dis" to the undissable Ovitz.

Puttnam's next sacrifice was another Ovitz client and another of Columbia's sacred cows. Bill Murray had made a fortune for the studio with *Ghostbusters,* on Frank Price's watch. Now *Ghostbusters II* was in the works. Sequels were Hollywood's idea of pennies from heaven but Puttnam's idea of uncreative hell, the lifeblood of

the vampire agency CAA, whose famously expensive star packages Puttnam denigrated every chance he could. The new studio
head chafed at having to do something so blatantly commercial as
*Ghostbusters II.* To him it was almost pornographic, without redeeming social value. He railed particularly against Murray's guaranteed take and his refusal to defer his compensation based on the
sequel's supposedly guaranteed success. Not that Puttnam himself
had tied his own salary to Columbia's performance.

As reported by "Page Six" in the *New York Post,* Puttnam made
the unforgivable gaffe of comparing Murray unfavorably to Robert Redford. Redford, Puttnam told a British Chamber of Commerce luncheon at the Beverly Hills Hotel, was a giver, with his
Sundance Institute. Bill Murray, on the other hand, was a taker.
What had he done charitably with his *Ghostbusters* gross millions?
Puttnam naturally excoriated the tabloid and denied he ever said
this, but there were several Hollywood lawyers at the luncheon,
including Bill Murray's, who swore that was what he said. It was
no accident that the *Ghostbusters* sequel did not proceed until
1988, after David Puttnam had left the building.

It wasn't just mindless comedy sequels that David Puttnam was
loath to green-light. He also rejected the arguably sure-money
sequel to *Jagged Edge,* the grisly courtroom whodunit starring
Glenn Close and Jeff Bridges. Its producer, Martin Ransohoff,
had been a long-term friend of the Allens, if not Ray Stark, and
had a three-picture deal at Columbia, a crony deal that stuck in
Puttnam's craw. Puttnam tried to make the most out of it by getting a first-time directing job for a British friend, Ben Bolt, the
son of august *Lawrence of Arabia* screenwriter Robert Bolt, on one
of the Ransohoff films, *The Big Town,* starring Matt Dillon. This
caught Puttnam lots of flack for signing an unproven Brit to direct a period piece of Chicago-set Americana.

*Big Town* seemed dead before its arrival, but contrarian Puttnam seemed to abhor success for its own sake. Hence he stuck to

his guns in stonewalling *Jagged Edge II,* which was doubly insulting to Ransohoff, since the story credit for the new film was going
to go to his lawyer son, Steve. Again, like Bronfman and Fayed,
Ransohoff was a proud and doting father who wanted to give his
progeny the gift of celluloid. Inside every Hollywood lawyer was
a writer struggling to get a credit, and here was David Puttnam
bottling up the ambitions of this budding Hollywood prince.
Puttnam was not only a franchise killer, he was a butcher of
dreams—in this case Ransohoff dreams, which normally always
came true. Treading on the man who brought the world *The Beverly Hillbillies* was a high-risk strategy.

The most sacred of all Columbia's Brahma bulls was, of course,
Ray Stark, and even there Puttnam gave Stark the Rodney Dangerfield treatment. Stark had actually reached out to Puttnam
when he arrived in Los Angeles, inviting him to his Holmby
Hills estate to show off his museum-quality collection of Henry
Moores, Braques, and Légers and to seek assurances from Puttnam that his special relationship with Columbia would continue
to be honored. Puttnam did not tell Stark what he wanted to hear;
rather, he delivered his soapbox rant that, to him, everything depended not on the producer, but on the script. There would be no
blanket "puts," wherein Columbia would make anything Stark
wanted.

Puttnam quickly put his mouth where his money was by turning down Stark's new project *Revenge,* from a Jim Harrison no-
vella, plus rubbing salt in Stark's wounds by telling him that if
Stark couldn't place the project with another studio within ninety
days, Columbia, for the $600,000 development costs it had already
put up, would own the project outright. The grapevine told Stark
that Puttnam was going to give *Revenge* to his British friend Alan
Parker to make. This was not only lèse-majesté, it was un-American.
Stark went on the warpath, claiming Puttnam was stacking the
Columbia deck with all his British advertising cronies. Puttnam,

Stark ranted, was taking the studio so far out of the Hollywood mainstream that it should be renamed "British Columbia." Stark was not known for his bon mots, but this time the name entered the showbiz lexicon.

Pissing off Ray Stark was bad enough, but pissing off Bill Cosby was far, far worse. Cosby was the biggest television star in America. His NBC *Cosby Show* was the highest-rated program on the air. Eddie Murphy may have been hot, but Cosby was *God.* Thus when Columbia executive Steve Sohmer, another Yale man who had been passed over by Fay Vincent in favor of Puttnam, landed Cosby to do a feature film at Columbia, Sohmer's "get" was the coup of the year. Television used to be the curse of the big screen. Crossover was almost impossible. Now television was the blessing. If Eddie Murphy could pack the cineplexes, just think what Cosby could do.

The project Cosby wanted to make was called *Leonard Part 6,* a parody of espionage films, which, of course, harked back to Cosby's own interracial breakthrough of the 1960s, *I Spy.* Cosby had developed the idea with off-Broadway playwright Jonathan Reynolds, yet another privileged Lawrenceville Jew and an underachieving teen who had been a classmate of Michael Eisner's at safety school Dennison. But as Ginger Rogers had sung, "Ho, ho, ho, who's got the last laugh now?" Reynolds was writing for Cosby, while all the guys who made it to Princeton were writing boring prospectuses for First Boston. The plot line featured Cosby as Leonard, an ex–CIA spy who has to save the world from an evil female vegetarian who brainwashes animals into killing people in grisly ways. No, it didn't *sound* funny, but who was going to second-guess the most respected funny man in America? Those tens of millions of TV viewers could not be wrong.

When Cosby met Puttnam, the star assured the chief that this was going to be family entertainment par excellence, the monster

hit of the 1987 holiday season. Chief cheerleader for Cosby at Columbia was VP Steve Sohmer, a perfect example of the Ivy League
yuppie who had become seduced by show business. In his twenties, Sohmer had written an acclaimed novel about post-Ivy mal-
aise. He would cure his own by going to work in television,
which was much more permeable than features, where you had to
know Ray Stark to get a job.

Sohmer became a marketing maven at CBS, which he parlayed
into his top job at Columbia. He drove a Rolls-Royce, which discomfited Puttnam, who made do with an Audi. Sohmer also married soap opera star Deidre Hall from *Days of Our Lives.* What
more of a pinnacle to the Hollywood dream could he reach than
spearheading the comeback film for Bill Cosby, who owned his
own Coca-Cola bottling plant and had been a Coke spokesman,
or Cokesman, for years, at an annual stipend of $4 million? Fur-
thermore, Cosby was the dear golfing buddy of Goizueta's chief
operating officer, Don Keough, a hale and hearty Irish American.
Cosby, America's favorite family man, was a charter member of
the Coke family. Corporate synergy never had it so good. Roberto was happy. Fay was happy. David had better be happy, too,
at least this time.

Puttnam knew full well his own limitations in judging what
would play in Peoria. But as draft after draft of the script came in,
Puttnam got an increasingly sinking feeling. To cover his gaping
downside (the budget was $25 million and rising, Puttnam's big-
gest film by far), he did the thing that seemed to goad Hollywood
the most: he brought in still another British commercials director, the untested Paul Weiland, to helm the picture and Alan
Parker's longtime producer Alan Marshall to line produce it.
Having quickly inked feature deals with such British helmers as
John Boorman, Bill Forsythe, Ken Annakin, and Ridley Scott,
not to mention a raft of Brit screenwriters and his old partner

Sandy Lieberson, David Puttnam was criticized as operating Columbia as a British employment agency, proof that he played the crony game as well as Ray Stark did.

The greatest masters of the Ealing comedies could have done nothing to save *Leonard*. The finished product was so bad that Cosby himself went on *Larry King Live* and abashedly warned his countless fans to avoid it. Implicitly, he blamed Columbia's alien Brit pack, who didn't comprehend the sheer all-American genius of Cosby's original concept and had ruined the film. *Leonard* grossed well under $5 million, a fifth of its cost and less than Cosby's salary. Even *Ishtar,* at $15 million, had done better. After these two megaflops, Atlanta was badly in need of Mylanta.

Puttnam critics were quick to point out that for all his populist grandstanding, the prophet of budget had ceased to practice what he preached. In addition to his own seven-figure salary, *The Mission,* Puttnam's latest film, cost $25 million; it had a big budget and a big star, Robert De Niro. Economy had nothing to do with it. Nor did taste. One film that stood out, like a sore thumb, on the list of Puttnam-initiated studio projects was a comedy by the German director Doris Dorrie called *Me and Him,* about a talking penis. Another was *The Beast,* a very violent movie about the Russian-Afghan war with large amounts of dialogue in Pashto. Would those play in Atlanta?

When interviewed about his "vision" and conflicts with entertainment's big boys by London's *Daily Telegraph,* Puttnam adjusted the chip on his Cockney shoulder and unleashed a barrage of attitude: "I like a scrap. It's a working-class thing. Screw you. I don't need any of you. . . . If I make good movies and they don't work, I will go with my head held high. Suck it and see." Puttnam sounded less like a Harvard professor than one of the Krays, those celebrity twin gangsters of sixties London.

Not that Hollywood was Anglophobic. Just the opposite. "Dress British, think Yiddish" was the philosophy of both the garment and movie industries. Morton's, the power restaurant where studio heads ritually gathered on Monday nights, was a transplanted Berkeley Square private dining club, where waiters earned over six figures a year in tips. Hollywood worshipped British talent, Hitchcock, Lean, Cary Grant, Vivien Leigh, Laurence Olivier, on down to Hayley Mills and Dudley Moore. Hollywood even liked Puttnam's ad director mates, the Scotts, Parker, Lyne, liked them a lot. It just didn't like David Puttnam. It was personal.

If Puttnam was despised outside Columbia, he was emasculated within. The reason for the latter was that Columbia wasn't the only film studio in the Coca-Cola portfolio. Columbia Pictures Industries, Coke's umbrella entertainment division, also owned a major share of Tri-Star Pictures, which had been formed in 1982 as a joint venture of Columbia, HBO (owned by Time Inc.), and CBS in an attempt to synergize the newly booming cable business. To get an exclusive on Columbia films, HBO, under the deal, agreed to put up 25 percent of the budget of those films, with no ceiling whatsoever on that budget. CBS would kick in millions more per film for the right to exclusive showings on the network. It was the kind of deal that David Puttnam, the oracle of low-budget filmmaking, considered anathema. Tri-Star, as one might expect, was the brainchild not of any auteur, starving or otherwise, but of the two top lawyers in the company, Fay Vincent and Victor Kaufman, the latter a very unflashy, backroom-type, Queens-born, NYU-trained staff attorney who had survived the Begelman fiasco and, remaining away from the L.A. fray in corporate New York, successfully slithered through the gauntlet of successive studio heads.

Now Kaufman, still in Manhattan, was the head of Tri-Star, which had had its biggest hit with a sequel, naturally, *Rambo: First Blood Part II*. They also did *Meatballs Part II*. David Puttnam, whose most important goal was to be a class act, was understandably appalled at sharing the Columbia umbrella with Tri-Star, especially because there was always the threat, often issued by Martin Ranso-hoff and others, that if Puttnam was too lofty for a project, the lowbrow moneyman Kaufman would pick it up, and it would become a Columbia picture anyway. In your face, David Puttnam!

Victor Kaufman's bottom-line-oriented second in command was a Boston native and Harvard Business School product named Jeff Sagansky, who had risen through the ranks of NBC and was very close to both of Puttnam's nemeses, Bill Cosby and Ray Stark. Notwithstanding his two Harvard degrees, Sagansky had a name that was associated with Mob royalty. Harry J. "Doc" Sagansky was a dentist turned loan shark who was both beloved and feared as the Godfather of Boston's Jewish Mafia. Even if Jeff had no blood tie to Harry, the name alone would have garnered respect in Beantown.

Doc Sagansky was the silent partner of Michael Redstone, whose New England theater chain became the cornerstone of Viacom, the media empire built by his son Sumner (another two-degree Harvard man) that would eventually take over Paramount in the early nineties. Viacom syndicated *The Cosby Show,* of which Jeff Sagansky was the network champion, and Redstone was a charter member of the Jewish moguls club that included the Allens and Ray Stark. It was a tight, insular world of tycoons that poor north London Jew David Puttnam couldn't have been more alienated from.

In the end—and the end came barely a year from the beginning, in the fall of 1987—David Puttnam, stranger in a strange land, felt he had no choice but to fall on his sword and tender his resignation. It was a bitter pill, made considerably sweeter by his $3 million golden parachute. Coke might have fought the payout, on grounds that Puttnam was weaseling out of his contract. But Coke was delighted to see Puttnam go. Three million dollars was a bargain not to have him trashing Hollywood and, by extension, trashing America itself.

Fay Vincent, too, left the studio, kicked upstairs to run Coke's bottling operations. Ruling the roost was the faceless, voiceless Victor Kaufman, who was too lawyerly discreet to ever antagonize anyone. Nothing ventured, nothing lost. Ray Stark had won, as he always won. In the end, it came down to size. Whose was bigger, Ray's or David's? Box office, that is. It was no contest. Stark's films had grossed in the billions; Puttnam had had only one bona fide hit, *Chariots,* and that had made far less than Stark's *Smokey and the Bandit.*

Victor Kaufman, who would always have the requisite soft spot in his heart for Stark, would now be the studio head of the "two Columbias." Working under Kaufman to clean up the Augean stable of bad will Puttnam had left behind was Paramount's Dawn Steel, she of *Flashdance* and the Gucci toilet paper. Aside from having taken the money and run, Puttnam did enjoy a last laugh of sorts when the one picture he had picked up for Columbia that he was most proud of, the British production *The Last Emperor,* swept the Academy Awards in 1988. Puttnam didn't attend, and not a single one of the winners of the film's record nine Oscars, many of them English, either thanked or even mentioned David Puttnam.

In fact, just about the only person in all the American media to speak up for David Puttnam and his ostensibly unimpeachable desire to make better movies was Tina Brown, then editor of *Vanity Fair.* Then again, Brown was British, the chief cheerleader for Brits in American media. She had become the dominant force in glossy magazines, an effort David Puttnam surely wanted to replicate in the movie business. In a seemingly endless article in her April 1988 issue, Tina Brown laid it all on the traumas to Puttnam of being on the wrong end of the British class system. Puttnam had cockney sensibilities and sixties idealism. How could he *not* despise the fat-cat capitalist pigs of Hollywood? As the fattest and piggiest of all, Ray Stark was the villain of Brown's piece.

She blamed the whole sorry Puttnam affair on Stark; the screed was her *Raya culpa*. But all the words in *Vanity Fair* couldn't resurrect David Puttnam in America. The most high-profile studio head in show business had been reduced to a nonperson. Such is the power of Hollywood.

# CHAPTER 10
## MURPHY'S LAWYER

LIKE THE INMATES at San Quentin and similarly incarceratory institutions, who are fascinated by the legends of those who escaped from prison, the young alumni of Harvard Law School and similarly exclusionary institutions seem equally fascinated by the legends of those who escaped from the law. Why, one would ask, would you want to get out when you worked so hard to get in? At least that's what middle-class parents would ask, and that very question is what has kept their high-striving issue in a career where a Harvard Law degree gives you a union card, a free pass, to a prestige law firm or a prestige corporation. You've got security, you've got dignity, you've got a future. But the price of all that is that you become a technocrat, living in a world of fine print and excruciating details. You're set for life, but you're bored to death.

In Hollywood, even if you left the cocoon of a law firm, the best you could usually do was to get into the business affairs department of a studio, where you shuffled the same papers you did in the law firm. But by the late 1980s, many of the studio heads, originally furriers and junkmen, and later agents, were now lawyers. Only lawyers, and very smart lawyers at that,

could comprehend the minutiae of the complex financing necessary to make the blockbusters that had transformed the business.

Accordingly, Sid Sheinberg and Tom Pollock, both Columbia
Law men, were running Universal. Frank Wells, Stanford Law
'59, ran the new Disney with Michael Eisner. Victor Kaufman,
NYU Law '67, had replaced David Puttnam, Nowhere '63, as head
man at Columbia Pictures. But even at the top, these lawyers
weren't having much fun. They weren't picking the movies. That
was still done by the agents, the producers, the hustlers, the guys
who weren't impressed with Harvard, who thought Yale was a
lock to pick.

The studio head lawyers were too busy doing law to revel in
their moguldom. These chiefs, like most of the many lesser Ivy
League lawyers in Hollywood, stuck in firms or stranded in studio bureaucracies, were grueling detail men. They had risen to
the top mostly because they had hitched their legal wagons to the
right rising stars, like Tom Pollock to George Lucas. Their identity was through their clients. It was all vicarious, like being
"dentist to the stars." Jon Peters they were not. But Jon Peters
went to reform school, not law school. With nothing to lose, he
gained everything. With a downside to think about, you avoid
risk, but you also avoid having a wild and crazy career.

In the eighties, the Harvard Law escape list was a short one.
Heading it was a 1955 HLS grad named Alan Trustman, who had
been something of a cult figure in Cambridge folklore. He had
written the screenplays of the Steve McQueen classics *The Thomas
Crown Affair* and *Bullitt*, as well as the Sidney Poiter hit *They Call
Me Mister Tibbs!,* the sequel to *In the Heat of the Night.* A New En-
glander of privilege and achievement, Trustman had graduated
from Exeter and Harvard College before going to Harvard Law
School. He played the law game out of school and played it well,
making partner at the hoary old Boston firm of Nutter McClen-
nen & Fish. He had gotten his idea for the *Bullitt* vertiginous car

chase back in 1954 as a summer clerk at San Francisco's top firm, Pillsbury Madison & Sutro.

Between briefs and prospectuses, Trustman somehow managed to find the time to write the scripts to the Boston-set *Crown* and to *Bullitt* while still at his firm, but after both films opened well in 1968, he quickly retired. His Hollywood career lasted less than a decade, terminated by the 1976 flop *The Next Man,* starring Sean Connery as an Arab diplomat trying to make peace with Israel, a bridge way too far for James Bond. Still, Trustman was revered by Harvard men as one who got away, perhaps not as far as Harvard's ultimate escape artist, Michael Crichton (B.A. '64; M.D. '69), but far enough to admire.

Trustman's counterpart in the 1980s was Ron Bass, who had shared the Best Screenplay Oscar for *Rain Man* and quickly became the hottest writer in the business. Bass, an L.A. native who had gone to Stanford before Harvard Law (J.D. '67), had, like Trustman, moonlighted with his writing while slogging up to partner at one of the leading entertainment firms, Armstrong Hendler & Hirsch, whose senior partner Barry Hirsch made himself unique by having two practices, one as a lawyer and another as a psychologist. Another name partner, Gary Hendler, Harvard Law '62, did wonders for his partner Bass's screenwriting ambitions when Hendler, whose juice came from his top client, Robert Redford, was chosen by fellow lawyer Victor Kaufman as president of the new Tri-Star Pictures in 1983. Redford quickly made *The Natural* as Tri-Star's inaugural film.

In his spare time, Bass had published, with zero fanfare, several novels, including a paperback spy thriller called *The Emerald Illusion* that was actually made into a straight-to-video film, *Code Name Emerald,* starring Ed Harris, in 1985. But now, with Hendler in a position of major power, Bass in 1987 ended up with a credit on Francis Ford Coppola's *Gardens of Stone,* a military drama about life in the States during the Vietnam War, starring

James Caan and Anjelica Huston. It didn't matter that the movie bombed. In Hollywood, a credit on a Coppola film was still something you could take to any studio, and the big-bearded Bass, who resembled a brainy anteater, would take it so far (with credits like *My Best Friend's Wedding*) that he broke the bank. Hendler died of cancer in 1989, but Bass, free of the shackles of the law, would write on and on and on, becoming notorious for his writing factory of mostly women, called the "Ronettes," who assisted him on his endless backlog of assignments.

It was hard to replicate Ron Bass's connections, even harder to replicate those of Sumner Redstone (Harvard B.A. '44; LL.B. '47), who had a flying start in the entertainment business with his father's powerful New England theater chain, used by Redstone to devour Viacom and eventually Paramount. Bert Fields (Harvard Law '52) wrote pseudonymous novels on the side, but his identity was unmistakably that of Hollywood's fiercest litigator. One unconnected self-made Harvard Law man who made it in the arts was Phil Kaufman, who directed *The Right Stuff* and the remake of *Invasion of the Body Snatchers*. But Kaufman spent only a brief year at the law school, 1958–59, before discovering his muse and dropping out. The lawyer most Harvard lawyers wanted most to be like was Peter Guber, who had gone to NYU. No drudgery for that man. But Peter Guber had married a deli heiress. He was connected, a made man. His career path couldn't be replicated. Heiresses were rationed. *Tant pis,* as the French would say. Tough luck.

Which all leads to the Harvard Law man with the coolest job in the world in the eighties, Robert Wachs (LL.B. '64), the up-from-Brooklyn attorney who was instrumental in creating, from whole cloth, the biggest star of the decade, Eddie Murphy. It was the odd couple of all time. Wachs was Murphy's Svengali. Murphy's idol, the man he wanted to replicate above all others, was Elvis Presley. If Murphy was Elvis, Bob Wachs was Colonel Tom

Parker. But Colonel Parker was a phony colonel, a carnival huckster, a total con man. Bob Wachs, on the other hand, was a total straight man, and a Harvard Man to boot. That he could make it, and make it to the very pinnacle, in the carnival of Hollywood gave hope to us all.

Although unconnected in the film business, Wachs grew up A-list in the rag trade. His father was a partner in Larry Aldrich, one of the premier women's dress designers of the 1950s, in the same American couture pantheon as Geoffrey Beene and Pauline Trigère. Larry Aldrich himself was a colorful character who wore spats and sported a walking stick. Perhaps setting a precedent for Wachs, Aldrich had forsaken Columbia Law School for Seventh Avenue. Once he made his fortune in dresses, Aldrich became a major modern art collector, with notable works by Rauschenberg, Johns, Stella, and Twombly. In 1966 he closed his dress business, sold all his Picassos, Monets, and Gauguins, and founded his own modern American museum in Ridgefield, Connecticut.

By then Bob Wachs had graduated Harvard Law School and was already chafing at the career Harvard had prepared him for. Even as a teenager, he was fascinated by show business, taking the train in from his upscale Belle Harbor, Queens, home to go hear jazz at the Astor Roof and the Blue Angel and to stuff himself with moo goo gai pan and egg foo yung at the China Bowl. At Poly Prep Country Day School in Brooklyn his best friend was pop music impresario-to-be Richard Perry (Tiny Tim, Captain Beefheart, Manhattan Transfer), who took Wachs to Alan Freed rock shows at the Paramount Theatre.

Wachs, a fair-haired, blue-eyed WASPy Jew whose style was privileged and preppy, planned to go to Princeton, for which he totally looked the part. But Princeton, notoriously and historically short on Jews, had other plans. Wachs ended up at William & Mary, whose southern gentlemen numbered even fewer Hebrews than Princeton. Undaunted, Wachs was active in student

theatricals and wrote a play with classmate and future star Scott
Glenn that got performed at the Yale Rep. He also deejayed a
radio show on the school station, spinning show tunes. Again he
was inspired by Larry Aldrich, who was a Broadway angel and had
*Variety* sent to Wachs in Williamsburg to remind him there was
life after academe.

Wachs graduated Phi Beta Kappa and went on to Harvard
Law, where the grind almost made him forget Aldrich's exhorta-
tions. He sought solace in the bars of Boston's small theater dis-
trict, where shows tried out before they moved to the Great White
Way. The celebrity highlight of his Harvard years was dating
Lainie Kazan when she was understudying Barbra Streisand in
*Funny Girl*. He hated Harvard, but he did well nonetheless, win-
ning a prize for the best brief in the school's gauntletlike Ames
Moot Court Competition.

Wachs decided he wanted to be an international lawyer, which
meant he wanted to see the world and have more fun than would
be afforded by the inevitable Harvard destiny of Wall Street or
its equivalent. To further this goal, Wachs found a summer in-
tern job in an American firm in Tokyo, but that summer went
up in smoke when his father died at fifty-three, leaving dutiful
Jewish son Wachs to care for his very dependent mother in Belle
Harbor. Instead of boulevarding on the Ginza, Wachs had to
downgrade to a post as a local day camp counselor. After graduating from Harvard, Wachs continued to live at home with Mom,
commuting to his first post–Harvard job as a staff lawyer at ABC,
overseeing contracts for Saturday morning cartoons. Wanting to
avoid Wall Street, Wachs had tried to land an associate job at one
of New York's so-called entertainment firms, whose work was
primarily in copyright and which were mostly quite small. These
weren't geared up to hiring Harvard men, not like Cravath or
Sullivan; the best way in was the Hollywood way, through family ties, which Wachs lacked. So he went into cartoons, at an

annual salary of $7,500. He was in show business, albeit nearly beyond the fringe.

Six months into his ABC job, Wachs got a call from the office of one of New York's most august jurists, the Honorable Harold Medina, who needed a research assistant for a bar association study he was heading entitled "Trial by Newspaper," to determine how press coverage could prejudice the right to a fair trial. Medina's assistant had discovered Wachs's résumé at Harvard and thought he was an ideal candidate. Wachs balked, but Wachs's mother, impressed by Medina's fame, insisted her son hitch his wagon to this legal star. Medina raised Wachs's salary to $7,800. More important, when the study was finished and published by Columbia University Press, Medina got Wachs a job at Paul, Weiss, Rifkind, Wharton & Garrison, a white-shoe firm that boasted New York law's preeminent entertainment department.

Wachs worked under such giants of the showbiz bar as John Wharton and Robert Montgomery, handling the estate of Cole Porter, who had just died in 1964. Wharton had represented David O. Selznick on *Gone with the Wind,* and Montgomery seemed to represent every important entertainment figure in New York, except maybe Woody Allen. Marilyn Monroe, Mike Nichols, Louis Malle, Arthur Penn, and Lauren Bacall were all his clients, as was Andy Warhol. Bob Wachs was in star heaven, traveling to Rome to babysit Jason Robards, taking his first trip to Los Angeles to sell the *Kiss Me, Kate* catalog to Lawrence Welk.

By 1971, Wachs was up for partnership. Alas, it was to be not in the entertainment department, but in corporate, where Paul, Weiss needed a brain like Wachs to sort out the incomprehensibilities of Calgary oil leases for one of their high-paying petroleum company clients. Showbiz was fun, but bigbiz paid the rent. Having been bitten by the entertainment bug, Wachs decided to leave and go out on his own. He had gotten married to a Boston University girl he had dated at Harvard, if only to get an excuse to move out of his mother's house. Now he had a family to support, and leaving the safety of Paul, Weiss for the nothingness of a fleabag office on Eighth Avenue and Fifty-seventh Street was a bold move most Harvard men would have deemed suicidal.

Somehow Wachs got clients, the documentarian D. A. Pennebaker (*Don't Look Back, Monterey Pop*), the artist Larry Rivers, and a lot of literary agents who hung around Elaine's. Wachs became a full-fledged showbiz lawyer, hardly in the league of Bob Montgomery but holding his own. Then he met Richie Tienkin, a streety Bronx thirty-year-old, who with his shorts, sneakers, and cooler full of beer looked much more like a bleacher bum than a wannabe music mogul. Tienkin, the flip side of the Ivy Leaguer, found his way to Wachs to negotiate a contract with singer Bobby Hebb ("Sunny"), and the two opposites attracted.

Tienkin, who with his partner, John McGowan, owned a bar in the Bronx catering to a nearby police precinct house, had decided to make the move into Manhattan by starting a comedy club. The brainstorm came when Tienkin went to Manhattan's Catch a Rising Star on the Upper East Side to see one of his policeman patrons trying to start a stand-up career as an impressionist. Although the club opened at ten, by one thirty in the morning, the cop was still waiting to go on. Tienkin complained to the owner, who told him the cop could wait and that Tienkin could leave. He had a full house and he didn't need Tienkin's business. Enraged, Tienkin noted the crowd and the packed bar and, with sugarplum visions of liquor sales, decided to start his own comedy club. To teach Catch a Rising Star a lesson, he found a location in a shuttered Irish bar a few blocks away, named it the Comic Strip, and made Bob Wachs a partner in return for doing all the leases, licenses, and other legal work. Now Wachs was truly in show business, in its dirty heart of darkness.

Soon the Harvard lawyer was hanging coats on Saturday night, placing ads in *Backstage,* and auditioning new comic talent that included Jerry Seinfeld, Paul Reiser, and Carol Leifer. The Comic Strip opened in 1975. By 1977, Bob Wachs was divorced. Comedy was an even more jealous mistress than the law. In 1978, a teenage black comic came to the Comic Strip on open microphone night and tried to push his way to the front of the other wannabe stars. Wachs told the boy to wait his turn. When the boy refused, Wachs threw him out. The boy was Eddie Murphy.

Edward Regan Murphy wouldn't take no for an answer, even from an intimidating Harvard gatekeeper. The seventeen-year-old lived in Roosevelt, Long Island, a largely black suburban community whose most famous product was basketball great Julius "Dr. J" Erving. (Howard Stern was second, but he was famous only after Murphy was.) Murphy had been born in the tough Bushwick section of Brooklyn. His mother, Lillian, was an operator for New York Telephone. His father, Charles, was a Manhattan Transit Authority cop who had his own dreams of comic stardom, working the New Jersey stand-up circuit in hopes of being discovered. Charles was also a wannabe playboy. His affairs cost him his marriage when Eddie was three. Five years later, when Eddie was eight, one of those affairs cost Charles Murphy his life. He was stabbed to death by a twenty-one-year-old who was convicted of manslaughter but served only five years' probation. At an early age, Eddie Murphy saw that life was both short and unfair.

After his parents' divorce, Eddie's mother got very ill, forcing Eddie to spend several Dickensian, or Jon Peters–ian, months in a foster home, where he has described his foster mother as a "black Nazi." It was an ordeal that he later credited as the source of his sarcastic sense of humor, as a defense mechanism. In elementary school, he learned to do impressions, Bugs Bunny, Speedy Gonzales, Road Runner. Funny was Eddie's identity. The year his father was murdered, Eddie's mother remarried, to an ice-cream man named Vernon Lynch, who worked the loading dock at a

Breyers plant. It wasn't stardom, but the Lynches' double income was a living that enabled them to move out of the Brooklyn ghetto to Roosevelt suburbia, where Eddie developed his obsession with Elvis Presley, whose routines he practiced incessantly in his basement rec room, much the same way Robert De Niro's Rupert Pupkin character practiced Jerry Lewis in Scorsese's *King of Comedy*.

Murphy did far better than Pupkin. He began working the local clubs and even made it out to his father's old haunts in New Jersey. At fifteen, Murphy actually landed an agent, whom he found in the yellow pages. The man was Irving "King" Broder, a small-timer who was straight out of Woody Allen's *Broadway Danny Rose*. Broder specialized in Borscht Belt comedians, tummlers he would try to get gigs for at resorts like Grossinger's. Although the Borscht Belt wasn't the market for black teen impressionists, Broder saw something in Murphy and acted as his mentor until he could legally sign the boy at eighteen.

Broder then teamed Murphy up with two white comics to create an act called the Identical Triplets. The incongruous name was probably the funniest thing about the trio, which didn't last long. Meanwhile, Murphy was adding all sorts of characters to his solo impressions act, from Laurel and Hardy to Martin and Lewis, Al Green to Jackie Wilson. He was an equal opportunity mimic. But he hit paydirt when he fixated on Richard Pryor, who was his psychological antecedent. Murphy was Pryor Sweet, the humor minus the anger. What Bob Wachs didn't see, Richie Tienkin managed to spot. Tienkin and McGowan had opened a branch of the Comic Strip in Fort Lauderdale, where Tienkin sent Murphy to polish his act.

It was 1980. A funny thing happened to Eddie Murphy on his way to enroll at Nassau Community College, where the Lynches wanted him to exorcise his unrealistic comic demons and foolish dreams of fame. Back in Manhattan, *Saturday Night Live,* off the

high of its initial Lorne Michaels glory years, was looking for a
black comic to replace Garrett Morris in the token "ethnic" spot.
Wachs supplied them with a Comic Strip regular named Charles
Barnett, who was street funny but too street, in that he was literally illiterate and couldn't read the show's cue cards.

Wachs was desperate to fill the void. It would be a major feather
in his cap. He thus called on *SNL*'s Joe Piscopo, who had been a
Comic Strip act, to work with Murphy and try to make him look
good. Piscopo did the job, and also became Murphy's best white
friend. Wachs negotiated a deal with *SNL* that would pay Murphy the (to him) princely sum of $750 a week. Wachs muscled out
King Broder and signed his new star to an ironclad management
contract with him and Tienkin. Broder sued, and Wachs settled for
what turned out to be chump change. That was where the Paul,
Weiss in him came to the fore.

Ironically, Wachs did not initially feel that Eddie Murphy was
funny, either at the club or now on the air. Murphy was a percentage, and unlikely to be a long-term one. Then in September
1981, *SNL* producer Jean Doumanian, then Woody Allen's best
friend, had so little material for the show that she found herself
with five extra minutes at the end. Scrambling, she told Eddie
Murphy to go out there and do his routine. Bob Wachs was at the
show, with his old Poly Prep classmate Richard Perry. Somehow,
Murphy that night suddenly evolved from mimic to genius. "The
game is over!" Wachs declared to Perry. Wachs had an epiphany.
He was possessed with visions of not only television stardom but
also movies, records, products. He saw a whole career before him,
a grand slam.

The division of labor between Wachs and Tienkin was that
Wachs was the "day guy," Tienkin the "night guy." The reality
was that they were both all over Eddie Murphy, or at least his
career, 24/7. Wachs's first big career moves were to get Murphy
on Johnny Carson and then secure him a $100,000 record deal,

where he could say all the expletives that were barred on not-for-prime-time. That $100,000 record deal provided the fiscal "quote" to get Murphy a $200,000 movie deal at Paramount for *48 HRS.* The *48* deal came about after Wachs placed Murphy at ICM with a young agent named Hildy Gottlieb, whose uncle was Broadway impresario Morton Gottlieb (*Sleuth, Same Time, Next Year*). Wachs knew Morton Gottlieb through Paul, Weiss. He knew *everybody* in New York through Paul, Weiss, but he was not in the L.A. loop at all.

Although ICM itself was doing nothing for its new client to fulfill Wachs's grandiose dreams, Hildy Gottlieb did have one major connection. This was the director Walter Hill, who was her live-in boyfriend. Hill had helped develop the *48 HRS.* project years before, originally for Clint Eastwood and Richard Pryor and later with the idea of reteaming Pryor and Gene Wilder in the wake of their odd couple comedy *Silver Streak*. It hadn't taken, and the project was all but dead until Gottlieb met Murphy and the lightbulb of lucre clicked on in her head. Although Paramount exec Don Simpson was unimpressed with Eddie as a "TV guy" and wanted to cast Gregory Hines, Simpson was soon fired for his excesses, and boss Michael Eisner, a TV guy himself, was all for Murphy, even though his retriever Jeff Katzenberg shared Wachs's initial assessment that Murphy wasn't funny and wanted to fire him several weeks into the San Francisco shoot.

He didn't, and when *48 HRS.* turned out to be a smash, Katzenberg reversed course and became Eddie Murphy's biggest champion, yielding to Wachs's relentlessly escalating demands that would see Eddie Murphy earn $8 million per picture, plus a percentage of Paramount's gross receipts, by the time he made *Coming to America* in 1988. Only a very few stars like Stallone, Streisand, and Redford were in that stratosphere, and Murphy was only twenty-six at the time. In addition to helping make Murphy a fortune, Wachs took credit for saving Murphy's beloved brother,

Charles, who was in the navy and about to be sent to powder-keg Lebanon, which was certainly in harm's way. Wachs leaned on Senator Al D'Amato, himself a Long Islander, to help his constituent, with the quid pro quo that Eddie Murphy write funny material for D'Amato and his fellow Republican Rudy Giuliani. When Charles was discharged and joined the entourage, Eddie Murphy would constantly joke that he should have left him in the navy.

For all his fruitful efforts on Murphy's behalf, Wachs was never sure Murphy actually *liked* him. Why should he? Aside from being born in Brooklyn, growing up on Long Island, and having very high IQs, the two men had nothing in common. While Wachs was a cosmopolitan gourmet who loved to travel and talk ideas with all the famous people who now were dying to talk to him, Murphy liked nothing more than to hang out at "Bubble Hill," his Graceland-copycat mansion in Alpine, New Jersey, a town near the Palisades that was also home to buddy Joe Piscopo, as well as to Stevie Wonder.

Trying to replicate Elvis Presley's "TCB" Memphis Mafia, Murphy had his own entourage of old Roosevelt High School chums with names like Fruity, Sweetmeat, Cousin Bert, and Mabuddah. The ringleader was Eddie's uncle Ray, who had done time in Canada. The good uncle was a smooth operator who was great at using his nephew as star bait to pick up gorgeous on-the-make women at nightclubs. Armed with a sheath of "contracts" to appear in Murphy films, Uncle Ray would invite the aspirants up to what was known as the "hostility suite" (a play on "hospitality," Murphy style). Few women refused. Saying no to Eddie was like saying no to Elvis.

Murphy needed a lot of volume, since, according to Wachs, he was the toughest of customers. He wanted more than mere beauty; he wanted perfect, tiny feet. He would have loved imperial China. If a woman's feet were wrong, out she would go. And if

she seemed at all less than pristine, he would exclaim, "Nonspe-
cific," as in urethritis, which was a signal to Uncle Ray to send her
packing. Murphy hated to travel. In Israel, where he spent several
weeks at Jeff Katzenberg's beseeching doing a cameo (for $1 mil-
lion) opposite Dudley Moore in the loser arms-dealing comedy
*Best Defense,* Murphy holed up with his posse in the Jerusalem
Hilton and never even visited the Wailing Wall or the Via Dolo-
rosa, his purported serious cross-wearing Catholicism notwithstanding. It was the same wherever he went outside New York,
sequestering himself in hotel suites and, between starlet foot in-
spections, watching *Star Trek* reruns. Murphy didn't smoke, drink,
or do drugs; his podiatric obsession was a minor vice that could be
tolerated.

Even in Los Angeles, where Murphy would have been at the
top of the Hollywood A-list, he only wanted to replicate Bubble
Hill. He and Wachs would have business dinners at Carlos'n
Charlie's on the Sunset Strip or at Murphy's favorite haunt, Ros-
coe's House of Chicken'n Waffles, but he preferred to hole up in
the mansion Wachs rented for him in Benedict Canyon, near the
site of the Charles Manson murders of Sharon Tate and her entourage. The house had previously been rented by the star formerly
known as Prince. For whatever reason, Prince, Manson, or something else, Murphy, according to Wachs, demanded that Wachs
do a formal exorcism on the house. Anyone else might have
thought Murphy was joking, but Wachs believed that the comedian was always serious about his demands. Accordingly, Wachs
hired a priest and nuns, armed with holy water and other tools of
the trade, who said their prayers and sprayed their incense. "It's
done," Wachs told Murphy, and only then did Murphy assent to
moving in.

Another time, Wachs had to exorcise the increasingly uncon-
trollable Don Simpson. Simpson mortally offended Murphy by
answering a press query as to what Murphy brought to *Beverly*

*Hills Cop,* "A watermelon and a jug of wine." Murphy didn't get the joke. While portraying himself as an equal opportunity offender, Murphy had won the enmity of feminist and gay rights groups with his riffs and rants about "hos" and "homos." However, Murphy drew the line at racist humor, even if it came from the coked-out mogul who was making him wildly rich. It took all of Wachs's negotiating skills to wring an apology out of the profane superproducer.

Wachs, who with each Murphy hit decided he wanted to be a superproducer himself (and not just a supermanager), allowed himself his own Hollywood indulgences, renting Linda Evans's mansion in Coldwater Canyon a few blocks from Don Simpson, buying a big Ferrari like Simpson's, and commandeering a big table at Morton's like Simpson's. He still kept his base in New York at 232 East Sixty-third Street, but that was more a Manhattan clubhouse for Murphy's Roosevelt Roundtable. Wachs's big work was on the coast, making Murphy the biggest star in the world.

Wachs and Murphy's idea of having fun together was making serious bets on the future grosses of their films. Wachs's overoptimism on *The Golden Child* cost him a BMW for Eddie. Eddie's too-low guess on *Beverly Hills Cop II* won Wachs a black Rolls convertible, which Murphy gift-wrapped with a giant red bow, with a note: "Get you next time, you prick." For all their dissimilarities, Wachs was certain that Murphy appreciated having "smart Jews" doing his business for him. When Murphy and Richie Tienkin fell out in 1987 over party-boy Murphy's intolerance of Tienkin's substance-fueled own party habits, Murphy fired him and replaced him as Wachs's management partner with his supersquare long-term CPA, Mark Lipsky, another "smart Jew" who would provide a check and balance to Wachs's mounting power as the most important manager in Hollywood.

Still another "smart Jew" who smarted at Wachs's Svengalian

influence over Murphy was Jeff Katzenberg, who Wachs was convinced despised him. Katzenberg was Paramount's point man for Murphy, and every million Wachs wrung out of Paramount was a million Diller and Eisner surely wrung out of Katzenberg, at least psychologically. Katzenberg may have felt that Wachs was getting too greedy, except that whatever Wachs got Paramount to pay Eddie Murphy always proved to be vastly more than worth it, even in critically savaged duds like *The Golden Child,* an un-funny comedy of miracles that Wachs had to wrest away from Mel Gibson, whom Paramount had intended it for. In fact, Wachs felt that for all the millions, Paramount was still not giving his client, or himself, due respect. *Beverly Hills Cop* was intended for Stallone; Murphy was a last-minute replacement.

On *Beverly Hills Cop II,* Paramount did its best to deny Wachs the story credit and attendant royalties that credit would entitle him to. According to Wachs, they didn't even submit his name to the Writers Guild for credit arbitration. But Wachs, a man of a thousand eyes, managed to find out about the arbitration and flew in by private plane to make his case to the guild, successfully. Crowned with his creative credit, the dutiful Jewish son took his mother, the queen of Belle Harbor, and her sister to meet the queen of England at the royal premiere of *Cop II,* where Don Simpson, with coke-fueled disrespect, refused to bow before the monarch. In his mind, she should have bowed to him.

The biggest bullet (an artillery shell, actually) that Bob Wachs would take for Eddie Murphy was in defending the honor of his client in the highest-profile Hollywood lawsuit of the decade, *Buchwald v. Paramount.* In the protracted litigation, Paramount (and Murphy) was accused of ripping off America's best-loved syndicated columnist. In 1983, Art Buchwald had sold Paramount a treatment for a comedy, ostensibly perfect for Eddie Murphy, called *King for a Day.* In his story, an African king is deposed while visiting Washington, D.C. He winds up broke in the D.C.

ghetto, where he ultimately finds an American bride. After languishing in development hell for several years, Paramount dropped the project.

In 1988, Buchwald saw *Coming to America,* in which an African prince comes to the Queens quasi ghetto and goes undercover in search of an American bride. His blood boiled, for what he felt he was watching on the screen was a very bad execution of what he thought was his very funny idea. Wachs's position, and that of Paramount, was that *Coming to America* was the sole creation of Eddie Murphy, uninspired by anyone and anything other than Murphy's own comic genius. In a way, Eddie Murphy was the movie version of Art Buchwald, the funniest man on screen, just as Buchwald was the funniest man in print. Eddie, the ultimate mimic, was being accused of mimicking Buchwald, of imitating Art. What ensued was a clash of the comic titans, with Bob Wachs playing straight man in a legal farce.

Buchwald had first pitched his idea to his best showbiz friend, Alain Bernheim, a major French film and literary agent who had represented such Americans in Paris as James Jones and William Styron. The *King* story had its genesis years before; B&B, as the pair were known, loved sitting at Fouquet's on the Champs-Élysées, watching oil-rich African potentates with their entourages of bodyguards, yes-men, and Madame Claude's *filles de joie.* In 1979, Bernheim himself had come to America, having married a wealthy, jet-setting Beverly Hills playgirl, and had switched from agenting to producing.

Bernheim had quickly gotten three big pictures on-screen, all flops. The first was Billy Wilder's last film, *Buddy Buddy,* a remake of a French farce about a Mob hit gone awry that neither the great Wilder nor his great stalwarts Lemmon and Matthau could salvage. The second film, *Yes, Giorgio,* like *Buddy* was green-lighted by Francophile David Begelman at MGM. Starring Luciano Pavarotti as basically himself, *Giorgio* had European sensibilities that were lost on American audiences and, later, on European ones as well. The third, *Racing with the Moon,* a coming-of-age period piece starring Sean Penn and Nicolas Cage, got good reviews but was lost in the box office shuffle. Nevertheless, in Hollywood, failure was relative. Bernheim was getting films made, which was a herculean success in and of itself. Bernheim was making deals with the big guys like Begelman, whose tarnish in L.A. became a patina. The Frenchman was thus considered a player.

Paramount had produced Bernheim's *Racing,* and Paramount had a hot new star in Murphy, so it was there he took Buchwald's eight-page treatment, originally entitled *It's a Crude, Crude World,* because its African royal ruled a major source of petroleum, like Nigeria. Before coming to Paramount, Bernheim had developed the idea with the French auteur Louis Malle, who had tried but failed to get his playwright collaborator John Guare to write the script. At that time, before Bob Wachs had introduced Eddie Murphy into Hollywood's consciousness, Bernheim's casting targets were Richard Pryor, Bill Cosby, and even Garrett Morris. But by the fall of 1982, when Bernheim pitched Buchwald's concept to Jeff Katzenberg, Paramount was waiting to see if *48 HRS.,* due out in February 1983, would make Murphy bankable, hence castable. In February, Murphy became a movie star and Bernheim and Buchwald got their development deal.

Paramount liked the idea so much that after a false start with a first-time writer who was discovered at a 7-Eleven by one of Katzenberg's myriad subretrievers, the studio hired Bernheim buddy and French heavyweight comic auteur Francis Veber, who had written the French movie from which *Buddy Buddy* was remade and, more positively, whose *Le Cage aux Folles* was a global smash, for the then huge fee of $300,000 to write the script, with $1 million more to eventually direct it. Ultimately, alas, Veber's draft didn't translate. Bob Wachs, for one, hated the idea. Buchwald's treatment described the king as a "despot" propped up by the CIA and ultimately deposed by the agency. One of Wachs's rules was for his star to stay away from anything "political." Everything about D.C.-based Buchwald was political.

By the same token, Wachs also nixed a convoluted pitch by soon-to-be-esteemed author Jim Harrison (*Wolf, Legends of the Fall*), whose agent had been one of Wachs's legal clients, that was both similar to the Buchwald idea and similarly political. Harrison had Murphy playing an aide to a corrupt southern senator whom mobsters finger as a man who knows too much and want to kill him. He goes on the lam, buying sunglasses and a sable coat from a pimp to look like royalty, and buys a plane ticket to Africa. At the airport, he meets a real African prince en route to an exchange year at the University of Texas who would prefer to spend the time with his girlfriend in Paris. Eddie talks the prince into trading places with him and escapes to Austin, with the expected comic consequences.

Wachs diplomatically slithered out of insulting Harrison by resorting to the old Hollywood cliché that Paramount already had a "similar" Eddie Murphy project by Buchwald in development. What he didn't want to say was that in addition to avoiding politics, he also avoided anything that smacked of racism, and the sable coat pimp act was, to Wachs, as stereotypical and racist as it got. Not that Eddie Murphy was a complete stranger to pimps and hos in his profane act, but as his gatekeeper, Wachs held himself to a vastly higher standard, a lawyer's inculcated caution and an educated liberal's sensitivity. His own position, and his fortune, depended on his not pushing the envelope.

Francis Veber had desperately wanted to meet Murphy so he could tailor his script to the star he was writing it for. But the meeting never came to pass. Murphy's hit song "Party All the Time" was also his anthem. Paramount's approach to its hottest commodity was basically "Do not disturb." Scripts, even $300,000 scripts, would not be presented to Murphy until they were a hundred percent ready to shoot, which, in the bowels of development hell with the endless tinkering by everyone from Katzenberg down to the lowliest d-boy or d-girl, usually meant never. The last thing in Hollywood you want to do to a star is ask him or her to *read* something, particularly something that isn't green-lit with a major director attached. This was a business of pictures, not words. Words were hard work, forced labor, something to be avoided. Even yours, up yours, Art Buchwald.

The challenges to Buchwald, Bernheim, and Veber became insuperable after the "Tuesday Night Massacre" of September 1984, when Barry Diller, finding himself incompatible with Charles Blühdorn's very corporate successor, Martin Davis, defected to work for another Davis, the behemoth Marvin running Twentieth Century Fox. Meanwhile, Eisner and Katzenberg, stung by Davis's appointment of marketing chief Frank Mancuso as studio head over Diller's supposed successor Eisner, also defected to run the new Disney. *King for a Day* had thus been orphaned. In February 1985, Paramount's new production chief, Ned Tanen, another Hollywood musical chair who had previously run Universal, called his supposed buddy Bernheim to inform him that Paramount was dropping *King*. Tanen gave Bernheim the standard year in turnaround to place the project at another studio and pay Paramount back the $500,000 it had spent on a project for Eddie Murphy that no one really knew whether Eddie Murphy had even heard of. Party all the time.

The indefatigable Bernheim hit the pitch trail. If you couldn't get Eddie Murphy, his spiel went, I've got the perfect project for the *next* Eddie Murphy. This wasn't Halley's Comet. New comics were being minted every night at places like the Comic Strip. Just ask Bob Wachs. Or maybe don't ask Bob Wachs, who, pre-massacre, had insulted the formal Bernheim by calling him "Al" and brushing him off with the standard escape clause that Veber's opus, which Wachs later admitted he hadn't read, "needed work."

If there was going to be a new Eddie Murphy, Bob Wachs was hell-bent on being his manager. Already on the case, he had signed up his second management client in Murphy's new best friend and favorite sidekick, Arsenio Hall. Hall, an Ohio native and Kent State alumnus, had moved to L.A. to hit the stand-up trail. Bob Wachs saw him and found him infinitely funnier than he had initially found Eddie Murphy. After making his mark as the opening act for Patti LaBelle, Hall got his big break as a guest host on the ill-fated *Late Show Starring Joan Rivers,* Fox's feeble attempt to challenge Johnny Carson.

Although Joan Rivers *was* killed, Arsenio Hall *killed.* Fox offered Hall the show for himself; Wachs told him to turn it down, at which point Hall signed with Wachs, who set up Hall's own syndicated show, which was a smash. Wachs was proud that he took Hall from making $120,000 a year to making $20 million virtually overnight. He also arranged to get the untried Hall cast as Murphy's sidekick, the Hope to Murphy's Crosby, in *Coming to America,* on which Eddie Murphy demanded and got story credit, with neither a nod nor a wink to Art Buchwald. The film cost nearly $40 million. It grossed over $300 million worldwide. It was huge. B&B felt robbed.

Hence the lawsuit. Paramount marshaled a phalanx of its own lawyers and outside counsel to crush the efforts of B&B, who got the L.A. branch of the New York firm Kaye Scholer to take the matter on contingency. Because B&B were still on the hook for costs (as opposed to the actual lawyers' time), Paramount figured that it could spend B&B to death, driving those costs into the hundreds of thousands. Paramount's millions in fees were covered by its massive insurance policies. Despite Buchwald's fame, he was still the David to Paramount's deep-pocketed Goliath.

Paramount's position was that its top star Eddie Murphy basically had no awareness of Buchwald's project, other than a brief mention on a long list of possibilities once at a 1983 Ma Maison dinner with Katzenberg, Murphy, Wachs, and some creative underlings, probably between courses of its famous *caneton deux façons.* Everybody seemed aware of the limits of Eddie Murphy's attention span, but many people in the film industry felt that the notion that the genesis of *Coming* was pure Eddie was as big a fiction as Paramount's other franchise *Star Trek.*

Even harder to swallow was Paramount's despotic definition of net profits, of which B&B claimed to be entitled, per their Paramount contract, for up to 40 percent. In the gospel according to Paramount, B&B's points were worthless, because studio accounting showed that *Coming,* one of the thirty top-grossing films of all time, was still in the red and would probably always be in the red. Who, then, got the money? The "gross players," starting with Eddie Murphy and including director John Landis, who had nearly come to blows with his star over Murphy's refusal to support him in his *Twilight Zone* manslaughter trial. Again, the blessed peacemaker was Bob Wachs, whose own management percentage came out of Murphy's gross. Net points were known as "monkey points." They were for writers, the "schmucks with typewriters." Things hadn't changed since the moguls made the rules. The trial was a dispiriting lesson on who mattered in Hollywood, though it was no surprise that nice guys, and writers, even famous writers, finished last.

At the 1990 trial, Murphy did not bother to appear to testify. The judge held for B&B and awarded them $900,000 for their years of trouble: $150,000 for Buchwald's eight pages of inspiration and $750,000 for the producer's reward Bernheim should have earned. Again, between writers and producers, the priorities of the business were clear. But neither man made it to the bank. Kaye Scholer, which was out $2.5 million in lawyers' hours, amortized a mere $360,000 of that with its 40 percent contingency fee. Another $500,000 went back to the law firm for costs it had advanced. B&B were left with $40,000, enough to celebrate their Pyrrhic victory at Spago, if they weren't blacklisted from getting in.

What the case showed was the immense power of Eddie Murphy, the star of the decade. All the negative reviews in the world (and they were vicious) could not deter Murphy's world of fans from *Coming to America*. In truth, Murphy didn't need Art Buchwald. He didn't need ideas. He just needed to get on-screen. If he made it, they would come. After the *Coming* lawsuit, Murphy decided that despite his manager's foot soldier loyalty, he didn't need Bob Wachs. Murphy may have taken a cue from his soul mate Arsenio, who was the first to cut Wachs out of his booming career. It may have also had something to do with the Wachs-produced *Harlem Nights,* a Roaring Twenties period piece à la Robert Evans's ill-fated *Cotton Club.* Murphy's next film after *Coming, Harlem,* which Murphy also directed, was a fantasy project teaming him not only with Arsenio Hall but with his idols and antecedents Redd Foxx and Richard Pryor. All the generations of comic talent couldn't save the film, which, while still profitable at $100 million world gross, made less than a third of what *Coming* did.

Murphy decided he didn't like his gross deal that much more than B&B liked their net. Once he learned that both Schwarzenegger and Stallone had better deals on their films, it was curtains for Bob Wachs. The supermanager got a Dear Bob letter from Murphy's new lawyer, Skip Brittenham, curtly informing Wachs that his services were no longer necessary. Wachs appealed to Katzenberg, but that was like Jesus appealing to Pontius Pilate. Katzenberg, now at Disney, told Wachs that Eddie Murphy needed to be his own man. The next day, as if by telepathy, Wachs found himself locked out of his Paramount office suite and barred from the lot. Thanks a lot, for eight huge hits, he thought to himself.

Wachs suddenly realized he wasn't going to be Don Simpson. But he soon took a consolation prize in marrying Don Simpson's favorite d-girl, Tess Haley, who meant more to Simpson than all of Madam Alex's hookers. Wachs may have lost the biggest prize in Hollywood, but loving well was the best revenge.

# CHAPTER 11
## ARISTOCRATS AT THE GATE

BOB WACHS WASN'T THE ONLY IVY LEAGUE LAWYER having big-time adventures in Hollywood. But he was one of the rare prestige yuppies living in the world of talent. There was an exponential growth of Ivy in the eighties, but almost all of it was in the business of show business, and much of this was in New York, which became the new heart of Hollywood. Allen & Company had always ruled Columbia Pictures from its Fifth Avenue suite above La Côte Basque, and Steve Ross ruled Warner's from New York in a way Charles Blühdorn never ruled Paramount from his Gulf+Western tower at Columbus Circle. But Blühdorn was a seventies phenomenon, when movies were still in the last gasp of being movies. Now they were "product" that demanded the legal sophistication and complex financing possessed exclusively by the wizards of Wall Street.

Two of these wizards had succeeded Bob Wachs in the entertainment division of Paul, Weiss, Rifkind, Wharton & Garrison and ended up on their own and as essential to the success of Disney as Wachs was to the success of Paramount. The two soon-to-be ex-lawyers were both Yalies of great privilege and connections, Tom Bernstein and Roland Whitney Betts, whose fathers, respectively, ran Random House and the Vincent Astor Foundation. Already pretty much owning New York, they needed another mountain to climb, and that mountain was Hollywood. Tom Bernstein's father, Robert, himself a Harvard man, was Bennett Cerf's heir apparent at New York's leading publishing house, as well as one of the country's preeminent human rights activists. Bernstein, a golden boy at Scarsdale High and a summa, as well as *Law Journal,* at Yale, grew up in a Gotham überworld of Updike and Roth, Comden and Green, Kirkland and Nureyev, Sakharov and Havel. Eisner and Katzenberg had to have been an anticlimax.

While Bernstein tagged every base of the American achievement game at the highest level, his partner, Roland Betts, was totally unorthodox in his route to the top. Raised in Oyster Bay in the WASPiest precinct of Long Island, Betts went on to St. Paul's School, where he played hockey with John Kerry and followed him to New Haven, Betts's father's alma mater. At Yale, his best friend and roommate was George W. Bush. They both joined Delta Kappa Epsilon, Yale's *Animal House.* The lyric of the college party song "Hot Nuts," "See that man, he's a DKE. His nuts hang below his knee," was a call of the wild that every chapter of the Greek letter outfit strove to live up to. The hallmark of the DKE was that he was well-endowed, socially, economically, physically. In 2011, DKE capped a long tradition of reprehensible high jinks by being suspended from the Yale campus for conduct unbecoming, in particular a war chant required of pledges, "No means yes, yes means anal." Roland W. Betts rose to become DKE's rush chairman, George W. Bush its president.

After Yale, Betts, a jock who looked like a bear, albeit a bear with a pedigree, would have normally been bound for Wall Street. Instead he took a detour to 125th Street, where he became a schoolteacher in Harlem. The move wasn't totally altruistic. Betts had graduated in 1968 during the Vietnam War; teaching provided a deferment that would enable him to beat the dreaded draft. Nevertheless, Betts not only loved teaching but fell in love with a fellow teacher, a woman named Lois Phifer. Betts's presumed inamorata would have come from Bedford and gone to Miss Porter's. Betts, however, confounded expectations. Lois Phifer was not the hockey mom type. She came from New Jersey, from a poor black family of fourteen children. She had gone to Adelphi. Opposites had clearly attracted.

The Bettses had two girls and lived on the Upper West Side. Of course, 102nd Street was no-man's-land for an Oyster Bay preppy, but the big, burly Betts was anything if not intrepid. In 1975, the war avoided, Betts decided that to better support his family he would go back to school, to Columbia Law. While there, he wrote a book about his life as a teacher, called *Acting Out: Coping with Big City Schools,* published by Little, Brown. In the book, Betts set up a dramatic contrast between his *Blackboard Jungle* day job and his weekend trout-fishing idylls in the Adirondacks, DKE-ishly washing down his catch with fresh spring water mixed with bourbon and Scotch. Some of the coping strategies Betts described also had a distinctively DKE air, like explaining how to break wind in class and still maintain the respect and control of the students. His solution was what he termed a "deposit and run" strategy, dropping the bomb at the blackboard, then dashing to the other end of the classroom in the guise of Socratically (as opposed to olfactorily) challenging one of his charges.

Betts's preppy humor was lost on the public; the book barely sold. There would be no career as a writer. However, his years in the Harlem schools probably brought him closer in touch with the youth audience for the Disney films he would one day finance than any other big player in the movie business, other than Jon Peters. When Betts graduated from Columbia Law in 1978, he once more opted against type and went not to a rock-ribbed Republican firm like Sullivan & Cromwell, but to the archliberal Democratic firm Paul, Weiss. There he met the Jewish prince of

the city Tom Bernstein, as both men were tapped by the Boston
Brahmin Bob Montgomery to work for him, as Bob Wachs had,
in the coveted entertainment department.

If Bob Montgomery was New York's top entertainment lawyer, its top agent of the times was yet another Ivy Leaguer, Sam
Cohn, the head of ICM's Manhattan office. A graduate of Princeton and Yale Law School and the product of a rich Pennsylvania
oil family, Cohn had such clients as Mike Nichols, Woody Allen,
the emerging Meryl Streep, and just about everyone else in the
Broadway-Hollywood firmament. Cohn was an eccentric, holding court at the Russian Tea Room in his preppy tattered Shet-
land sweaters and rumpled khakis and nervously chewing strips
of newsprint between slurps of borscht. Between Montgomery
and Cohn, who often worked closely on deals, Bernstein and Betts
got their Hollywood education without having to go west of the
Hudson.

Even at Paul, Weiss, entertainment law was still a long slog. It
was much more law than entertainment. Bernstein and Betts, like
most lawyers, were looking for a better way. The B boys saw how
obsessed the public in the eighties had become with the business
of movies. Their epiphany, and their ticket to freedom and fortune, was to give the public an opportunity to put their money
where their fantasy was. Let the masses become producers. The
idea was something out of Mel Brooks. The B boys began working with their numbers-men friends on Wall Street to create a
financial instrument to give the people what they wanted, P. T.
Barnum goes to Drexel Burnham (or, in actuality, E. F. Hutton).

The result was Silver Screen Management, a virtual studio that
would fund movies with proceeds from lay investors who bought
shares of a partnership, called Silver Screen Partners. The beauty
part was that it seemed risk-free. After five years, the partners
were guaranteed to get their principal back. What could be better,
and more of a wild pipe dream, than making movies and never

losing a cent? Unheard of. What the poor partners—or suckers, as Barnum might have called them—didn't realize was that although they might not be losing their money, they might not be making anything on it for five long years. In those inflationary times, that amounted to losing money, and plenty. Furthermore, if there turned out to be any profits, the fine print on the deal relegated the Silver Screen investors to the back of a long, long line of eagle-eyed showbiz veterans.

The B boys' first offering, Silver Screen Partners I, in 1983, raised $75 million for HBO from about twelve thousand investors. It was a big flop. Here the B boys teamed up with the rising star of the film business, Home Box Office, presales of rights to which was a key element of how Hollywood movies, particularly independent movies, in the eighties got funded. HBO now had the bright idea of producing their own films rather than buying Hollywood's, and the B boys stepped up to become their enablers. They were all in New York, all lawyers, and all spoke the same language, so the match seemed perfect. Refusing to remain backroom paper shufflers, Bernstein and Betts insisted on being fully involved in the creative process. The fatal flaw was that they weren't creative, at least when it came to the screen itself. Their creativity was the deal, and nothing more. In the Silver Screen–HBO effort, all the parties involved had the cautious, risk-averse tastes and instincts of lawyers, not showmen, and the seven movies they made were all not just awful, but awful in uncommercial ways.

Typical was the HBO–Silver Screen maiden effort, *Flashpoint*, starring Kris Kristofferson and Treat Williams as border guards who get in deep trouble when they stumble upon proof of the government conspiracy to assassinate JFK. Distributed by the new HBO-part-owned studio Tri-Star, the film had a TV director, was low-budget ($8 million, less than half the average studio picture), and pretty much belonged on the small screen, not the

large, which was the case with all the forgettable films on the B
boys' slate. The idea was for the investors, who usually put up
$2,000 or more (up to $500,000), each to "get into movies," to go
see a *Flashpoint* and exclaim, "That's *mine*. That's *my* movie! I put
up the money for that." But it didn't work that way. The investors
were too ashamed of the product to claim credit. Roland Betts's
instincts in this package were less attuned to Columbia Pictures
than Columbia Law.

Not that the Silver Screen bomb was a blot on the HBO image, which was unblottable, with over thirteen million subscrib-
ers and growing. The head honcho here, Michael Fuchs, was still
another yuppie lawyer cut of the same mold as ascendant yuppie
lawyers Peter Guber and Victor Kaufman of Columbia and Jonathan Dolgen of Paramount, all of whom were fellow alumni of
NYU's increasingly prestigious law school. Fuchs was born in the
Bronx, where his father owned the Concourse Plaza Hotel, across
from Yankee Stadium. The hotel was the scene of *The Catered Affair,* the 1956 Bette Davis–Ernest Borgnine follow-up to *Marty.* It
was the ten-year-old Fuchs's first taste of Hollywood. Fuchs, a
Union College alumnus, didn't have the Ivy résumé to get to
Paul, Weiss and settled for a post-NYU job at a lesser entertainment firm, Marshall, Bratter, Greene, Allison & Tucker, which
nonetheless had such important clients as Goodson-Todman, Merv
Griffin, and Dick Van Dyke.

After a few years, Fuchs went to a smaller entertainment firm
made up of former Paul, Weissers who didn't make partner there.
The firm did some work for Dino De Laurentiis, who took a liking to Fuchs, who was almost his petit size, and offered him a job
to work for him in his new Los Angeles operation. But Fuchs was
true blue to New York, subscribing to the Woody Allen philosophy that L.A.'s only cultural advantage was being able to turn
right on a red light. Fuchs turned De Laurentiis down, one of the
few. He worked briefly in business affairs at the William Morris

Agency's Sixth Avenue headquarters before hustling a new job down Sixth Avenue in the Time-Life Building as the then fledgling HBO's chief of programming in 1976.

Fuchs was the sharp Bronx boy in Time Inc.'s smooth Greenwich culture. The Ivy Leaguers there had no real idea what to do with HBO, whose naughty late-night movies made them extremely uncomfortable. Fuchs did, which was to do things that network TV could not, like talking dirty. He made his first mark with a string of comedy specials, featuring George Carlin, Steve Martin, and Bette Midler, followed by a string of concerts starting with the three Neils—Young, Diamond, and Sedaka. With Ray Charles, Gladys Knight, and Sammy Davis Jr., Michael Fuchs turned American living rooms into Las Vegas lounges, softening up those homebodies to watch movies on HBO as well. A discomfited Henry Grunwald, the highbrow editor in chief of *Time,* called Fuchs a "Visigoth," which in an era of barbarians at the pearly gates was the ultimate compliment.

Michael Fuchs wasn't thrilled with HBO's Silver Screen debacle. He ridiculed the Silver Screen partnerships as "deals for dumb dentists." But that didn't stop Bernstein and Betts from trying again. Soon they were on to Silver Screen Partners II, which was like a Hollywood sequel. Normally, though, Hollywood didn't make sequels to a flop. But this one was a fresh start, with a new take on an old studio, Walt Disney Productions, which had fallen on the hardest of times since its last big live-action feature hit in 1974, *Herbie Rides Again,* the sequel to the even bigger *The Love Bug.* One reason the new Disney gave the B boys a second chance was that Bernstein and Betts promised to stay completely out of the creative process this time and stick to business.

The new Disney was all about business, much more so than any other studio. Michael Eisner and Jeff Katzenberg felt right at home with Tom Bernstein and Roland Betts, and rightly they should have. They were all cut of the same Park Avenue silk, although the B boys' academic credentials put to shame those of the D boys. Like the B boys, the man who put Michael Eisner in the Disney driver's seat was yet another Yalie, and an Andover man, precisely in the Texas mode of Betts's best buddy George W. Bush.

This was Sid Bass, the Fort Worth billionaire who in 1984 had rescued Disney from greenmailer Saul Steinberg. Bass insisted on putting Eisner at the top of the Mouse House, over the snobby objections of the very un-Jewish, Pasadena-intensive Disney board, who preferred one of their own, namely, Annapolis man and Rhodes scholar Dennis Stanfill, who had held a similar helm at Fox with desultory results. Bass's money talked, and the board had to settle for the Mormon Rhodes scholar and Stanford Law man, Frank Wells, who had been president of Warner's, to serve as Eisner's number two.

One might have thought that Sid Bass, himself a Stanford M.B.A., would have opted for Wells. But despite his low-key, clubby façade, Sid Bass was a maverick, while not quite as out there as Roland Betts, very much in the mold of the man who had made him rich, his great-uncle and namesake, oil wildcatter Sid Richardson. The West Texan Richardson had done his deals on pay phones and held court in a drugstore, pigeonholing investors in his wells from passersby on the street.

Sid Bass would make social headlines by leaving his perfect blond wife of twenty-one years, Anne, a Vassar alumna and *Vogue* fixture, in one of the most expensive divorces of the greed decade, to wed Mercedes Tavacoli, the darkly exotic Persian ex-wife of another rich man, the much older Francis Kellogg, prominent New York socialite, diplomat, and miniature-horse breeder. The joke went around Mortimer's that Sid Bass had paid $200 million for a used Mercedes.

Nobody, on the other hand, had a chance to joke about Sid Bass's investment in Disney. Michael Eisner turned the moribund studio around too fast, thanks to the aid of Bernstein and Betts's Silver Screen Partners II, which quickly raised $100 million that funded Eisner's out-of-the-gate hits *Down and Out in Beverly Hills, Ruthless People,* and, most appropriately, *The Color of Money.* To sell the issue, Betts arranged road shows in which he paraded out Eisner, Katzenberg, and Wells to pitch the issue to ballrooms of brokers around the country. Early on, Betts saw that Eisner and Wells, both imposing six footers, played in the investor heartland far better than Katzenberg, famously described in Eisner's redundancy as "the little midget." Katzenberg was thus kept in Hollywood to focus on high-concept projects, while the "dull guys," as Betts called the two top execs, became the poster boys for the "dumb dentists" targeted to buy the issue.

Like a *Star Wars* franchise, the Silver Screen partnership spawned several more sequels, until the B boys had raised over $1 billion for Disney, from over a hundred thousand wannabe, armchair producers, stoking its hit machine with such blockbusters as *Cocktail* and *Pretty Woman,* films that would have had Walt Disney spinning in his grave and their friend George Bush spinning in his vice presidential chair in the Reagan White House. They even put George W. Bush on their board, making him something of an honorary Mouseketeer and giving him his one taste of Hollywood, even though he had long stopped drinking cocktails and chasing pretty women. The B boys also got in bed with W by joining with him to purchase the Texas Rangers baseball franchise and installing him as president. President of DKE, president of the Rangers, and future president of the United States, with Roland Betts as best friend number one and Lois Betts the template for Condoleezza Rice.

Too bad for the Silver Screen investors that the big grosses for the Disney hits tended to be offset by the big losses from Disney flops, like *Adventures in Babysitting* and *Ernest Saves Christmas.* The "dumb dentists" never got rich on these deals, although Disney did. Roland Betts's proudest moment may have been that when the first Silver Screen Disney slate was announced on the front page of *Variety,* the lead film was *The Roland Betts Story,* the adventures of a prepster WASP in darkest Harlem. It was as high-concept as Jeff Katzenberg could ever want, a reverse *To Sir, with Love.* The grapevine quickly had it that Tom Cruise was in discussions for the lead.

Before Disney, Betts had raised some of the money for Richard Attenborough to produce *Gandhi.* Now he would have his own *Gandhi.* An A-list autobiographical film would be a fitting tribute to a man who raised all this money and raised Disney from the dead, transforming the brand from mouse to monster. Sadly, for all Betts's juice, the movie never got made, proof that even the greatest god of Wall Street, backed by the gods of Washington, was not immune from the mortality of Hollywood's development hell. By 1991, for all their success, the B boys would be out of Hollywood and into something more real—real property.

There was one New York Ivy League lawyer who was even more influential than Tom Bernstein and Roland Betts in determining the future of the entertainment business of the eighties. Walter Yetnikoff, a Columbia Law man like Betts, was as profane as Betts was polished, as militantly Jewish as Betts was understatedly WASP. Born very poor in 1933 in Brownsville, Brooklyn, Yetnikoff was the son of a house painter and a bookkeeper. He worked hard to get his Phi Beta Kappa key at Brooklyn College, a few years ahead of two other similarly motivated notable alumni, Alan Dershowitz and David Geffen (who would drop out).

Yetnikoff did so well, magna cum laude, that he was admitted to Columbia Law School, although his Lithuanian immigrant grandfather, a tailor who lived with his family, tried to get young Walter to pass on Columbia and follow him into tailoring. Grandpa's logic was founded in deep insecurity: if America deported the family, which he saw as a real possibility, being a tailor was a far more portable profession than being a lawyer.

Yetnikoff's mother pushed her son away from the needles and thread and up to Morningside Heights, where, walking in the legal footsteps of Columbians Theodore and Franklin Roosevelt, he continued to study like a dog and made *Law Review*. Still lacking the tone for Paul, Weiss, Yetnikoff did land a job at a major entertainment firm, Rosenman, Colin, Kaye & Freund, the firm co-founded by Franklin Roosevelt's brilliant speechwriter Samuel Rosenman, later a federal judge who happened to be a loyal Columbia man. Yetnikoff's Ivy tie got him in the door. The Colin of the firm was William Paley's lawyer, and Yetnikoff did lots of drudge work for Paley's Columbia Records division of CBS.

With roots going back to John Philip Sousa, Columbia Records was the pioneering and preeminent label that had recorded everyone, Bessie Smith, Duke Ellington, Benny Goodman. By the early 1960s, the label, famous for its Broadway cast albums, was now making fortunes on Barbra Streisand and Bob Dylan. Working alongside Yetnikoff at Rosenman, Colin was another Brooklyn Ivy man, Clive Davis, who had escaped the ghetto to go to NYU and then Harvard Law. Though more assimilated and less a super-Jew than the foot-in-the-old-world Yetnikoff, the two men had a great deal in common. When Davis left the firm for the law department at Columbia Records, he eventually persuaded Yetnikoff to join him, mostly on the grounds that Rosenman, Colin was unlikely to make either one of them partners.

When Davis brought Yetnikoff to Columbia Records, there was very little glamour in being a record lawyer. Music was the stepchild of the entertainment bar. For every Bob Montgomery handling the Cole Porter estate, there were dozens of Tin Pan Alley shysters chasing the unpaid royalties of one-hit wonders. Music, especially pop music, was a sleazy, fly-by-night business, rife with payola and Mafia strongmen. The original moguls of

Hollywood, crass though they were, were landed gentry compared with the bottom-feeding moguls of pop, men like Morris Levy, the godfather of rock and roll, who owned the jazz club Birdland and then "owned" most of the early stars of the genre. Even after the advent of Elvis Presley changed the entire meaning of what a star was, dealing with Elvis meant dealing with the ex-carny Colonel Tom Parker. Music law simply wasn't a suitable place for a nice young Harvard or Columbia man, not when he had the option of going to the paneled prestige of Wall Street.

Next to mobbed-up outfits like Levy's Roulette Records, Columbia Records was an oasis of civility. To begin with, no one in New York was more sought after than Bill Paley and his best-dressed wife, Babe. At the record division, Davis and Yetnikoff reported to president Goddard Lieberson, a refined Jewish Englishman from a shoe business fortune who himself had attended the Eastman School of Music and whose wife was prima ballerina Vera Zorina, the ex of George Balanchine. Lieberson's chief A&R man, John Hammond, who discovered Billie Holiday, Bob Dylan, and Bruce Springsteen, was a Vanderbilt blue blood who liked to hit the clubs. Talk about pedigree. Not that Walter Yetnikoff cared about such refinements. Inside the grindy *yeshiva bucher* lurked a rock-and-roll animal waiting to be uncaged.

Clive Davis ascended to the presidency of Columbia Records in 1967 and brought the company, kicking and screaming, into the rock era, signing Janis Joplin, Santana, Billy Joel, Chicago, Pink Floyd, and Aerosmith, among everyone else. That was all very cool for a Harvard guy and won Davis legendary status on campus in the sixties and seventies. However, in 1973 Davis acquired a new kind of Harvard notoriety by being fired for the alleged defalcation of using CBS money to pay for his son's lavish bar mitzvah. The fete, at the Plaza Hotel, featured Skitch Henderson's orchestra and cost a then whopping $20,000. The CBS charges also included using $50,000 of company funds to decorate his Central Park West apartment but were never proven, though Davis did soon plead guilty to unrelated IRS tax evasion charges.

But record bosses, like studio bosses, are unkillable. As in the resurrection of David Begelman in Hollywood, Davis soon got funding for his own label, Arista. Meanwhile, Walter Yetnikoff stepped into Davis's big Gucci loafers as the new president of the entire CBS record division, which included Columbia and other labels. The party was about to begin. Even before he segued into his new rock persona, Yetnikoff assured his own tenure by winning the heart of Columbia's biggest cash cow, Barbra Streisand. She adored Yetnikoff's unabashed, belligerent Brooklyn Jewishness, which was just like her own.

Not surprisingly, Yetnikoff also found a huge admirer in Jon Peters. Peters's debut as a producer of *A Star Is Born* coincided with Yetnikoff's debut as a record czar. They were making each other rich. The *Star* sound track sold eight million copies and was number one on the *Billboard* charts for six weeks. No one had bigger, more preposterous dreams than Jon Peters, and he managed to hook Yetnikoff on his seemingly delusional but surprisingly often realized wavelength. Given that the entire entertainment business of the decade could be boiled down to six degrees of Barbra Streisand, it is not surprising that Jon Peters, who controlled access to Streisand, got as far as he did.

While producing the fashion world–set *Laura Mars* in New York, Peters was able to introduce the square Brooklyn lawyer to a world of glamorous models and starlets that the rock stars may have gotten but Yetnikoff assumed were off-limits to the backroom boys. Now he was in the front room, and Peters taught him how to sexually flex his corporate muscles. Sartorially, Yetnikoff let his hair down (literally) and got a fashion makeover, jettisoning his drab suits for gold chains and big-collared open shirts flashing lots of chest hair. While Clive Davis continued to look like Harvard, Yetnikoff became Disco Dan, the embodiment of

the new Tin Pan Alley. Yetnikoff's discovery of cocaine may
have helped him summon the courage to make his party moves.
Furthermore, Yetnikoff, Peters insisted, shouldn't limit himself to
music. He should get into the movie business, just the way Jon
Peters was getting into it. As Yetnikoff watched the ex-hairdresser
get bigger and bigger, he realized that Peters had a point.

Yetnikoff's other big enabler in his rise to power was a hemi-
sphere away. Before he took Davis's place as president of CBS
Records, Yetnikoff headed the company's international division.
As he was working his way up the foreign ladder, he had set up a
music joint venture with Sony in Japan and had become close
friends with the head of that division, Japanese aristocrat Norio
Ohga. Aside from being about the same age, the two men had
nothing in common. The descendant of a lumber dynasty, Ohga,
like Goddard Lieberson, was a classically trained musician. He
took it even further than Lieberson had, building a career in Europe as an opera singer and marrying a concert pianist before being recruited to a top post at Sony in 1959, when he was almost
thirty. Ohga, a rich boy who had everything, wasn't the typical
effete musician; he was also an accomplished jet pilot.

At Sony, Ohga was the point man on the development of the
Walkman and the compact disc, which revolutionized the record
business and brought him into close contact with Yetnikoff. Opposites attracted, and Ohga enjoyed the exotic *yiddishkeit* ambi-
ence of the Yetnikoffs' home in Great Neck, where Ohga liked
to stay, as opposed to the Sony bunkhouse, the Waldorf-Astoria,
on his continuous visits to New York. Ohga became president of
Sony in 1982, under its founder and chairman, Akio Morita, another aristocrat from a sake dynasty. Despite their countless successes, they remained haunted by the failure in the eighties of
their Betamax video recorder, which lost out to the VHS system
pioneered by JVC, a division of archrival Matsushita. They rued
never having bought, with all their surplus high-value yen, an

American film studio. That would have given them control of the software that could have been used to bludgeon consumers into buying their hardware (the Betamax). Won't get fooled again, they vowed.

Walter Yetnikoff gave his Japanese friends their second chance. But first they gave him the gift of buying CBS Records and making him their number one son. Despite his enormous eighties successes, none bigger than Michael Jackson, Yetnikoff felt he was getting no respect at the CBS parent, whose starchy CEO, Thomas Wyman, was denigrated by Yetnikoff as "the goy upstairs." The "goy" was always bumming out Yetnikoff's drug-fueled exuberance, not buying him a private jet and generally making him feel like a loser, especially since Yetnikoff viewed as his rival the highest liver in showbiz, that other dear FOB (friend of Barbra's) Steve Ross, still another Brooklyn boy made great. The big difference here was that Ross was the owner, and Yetnikoff was just an employee. Even little *pishers* like David Geffen and Irving Azoff were getting rich by being their own men. Yetnikoff, CBS's man, was rich by any other standards but his own, and it was making him crazy.

In 1986, the goy upstairs was replaced by someone Yetnikoff might have liked better, the Jewish philanthropist Laurence Tisch, who took over the company in an enormous stock play. But Tisch, a very straitlaced character, was uncomfortable with the world of rock and roll, especially by Yetnikoff's symbiosis with the likes of Morris Levy and Joe Isgro, the octopus-like record promoter at the heart of a major new federal payola prosecution that was dismissed because of government misconduct. Michael Jackson billions notwithstanding, Tisch concluded that all the music shenanigans proved a risk to the licenses of his television stations, which in the end were more valuable to CBS than music. Yetnikoff soon came to hate Tisch and began calling him "the kike upstairs" and "the evil dwarf."

Realizing that Tisch would be delighted to be rid of the "Jew downstairs," Yetnikoff set out to find someone to buy CBS Records and run it as a separate company. He didn't have to look further than his friend Norio Ohga, who had risen to president of all Sony. Yetnikoff made his initial pitch to Sony's head man in America, Mickey Schulhof, a Czech-born, seemingly nerdy Brandeis applied physics Ph.D., who had gotten his first non-science business job from Clive Davis at CBS Records before moving to Sony, where his high-tech background would be better utilized.

Like Yetnikoff, Schulhof was Jewish and lived in Great Neck, though unlike Yetnikoff, he had gotten there as a rich kid. Schulhof's immigrant father had made a fortune manufacturing Catholic greeting cards. *Sauve qui peut.* Like Ohga, Schulhof was a jet pilot who liked to fly the Sony planes. He was at Teterboro Airport when Yetnikoff pitched the sale of CBS, $1.2 billion plus a $50 million package for *mishpocheh,* Yiddish for the "family" of Yetnikoff and his trusted team, like Michael Jackson manager Frank Dileo, another promotional wizard who had risen to the peak of records from the back of his family's Pittsburgh sub shop. Schulhof called Tokyo and got Yetnikoff a yes in twenty minutes.

The "evil dwarf" Tisch backed out of the deal several times, jacking up the price to $2 billion, until the "Black Monday" stock market crash of 1987 jarred him into a fear-based submission. This marked the first wave of what would become in the next few years a Japanese "invasion" of corporate America, a shopping spree where no company was safe from a Rising Sun takeover. CBS was as apple-pie American as Sousa and Springsteen and Dylan, and Streisand, too. But nobody was asking the stars to don happi coats or kimonos. Their rabbi, Walter Yetnikoff, whose psychedelic craziness was as incomprehensible as most rock lyrics, was the new face, the Jew face, of the old company. But this was just the beginning. Steve Rechnitz, now Ross, had better watch out. Velvel (Yetnikoff's childhood name) was going to leave him in the dust. The next Brooklyn bullet train was leaving the station.

Just before the CBS Records deal closed, Yetnikoff was with Norio Ohga and his wife at the Salzburg Festival to see Ohga's favorite conductor, Herbert von Karajan, conduct *Don Giovanni*. To Yetnikoff, Karajan, who had Nazi associations, was a symbol of Hitler more than Mozart. The "never forget" Yet vowed to himself to refuse to join the inevitable standing ovation.

He didn't have to embarrass his host. That night, in the middle of the opera, Ohga, then in his late fifties, had the first of what would be a string of heart attacks. Still, he refused to be deterred from Sony's mission to colonize America, particularly with the dollar plunging against the yen. The coronary was an excuse for Ohga to leave Yetnikoff alone, to not try to micromanage their temperamental American genius. No sooner had the music deal closed than Ohga told Yetnikoff to now find a Hollywood studio for him to buy and, presumably, for Yetnikoff to run.

First choice might have been the august (for Hollywood), MCA-Universal, but Lew Wasserman, the shogun in residence, was still not ready to abandon his throne, whatever the price. MGM was a no-go, because it was a shell of its former self, and for Ohga, having to deal with owner Kirk Kerkorian was a fatal coronary waiting to happen. That left Columbia, which its parent, Coke, was more than willing to unload. Still reeling from the debacle of introducing New Coke in 1985, Coke had been further embarrassed by the abject failure of David Puttnam and his list of films like the talking penis *Me and Him*.

Puttnam's successor, Victor Kaufman, had fared no better. Kaufman's brainchild, Tri-Star, the studio that supposedly could not fail, was hamstrung by the lawyer Kaufman's conservative and boring film taste, taste that failed to win the studio the big hits it needed to put it on the map. While not a *Titanic* shipwreck, Tri-Star was a big blah. Kaufman's successor, Dawn Steel, unchivalrously dumped by Paramount after she got pregnant, was not only a bomb but also a bomber. Her cover of *New West*, labeling her "the Queen of Mean," Hollywood's answer to the psychotic and vicious Leona Helmsley, created the kind of bad publicity that was anathema to the all-American Coca-Cola, whose core business centered around selling uncomplicated good times through sugar and water. Those wonderful folks who brought us Pearl Harbor thus looked like saviors to the folks in Atlanta.

All that was left was to settle on the price. However, Yetnikoff thought putting Sony's Schulhof to the task against master negotiator Herbert Allen was akin to putting a Chihuahua into a dogfight with a Labrador. So Yetnikoff brought in the big dog of New York, the Blackstone Group, headed by former Nixon commerce secretary Pete Peterson, an American Dream success story whose Greek immigrant father had run a diner (cheeseburger, cheeseburger) in Kearney, Nebraska. Peterson's chief lieutenant was billionaire-to-be Stephen Schwarzman, another American Dream success story. Schwarzman's middle-class Jewish father ran a dry goods store in the Philadelphia suburbs. Schwarzman strived so hard in the public schools that he made it to the Ivy pinnacles of Yale, alongside Roland W. Betts, and to the Skull and Bones, alongside George W. Bush. He did not join Betts and Bush at DKE, perhaps out of an aversion to its hard partying, perhaps as an indication that upward mobility had its limits. Bones was honor, DKE was social. The hypersensitive Walter Yetnikoff probably would have jumped to the conclusion that the legacy boys saw the upstart Schwarzman as a "pushy Jew" to be excluded, but that was Yetnikoff. If Schwarzman wanted revenge, he more than got it in terms of worldly success.

Even though Schwarzman had proceeded to that other summit of Harvard Business School, nothing in New Haven or Cambridge had prepared him to deal with the nonschoolbook ways and means of Hollywood. Blackstone came up with a bid of close to $15 a share for Columbia's stock, which was selling for around $12. Herbert Allen wanted $35. He had gotten Coke to pay $70 a share for stock that had traded for $40. There was no reason to stop him from trying to break the bank, and then some, once again. While the two sides remained oceans apart, Ohga had several more heart attacks, and the deal process dragged on and on.

Aside from the money, there was also the key question of who would run Columbia if Sony did in fact acquire it. While Sony was pathologically distrusting and hands-on in their electronics business, they fully understood that any controls they might try to impose on the freewheeling movie business would be lost in translation. That was why they left Yetnikoff alone to do his thing in records, where the whims of rock stars were, if anything, even more abstruse than those of movie stars and star directors. Yetnikoff knew he could handle them all, but he didn't want to appear overreaching or avaricious. Accordingly, he had Sony retain the godfather of the New Hollywood, superagent Mike Ovitz, not only to help broker the deal, but to find the studio head for the prospective new operation.

Just as Yetnikoff saw himself at the helm of the "torch lady," as Columbia was known, so did Ovitz. Ovitz would have loved the job, which would make him far richer than even his percentages of just about every deal made in Hollywood. Part of the attraction here was that Ovitz was a complete Asiaphile, from requiring his foot soldier agents to study Sun Tzu's *The Art of War* to hiring I. M. Pei to design his minimalist CAA flagship in Beverly Hills. He saw himself as a model of Japanese Bushido warrior restraint. But the warrior Ovitz drew the line at kowtowing to Walter Yetnikoff, so he was stricken from Sony's wish list of leaders. The next candidate was Michael Eisner, who had accomplished a miraculous turnaround at Disney. Ohga found the top mouse to be a boring blowhard, so much so that the Sony prexy actually fell asleep as Eisner was pitching his elaborate high-volume, low-outlay corporate film philosophy, as he was wont to do.

By summer 1989, Sony was still without its key man. Walter Yetnikoff might have thrown his own hat into the ring had his doctor not insisted that he commit himself to Hazelden, the ne plus ultra addiction clinic in Minnesota, as beloved of the entertainment business on both coasts for substance abuse as Arizona's Canyon Ranch was for overeating. According to the doctor, it was do or die for Yetnikoff, who had been partying so hard that Roland Betts would have personally rushed him for DKE, bloodlines be damned. At Hazelden, ostensibly of a clearer, if not clear, mind, Yetnikoff came up with the brainstorm of Guber and Peters for Columbia.

True, they had never run a studio. True, Guber was conniving and Peters was a loose cannon. True, they had ridiculous matching ponytails, which the proper Japanese would find appalling. And true, they had just signed a seemingly ironclad deal at Warner's with the ironfisted Steve Ross, Yetnikoff's bête noir. On the other hand, they were both masters of taking all the credit where only a sliver was due (as well as denying all the debits of their flops) and, accordingly, had made themselves the I. M. Peis of the two most important movies of recent memory, *Rain Man* and *Batman*. They said they were geniuses, and damned if they weren't.

Furthermore, in the back of his new drug-free mind, Yetnikoff, even without the superman rush of cocaine, surely thought he was cleverer than both of them combined, cleverer than anyone on earth. Guber was weak, dependent on strongman Peters, and Peters was uneducated, in awe of the Columbia Law mastermind Yetnikoff. Yetnikoff surely believed that Guber and Peters, especially Peters, his bad-boy alter ego, would not only be beholden to him, they would ultimately be his tools, if not his puppets.

Walter Yetnikoff would rule Columbia, Columbia Records, Columbia Pictures, Columbia Law. As the Columbia College fight song went, "Roar, lion, roar." Maybe he'd pick up MGM, too, on his way to the Oscars.

Worried about the impression the irrepressible Jon Peters might make on the totally repressed Japanese, Yetnikoff arranged for Guber to meet Mickey Schulhof by himself. Guber turned on the charm, connecting with Schulhof on every level. They were the same age, forty-seven. They both were affluent suburban Jews who had gone to good schools. They were even both ham radio operators. Kismet. Schulhof, the Czech Chihuahua, was snowed by the Newton greyhound. Schulhof recommended Guber to his superiors, Ohga and Morita, who both interviewed Guber and were smitten by his fluent mogulese. Their ears weren't attuned to the Boston accent, so that didn't bother them. They concluded that if Guber hadn't run a studio before, it was high time he did.

Somehow Yetnikoff was able to finesse his dear friend Jon Peters out of the picture until the big closing took place in New York, wherein he and Guber would be agreeing to sell their shares in their Guber-Peters Entertainment company to Sony in return for a huge deal to run Columbia. Once Peters came on the scene, he turned on Schwarzman for trying to lowball the GPE share price. Schwarzman was talking $7 a share, Peters was talking $20. Furthermore, Schwarzman balked at doing any deal at any price until the Sony deal closed. What good was buying Guber and Peters if he had no place to use them?

Peters, who loved these deals even more than he loved movies, and just as much as he loved hairdressing, did his best to wrestle Schwarzman into submission, aided by his lawyer Terry Christensen, a tough-as-Peters ex-marine like Peters's late father. Christensen, who also represented tough-guy Kirk Kerkorian, would later be sentenced to three years in prison for the illegal wiretapping, with gumshoe-to-the-stars Anthony Pellicano, of Kerkorian's ex-wife. That was one of the rare times in Hollywood when tough guys finished last.

In the end, Sony paid $27 a share for Columbia, slightly under Herbert Allen's target but a cool $5 billion nonetheless. Allen & Company made over $100 million between selling its Columbia shares for $70 million and its $30 million banking fee. Mike Ovitz supposedly earned over $10 million for his "consultancy." Victor Kaufman, who may have been licking his creative wounds, was at the same time licking his financial chops. After redeeming his stock, he made out with $20 million. Dawn Steel got $7 million for her year of losers, as did Jeff Sagansky for treading water at Tri-Star.

Nobody did better than Peter Guber and Jon Peters, but here the road to riches was a rocky one. Peters and Christensen were able to bully Schwarzman into accepting a share price of $17.50 for GPE, getting them $200 million for a company that had lost nearly $20 million that year. Furthermore, Sony had to guarantee the two new moguls an annual salary starting at $2.7 million each, plus a bonus pool of $50 million, like Walter Yetnikoff's *mishpocheh* pool. No men were ever luckier in profiting from the devaluation of the dollar. The deal was a symbol of the excesses of the era of Mike Milken, whose own butt-boy Terren Peizer had started Jon Peters on the junk bond road to the company that he now was unloading for such a windfall. Peizer himself was too busy to celebrate, as he was in the process of saving his own neck by ratting out Milken to the feds, who were hot on Milken's funny money trail.

Before Guber and Peters could claim their unjust deserts, they had to get out of their Warner's deal. Steve Ross, abandoning all his undertaker solicitude, hit the roof and said no way in hell to these world-class ingrates. Ross, who had in 1989 just added Time Inc. to his empire, now called Time Warner, was feeling his oats

and now feeling very insecure that he was losing two of the biggest assets he had promised in the deal with Time. America itself
was feeling xenophobic, symbolized when *Newsweek* magazine put
the Columbia torch lady on its cover dressed as a geisha-hooker. At
Sony, Akio Morita responded to what he saw as blatant racism by
asking why no one got up in arms when the Australian Rupert
Murdoch bought Fox.

For all the angst around them, Guber and Peters were feeling
like foxes in the henhouse. While Ross was singing his sad song
about how valuable they were, to force Sony's hand into an outrageous settlement, they knew that Sony would have to settle in
order to have someone to run their new multibillion-dollar acquisition. The only question was how much more would Sony
have to overpay for the price of admission to the movie business.
The joke went around that the whole deal was Hollywood's revenge for Pearl Harbor, a revenge that, in the end, cost Sony an
extra billion dollars to get their ponytailed golden boys.

The biggest loser in the deal turned out to be its designer, Walter
Yetnikoff. The ham radio waves that bound Guber and Schulhof
turned out to be far stronger than the wild times that, pre-Hazelden,
may have bound Peters and Yetnikoff. Even all their nights together in Great Neck couldn't salvage Yetnikoff's friendship with
Ohga. The press all piled on Yetnikoff and fingered the once wild
man who had given them such great copy over the years as the con
artist who tricked Sony into the raw deal of the century, and all
for his own self-aggrandizement.

When it was time to realize that aggrandizement, in his being
made the overlord of both music and movies at Sony, as Yetnikoff
believed Ohga had promised him, Ohga deferred to Schulhof,
who protected Guber's power and reduced Yetnikoff to basically
consultant status. By 1991, Walter Yetnikoff was fired, barred
from his offices, and replaced at CBS Records by his subordinate
Tommy Mottola. He had hubristically assumed Mottola's loyalty,

just as he had assumed that of Jon Peters. But when Yetnikoff turned to Peters, in extremis at being fired, pleading to let him use his offices, Jon Peters could not accommodate him. He was Sony's boy now, not Yetnikoff's, and Hollywood's biggest icono-clast had to respect Sony's elaborate protocols. It wasn't that Peters had turned traitor. He had simply turned Japanese.

# CHAPTER 12
## ITALIAN RAPSCALLION

IN THE BULGING ANNALS of funny money in Hollywood, there is none funnier, or more absurd, than the filthy lucre surrounding the so-called financier Giancarlo Parretti, an itinerant Italian Horatio Alger from Orvieto who wanted to see the world. In so doing, he rose from a waiter on the *Queen Elizabeth II* to one at the Savoy in London and then to a job at a tuna cannery in Hong Kong en route to becoming chairman of MGM. Chairman of MGM? Yes, chairman of MGM. What's wrong with this picture? Everything. Yet rise Parretti did, in the most preposterously dizzying ascent that Hollywood had ever seen. Parretti, who bought MGM with $1.2 billion of somebody's money, was so unqualified for his position, even in this business of bogus résumés, that he made Jon Peters seem like Irving Thalberg. Parretti looked like Pagliacci, the mogul as clown, but he was the most successful clown to hit show business since Emmett Kelly retired. Unfortunately, the last laugh in the success story, the pinnacle and the end of eighties excess, was on Hollywood.

Parretti was one clown who didn't need makeup. He was his own best disguise, the most impenetrable tycoon to ever bestride Sunset Boulevard. He didn't bestride it much. Although he had the requisite mansion just north of Sunset on Coldwater Canyon, the first table at Madeo, the town's most authentic Italian restaurant, run by an authentic mobster from the Tuscan tycoon resort of Forte dei Marmi, and a starlet-filled prime banquette at Tramp, a branch of the London disco in the bowels of the Beverly Center run by Jackie Collins's husband, Parretti was usually more likely to be found on his Gulfstream IV.

Fascinated by MGM's absentee landlord, I tried to do a story on him, which took me to Rome and his papal offices in a grand palazzo in front of the Trevi Fountain. The Renaissance splendor of the place was an outtake of *Godfather III*. Parretti, in his late forties and bulging out of a dark Canali suit behind a completely unlittered, unlettered antique desk that probably belonged to Machiavelli, was cordial in the manner of a suspicious border guard. Part of the key to Parretti's sphinxlike aura was his inability or unwillingness to speak the King's English, or even that of Savoy room service. The linguistic gap seemed to belie his claim to have been Winston Churchill's favorite waiter at the Savoy Grill. Then again, lots of big claims were made by and about Parretti.

But who needed English when we could have an Italian lunch? Accompanied by his English-fluent young daughter, who wanted to be—what else?—an actress, we went in his stretch Mercedes limo with blackout windows to an unmarked, clearly exclusive trattoria near the Porta Pia, where an army of fawning waiters in tuxes served one of the great seafood feasts, its centerpiece a glistening whale-size *branzino* just flown in, perhaps on that Gulfstream, from Sardinia. This mogul knew food. Money? Funny money? He had nothing to say. Movies? He had even less, referring me to his newly installed studio chief, Alan Ladd Jr. Those Lucullan roast potatoes? He knew everything, from the spuds to the marque of olive oil, to the rosemary, even the salt. If the way to Hollywood's heart was through its stomach, maybe this was how this Pagliacci of pictures had stormed the gates.

The deliciousness of this *bouffe,* from the freshest baby clams to the freshest white peaches, distracted me from my frustrations at being unable to plumb the roots of Parretti's vast and unlikely success. From what little could be known, Parretti seemed like a one-man *Da Vinci Code,* with sinister connections to the Freemasons, to P2 (Propaganda Due), to the Vatican, to supercrook bankers Roberto Calvi and Michele Sindona, to Gaddafi, the Saudis, and many more persons of evil interest. How I wanted to delve into the relationship with his partner, Florio Fiorini, who was even more opaque and mysterious, not to mention more inaccessible, than Parretti. The Geneva-based Fiorini had not been a waiter or a canner. He was a highly educated economics whiz who had risen to become the all-powerful finance director of ENI, the Italian state-owned petrochemical giant. His brief was to place ENI's billions abroad in offshore accounts.

Since this was Italy, there was of course a dark side to this. Fiorini was involved in trying to save the notorious and floundering Banco Ambrosiano, where he had secreted a fortune of ENI funds that he couldn't afford to lose. Fiorini was close to Ambrosiano's chairman, Roberto Calvi, known as "God's banker" for his Vatican ties. Calvi was found hanged from London's Blackfriars Bridge in the midst of Fiorini's attempted rescue. In the ensuing scandal, Fiorini had to leave ENI. He somehow teamed up with Parretti to become the odd couple of Italian fiscal sleight of hand.

Parretti's inroads into the murky corridors of Italian power began when he left the Savoy in the early 1970s. Thirty-something, he went to work as a waiter in Sicily. There, in the cradle of the Cosa Nostra, he found himself attending to tables in one of several hotels owned by Graziano Verzotto, a powerful member of the Italian Senate. Like Fiorini a director of ENI, Verzotto was the owner of the Syracuse soccer team Calcio as well as president of a major state-owned mining company. Verzotto took a liking to his young waiter and took him on as his personal aide-de-camp.

In 1975, when Verzotto was indicted for embezzling $3 million from the mining company, he survived a Mafia hit and then fled to Beirut and later to Paris, leaving Parretti in charge of both his hotels and his soccer team.

*In loco Graziano,* Parretti began flexing his surrogate muscles. He began publishing Graziano's small but influential newsletter, *Il Diario,* which was the house organ of the PSI, or Italian Socialist Party, whose coalition with the Christian Democrats had ruled the country since the fall of Mussolini. Through the paper, Parretti formed the first of his unlikely political friendships, with Gianni De Michelis, a former chemistry professor and Socialist leader who oversaw ENI for the party and would introduce Parretti to the similarly intellectual Fiorini. Speaking of brains, De Michelis was the genius behind the notorious prime minister Bettino Craxi, the prime benefactor of Silvio Berlusconi. Craxi would eventually flee to Tunisia to avoid life in prison for his massive corruption. De Michelis made Parretti treasurer of the Socialist Party's youth organization, plunging the ex-waiter into the center of some very fast and loose company.

In 1982, Parretti ran into his first high-profile trouble. *Il Diario* was millions of dollars in debt and on the brink of bankruptcy. In addition, Verzotto's soccer team was facing an investigation over missing funds, suspicions over which had led to Parretti's arrest on two occasions, a brief prison term and the prospect of a far longer one on charges of massive bank fraud. Fiorini enabled Parretti to flee Syracuse and its legal sword of Damocles (Damocles, incidentally, had also been from Syracuse) by getting him the job at the Italian-run tuna plant in Hong Kong, home of many of ENI's Fiorini-controlled offshore accounts.

Parretti stayed in the Far East less than a year before relocating to Paris, where he became the PSI's formal secretary. With money-mad Craxi now in power, being the Socialists' man in the City of Light, its French Connection, enabled Parretti to meet some of the most powerful businessmen in France. The "Socialist" appellation was completely misleading where these supercapitalists were concerned.

Soon after ensconcing himself in Paris, Parretti made the short hop to the nearby tax haven of Luxembourg to set up his own shell company, called Interpart, with a mere $20,000 in capital. Within a year, the coffers contained $1 million. And within two years, during which Fiorini (who after leaving ENI had become an adviser to one of Muammar Gaddafi's Libyan banks) joined Interpart as Parretti's partner, those coffers were bulging with $60 million, whose provenance was endlessly questioned but never answered, thanks to the secrecy protections of Luxembourg.

In 1986, notwithstanding that $60 million, Parretti, whose Sicilian businesses were all bankrupt, was arrested at Fiumicino Airport in Rome, charged with trying to extort $20,000 from an Italian bank. But in Italy, justice is slower and more porous than just about anywhere else in the non–third world, and Parretti was never forced to have his day in court.

That the $60 million represented laundered Socialist funds was suggested by Parretti's first acquisition with $7 million of the money, the French Socialist paper *Le Matin,* which promptly went bankrupt by 1987. He also flipped the Melia hotel chain in Spain and bought a lot of abandoned condo high-rises on the Costa Brava, after which Spanish authorities issued arrest warrants accusing Parretti of illegally funneling money to that other tax haven of Andorra. He also started traveling to Liberia to do hotel deals with that country's strongman Samuel K. Doe, who was later killed by Liberian freedom fighters, thus silencing still another voice that might have explained where Parretti's millions came from.

It was inevitable that Parretti's unquenchable spending spree would lead him into the movie business. His first effort, *Bernadette,* about the Lourdes peasant girl who had visions of the Virgin

Mary, was anything but Hollywood, even though that role in the forties had paid off for Jennifer Jones with a Best Actress Oscar and marriages to David O. Selznick and Norton Simon. Parretti's *Bernadette,* produced in France in 1986, starred Nashville-born soap (*All My Children*) star Sydney Penny. The film was chosen to run in perpetuity in Lourdes itself and even won Parretti an audience with Pope John Paul II at the Vatican, which to an Italian was even better than winning an Oscar. For all his wheeling and dealing, Parretti was now sanctified, not to mention bitten, by the movie bug.

Driving home the sweet sting of cinema were the film's distributors, who would not have been invited to the Vatican. These were Menahem Golan and Yoram Globus, the Israeli "Go-Go Boys" who had become the kings of low-budget cinema in the 1980s. If Parretti was Pagliacci, the cousins Golan and Globus were variations on Jerry Lewis, showbiz as low comedy. In Giancarlo Parretti they had found an equally unlikely success story, not to mention a desperately needed source of capital. Here were two houses of cards, which, via the brilliance of Hollywood architecture, somehow managed to be each other's flying buttresses.

In truth, the Go-Go Boys were even more akin to the Festrunk brothers, *Saturday Night Live*'s two wild and crazy Czech guys played by Steve Martin and Dan Aykroyd, totally intoxicated by the American Dream as badly translated into their immigrant idiom. They didn't look like Hollywood, but they didn't look like Tel Aviv, either. They most resembled countermen, pastrami carvers, at Katz's Delicatessen on the Lower East Side. But as they say, one man's pastrami is another man's cinema.

Beginning their producing career with Israeli knockoffs of American hits, such as *Lemon Popsicle,* their tone-deaf take on *American Graffiti,* the Polish Israeli Golan and Globus discovered that the foreign audience to whom they sold their films was as tone-deaf as they were. Those foreigners, from Chechnya to China, loved the American Dream, too, and couldn't really discern the difference between the art of George Lucas and the schlock of Menahem Golan, who fancied himself a director as well as producer.

If there was a difference between Sylvester Stallone and Chuck Norris, the foreign market either didn't know or didn't care. They were happy to see Chuck Norris, so happy to see Norris that their happiness, in terms of ticket sales, made Golan and Globus rich enough by the mid-1980s to go out and hire Sylvester Stallone for $12 million, big-studio money, to make a movie for them. Alas, that movie was not a *Rocky*-type boxing epic but a very rocky road of an arm-wrestling story called *Over the Top,* whose commercial doom was doubly sealed when Menahem Golan, like a Festrunk brother, insisted on directing it himself. The cousins believed they were the next Goldwyn and Mayer, and everything they tried to do seemed to get lost in translation.

Typical and most egregious of their attempts at Americanizing their company, Cannon, was their great coup in signing none other than Katharine Hepburn to make a film for them. Of course, there were many catches. One, Hepburn was nearly eighty, although she had recently won her fourth Oscar for *On Golden Pond.* Worse was the project itself, a pet pipe dream of Hepburn's entitled *The Final Solution of Grace Quigley* that involved an aging woman's hiring of a hit man to euthanize herself as well as many of her elderly friends. Even with Nick Nolte, who would play the hit man, and director Anthony Harvey, who had served Hepburn so well in *The Lion in Winter,* the film was a hopeless case, a textbook example of what happens when two schlockmeisters try to buy class. The box office was close to zero.

The *Quigley* formula was repeated time after time, as the Go-Go Boys kept signing up aging or has-been stars to make pet projects that no studio, or even other independent companies, would think of touching. There was the Brooke Shields disaster

*Sahara,* the Bo Derek disaster *Bolero,* the Godard disaster directing *King Lear,* the Norman Mailer disaster directing *Tough Guys
Don't Dance.* They signed Dustin Hoffman to star in the Elmore
Leonard book *La Brava* but so embarrassed Hoffman by bragging
in giant ads how they had signed him that the sensitive actor quit
and sued the cousins instead for breach of contract, not to mention breach of his dignity.

Notwithstanding all these disasters, the Go-Go Boys still kept
making movies, making money, and raising money, particularly
from a starstruck Wall Street. Mike Milken's Drexel Burnham,
for one, got them over $200 million in appropriately named junk
bonds for junk films. The genius of Golan and Globus was a play
on H. L. Mencken: their ability to underestimate, time after
time, the starstruck idolatry of Wall Street and other banks around
the world. Big names meant big money, even if the projects were
dreadful. It was like Eddie Murphy in *Coming to America.* People
in the millions turned out to see Eddie Murphy, not the movie.

The difference, though, between a Paramount dud and a Cannon dud was that with the old stars Cannon rounded up, nobody
came out to see either the star or the film. But because the movies
were shot on such a shoestring budget, less than a third of studio
films, and because these films were presold, in advance of being
made, simply on the name of the attached star, to foreign distributors who were just as starstruck as the banks were, Cannon
never lost money. Or at least never lost it on the books, thanks to
typical Hollywood creative accounting and an SEC that was as
clueless as to incomprehensible movie profit definitions as it would
be toward the incomprehensible collateral debt obligations that
nearly bankrupted America in 2007.

Meanwhile, even though the audiences did not show up for
Cannon, the bankers did, and they kept on coming, putting their
money on stars like Charles Bronson, Robert Mitchum, Faye Dunaway, Shelley Winters, Elliott Gould, Jon Voight, Eric Roberts.

To Hollywood studios obsessed with Eddie Murphy and Tom Cruise, Cannon's stars might not be bankable anymore, but to the bankers they were. Even (to quote Norma Desmond) if the pictures had gotten small, those stars, at least in the memory of the bankers, were still as big as ever.

Those bankers were at least one or two generations removed from the growing teenage audience that was making the studios richer than they had ever dreamed. A Drexel banker's concept of a star, the knee-jerk awe akin to spotting a famous face at Elaine's or the 21 Club, was totally different from Jeff Katzenberg's, which involved putting teen asses in sticky theater seats. The Hollywood–Wall Street disconnect was what was keeping Cannon afloat, at least until Giancarlo Parretti came to the rescue. Just as the easy Wall Street money of the 2000s pushed the housing industry over a cliff, the easy Wall Street money of the 1980s pushed the independent film industry into the abyss. By the beginning of the 1990s, most of the big independents, Dino De Laurentiis, New World, Vestron, Carolco, and Hemdale, would all find themselves bankrupt or close to it

The one banker who had been the prime savior not only of Cannon but of all independents wasn't on Wall Street at all but in Rotterdam. The man was Frans Afman. Born in 1933, Hollywood's "Flying Dutchman" spent his formative career years at Rotterdam's Slavenburg Bank, which in the late 1960s had sent him to America to work at First National Bank of Chicago, a 20 percent shareholder in Slavenburg. Taken with America, and particularly American film, Afman created the bank's entertainment division to service one particular client, the indefatigable Dino De Laurentiis, who would do anything, fly anywhere, cut any deal, to get money for movies, especially after losing his Battistoni shirt on his Dinocittà studios in Rome. Introduced to Afman by Slavenburg client (but not for movies) Charles Blühdorn, De Laurentiis would become Afman's mentor in the ways of movies, and in return Afman helped him relocate to New York and finance his first American hits, *Serpico, Death Wish, Three Days of the Condor,* and the very big bucks *King Kong.*

Despite Afman's great work with De Laurentiis, by the 1970s Slavenburg's reputation had been nearly destroyed, with very un-Dutch scandals involving money laundering of drug money. Moviemaking was the least of the bank's vices, and Afman remained above reproach. Thus, when the French giant Crédit Lyonnais took over Slavenburg in 1981, renaming it Crédit Lyonnais Bank Nederland, the French owners were intrigued by Afman's entertainment niche and retained him to expand it. By then he had met Golan and Globus, who, thanks to his creative financings and support when the snobs of Hollywood and Wall Street would not return their Israeli-accented calls, became even bigger clients than De Laurentiis. Cannon produced more movies than anyone else in Hollywood, and every one of those films, schlocky as almost all were, was an exercise in high finance. In contrast with the matching tracksuited Go-Go Boys, the bald, dark-suited Afman looked like a gnome of Zurich, but he could wheel and deal with the fastest talkers anywhere.

Afman had his hits, but in the end—because his money party did eventually end—he had more flops. None of the latter was bigger than the Cannon-distributed, Roman Polanski–directed *Pirates,* which cost upward of $40 million (*Raiders of the Lost Ark* cost only $18 million) and domestically grossed downward of $2 million and not much more abroad. It was a far cry from Polanski's 1974 *Chinatown,* after which Polanski intended *Pirates* as his follow-up, even bigger knockout film, also starring his best friend and *C-town* star, Jack Nicholson, as well as himself as Nicholson's high-seas sidekick. One of Polanski's stated inspirations was the Disneyland ride Pirates of the Caribbean, an homage that brought the artsy Polanski ridicule back then and might have made him a visionary were he not so far ahead of his time.

The project failed to come together for many reasons, not the least of which were Jack Nicholson's salary demands. But more significant were the demands of law enforcement after Polanski was charged with raping thirteen-year-old Samantha Geimer at Nicholson's Mulholland Drive home. Polanski ultimately fled the country, and for all his genius, the studios were reluctant to back a presumed child molester's take on a Disneyland ride. Enter Tarak Ben Ammar, the thirty-something, Georgetown-educated, Paris-based, Nicolas Sarkozy–look-alike playboy nephew of Tunisia's progressive president Habib Bourguiba. What was Ben Ammar's ambition? To be a film producer. What else? Ben Ammar knew Polanski from the Castel-Bains Douches supermodel circuit; both men had an eye for pulchritude. Eventually, Ben Ammar talked Polanski into letting him make the *Pirates* dream come true.

Through his family ties, Ben Ammar was able to build Tunisia's first film studios. Parts of *Star Wars* and *Raiders* were both shot there. To those bragging rights, Ben Ammar added a prestige producer credit on Franco Zeffirelli's acclaimed 1982 filmed opera, *La Traviata*. Ben Ammar had grown up in Rome when his father was Tunisia's ambassador there. He was connected in Italy, to say the least, with access to all the lions of the arts like Zeffirelli. Universal having distributed *La Traviata,* Ben Ammar convinced that studio to finance and release *Pirates*. But Jack Nicholson was long gone. The Samantha Geimer connection was too damning for him to team up with Polanski again, on-screen or off-.

Ben Ammar needed a new Jack, but what he came up with was a very old one, in of all people the sixty-something, recently coronary-bypassed Walter Matthau, whom Ben Ammar met at a party for Gregory Peck and was totally charmed by. Both Ben Ammar and Polanski decided they had found their man, literally the last action hero. Universal dropped out, leaving Ben Ammar with a huge breach of contract suit. But soon Cannon, and Afman, stepped in. Cannon was obsessed with names, and now they had two big ones, notwithstanding the fact that Matthau's casting was a $40 million joke that only a dark humorist like Polanski would "get."

In the wake of the *Pirates* release in 1986 to the deafening sounds of silence, Tarak Ben Ammar couldn't have been more active in Hollywood. After all, he had a huge-budget Roman Polanski film, which gave him all the cachet he needed. I was impressed enough to sell him an option on a script of mine and even more impressed when he called me from Paris one morning asking me if I could fly to Rome the next day. He had a Zeffirelli project he needed a screenwriter for, a true story about conductor Arturo Toscanini's adventures in Rio de Janeiro as a young man. I wasn't a music man, I demurred. I knew very little about Toscanini. Neither do I, Ben Ammar assured me with all his considerable charm. "Listen, if Zeff likes you, you'll get a big job. If he doesn't, you'll get a fabulous week in Rome." With Rome as the consolation prize, it was an offer neither I nor many other writers could reasonably refuse.

I have to admit I really enjoyed Frans Afman's funny money, for it got me a first-class ticket and a room at the palatial Hassler Hotel atop the Spanish Steps. The day after I arrived, Ben Ammar took me out to a fancy gated compound on the Via Appia Antica, the Wilshire Boulevard of ancient Rome, to the grand villa of Zeffirelli, whose neighbors included the designer Valentino and Polanski's discovery Nastassja Kinski. Suffice it to say we got along famously, particularly since the Appian way to my heart was through my stomach, and I never ate as well as I did at Zeffirelli's. His cook, in her eighties, was something of the Julia Child of Italy, a treasure he had inherited from his mentor/lover Luchino Visconti. Zeffirelli, then in his sixties, was still an Adonis, a more refined version of George Peppard. How he stayed so imperially slim with his cook's Lucullan feasts could be the title of a diet book, *Italian Directors Don't Get Fat*. Every meal she made was the definitive version of the Italian classics that invariably took never less than three hours to consume, invariably in the company of local and visiting giants in music and the arts. It was a long way from Spago.

Between meals we talked about the Toscanini movie, which I managed to sum up as *The Graduate* in Rio in the 1880s, in which the Mrs. Robinson was a famous La Scala diva living in Rio as the mistress of the Brazilian emperor. Young Toscanini, then an itinerant musician, became her vocal coach/lover as well as her conscience. As a student radical, he was appalled that Brazil still had slavery and he used his affair to convince her to convince the emperor to free the slaves, which was done during a performance of *Aida* with all its Egyptian slaves on the stage.

It was totally strange but all true, and it was the antithesis of Hollywood's high concept. You could hardly sum it up in a page, much less a phrase. Don Simpson would have despised it. Thank heavens, I thought, for Frans Afman and the Crédit Lyonnais, when after a week of Roman feasts, Ben Ammar next flew me to Paris and installed me in the luxury of a Right Bank apartment next to the George V, where I would write the script, using his sumptuous offices in the former Admiralty palace at the Place de la Concorde for my secretarial needs. Say good-bye to Hollywood!

Despite his presumed access to Afman as well as to the Tunisian treasury, Tarak Ben Ammar was always hunting for money, whenever he wasn't hunting for models. One night he took me to a wildly expensive Paris sushi bar near the Palais Royal, where he was entertaining two Brazilian newlyweds on their honeymoon. Either the bride or the groom was heir to a São Paulo media fortune, some of which Ben Ammar wanted to tap for *Young Toscanini*. It turned out the couple were Orthodox Jews, an odd fit for Ben Ammar, who was also pitching me to write an epic biopic on Muhammad. No problem, it turned out, as Ben Ammar spent much of the meal joking with the couple in fluent Yiddish, the language of their parents, Polish Holocaust refugees who had gotten wildly rich in the New World. After we dropped the love-birds at the Ritz, I asked Ben Ammar about his cunning linguistics. He explained, without any irony, that he had a Jewish grandmother. So here he was an Arab with a Jewish grandmother who was educated by the Jesuits in Rome and at Georgetown. If anyone was the perfect producer for the foreign market, it was he.

After three months in Paris, my scripting idyll continued onward to New York, where Zeffirelli was mounting a lavish *Turandot* at the Metropolitan Opera but would work on my draft of the screenplay between rehearsals. I was billeted at the Westbury on Madison, around the corner from Zeffirelli's Fifth Avenue triplex, courtesy of one of his opera angels. In addition to script sessions, Zeffirelli spent a lot of time looking for his Toscanini and always included me in meeting the stars.

Including the writer in anything was not SOP in Hollywood, so this was a touch of dignity on top of the luxury. He went through Charlie Sheen, Matthew Broderick, and *Karate Kid* Ralph Macchio and somehow settled on C. Thomas Howell from Coppola's *The Outsiders,* a much lesser star than the others, but the actor who most resembled the young Toscanini. Zeffirelli was a production designer at heart; to him looks were everything. Zeffirelli saw himself as the main star of his shows, and Ben Ammar and Afman indulged his ego, something that Michael Eisner, who needed the insurance of a name, a young name, would never have tolerated.

For the diva/Mrs. Robinson, Zeffirelli considered such divas as Barbra Streisand, Shirley MacLaine, and Faye Dunaway, but he had his heart set on Elizabeth Taylor, with whom he had become close friends after directing her and Richard Burton in his big hit (for an art film) *The Taming of the Shrew.* The market had changed drastically since 1967, and Taylor had become box office irrelevant, if not box office poison. To the teen audience she was a

*Saturday Night Live* joke, a fat old hag (at fifty!) played by John Belushi, who choked on chicken bones. But to Zeffirelli she was the ultimate diva, and the teens were the ones who were irrelevant. Et tu, Katzenberg! Zeffirelli dispatched Ben Ammar and me to Los Angeles to get her.

The old hag who greeted us in a tiny bathing suit and a towel wrapped around her head looked spectacular, the last laugh at the now dead Belushi. Her opening line was, "I would normally do this in the nude, but I don't know you well enough." Then she winked and added, "Yet." Mrs. Robinson, I presumed. She had to look good, Taylor explained, as she was about to hit the road for a world tour to promote her new perfume line. She took us out to her pool and proceeded to pull down the top of her one-piece and tan herself with a triptych sun reflector. "What do you think of my body?" she asked. I wanted to say that her cups runneth over, but I was too in awe of her legendary stardom to risk the pun.

"It's some body," said Ben Ammar, the diplomat's son.

"Well, I want to show it off. This is the last time I'll ever be this skinny, and I want this for the record." At the time, Matthew Broderick was the front-runner for the male lead. She thought he was cute and liked the idea of having sex scenes with him. But she feared that the ever-tasteful Zeffirelli was "too prissy" to let her go what Nixon had called the hangout route. "You tell that old queen," she joked, "it's all or nothing." The once and, hopefully, future queen of the screen spoke like a stevedore, an X-rated Virginia Woolf. This, I thought, was the *real* Hollywood I had dreamed of as a boy, not coming up with three-word pitches for Don Simpson.

But, sad to say, the real Hollywood was the new, bottom-line Don Simpson Hollywood, and my experiences on *Young Toscanini* were an unreal, offshore Hollywood made possible only by the unreal ability of characters like Tarak Ben Ammar and Frans Afman to find massive sums of money for movies. Ironically, however, with the high-concept boys Eisner and Katzenberg now at Disney, the new Paramount, under Zeffirelli's buddy and *paisan* Frank Mancuso, had agreed to distribute the film in America. Elizabeth Taylor did sign on, and the picture did get made, shooting in Brazil, Tunisia, and Italy, although going five months and countless millions over budget as La Taylor got more depressed in Rome than she had since *Cleopatra* and fought a battle of the bulge with her weight that caused interminable delays so that she would look the same in every scene.

I wasn't on the set, and neither was Tarak Ben Ammar, who had had a terminal falling-out with Zeffirelli. There was a new Italian producer and there was a new writer, Frans Afman's fellow Dutchman Menno Meyjes, who was just coming off an Oscar nomination for Spielberg's (and Guber-Peters's) *The Color Purple*. Live by the word processor, die by the word processor, I consoled myself. However, just before the film was about to make its world premiere at the September 1988 Venice Film Festival, Zeffirelli called me and invited me to fly over for the festivities. He told me that I had received sole screenplay credit, which was going to be my ticket to big-buck studio heaven, as I would be more than thrilled at how the film had turned out. Zeffirelli was so ebullient that I was almost expecting Spielberg to be on the line next, beseeching me to pen his next opus.

First stop was Rome, where Zeffirelli was holding a pre-Venice screening of the film for his Italian friends, about two hundred of the most glamorous and aristocratic *principi* and *principesse* this side of the late noble Visconti. Sitting next to Zeffirelli in the theater, I was thrilled to see my name on the screen. But as the film unspooled, my heart sank, deeper and deeper, as the movie up there bore basically zero resemblance to the script I had written. I felt like Mia Farrow in *Rosemary's Baby* seeing her monstrous offspring for the first time. What's wrong? Zeffirelli asked me, noting my squirming. Jet lag, I lied. "I've made your career!" he whispered triumphantly. It wasn't my script, but whose was it? Maybe Menno Meyjes had refused the credit, and the production needed me as the fall guy.

Things got worse, far worse, in Venice. It started great, though. Zeffirelli was *the* man to be with in Venice, a prophet in his own country. He introduced me to Fellini, Sergio Leone, Marcello Mastroianni, and other legends. I joined his glamorous entourage riding sleek water taxis that cost rich tourists $100 for a ten-minute canal fantasy for parties at the Ca' d'Oro to watch the Renaissance regatta and at Peggy Guggenheim's to mingle with moguls among art masterpieces. I had Bellinis at Harry's Bar and linguini at off-beat trattorias known only to the cognoscenti. Producers who had given me the shortest of shrift back in Los Angeles now gave me the longest of shrift. Their radar had told them I was there, therefore I was "hot," and they started pitching "classy" historical projects to me over Camparis at hotels like the Cipriani and the Hôtel des Bains, where Thomas Mann had written *Death in Venice*.

*Death in Venice* was the right headline for what happened to *Young Toscanini*. To begin with, Elizabeth Taylor never showed up. She was always notoriously late, but this time late turned into never. She called in sick, but that call was a bad sign. Then Zeffirelli got into a contretemps with Martin Scorsese over Scorsese's showing at the festival of his controversial *Last Temptation of Christ*. In 1977, Zeffirelli had mounted a huge and acclaimed British-produced mini-series called *Jesus of Nazareth,* stuffed with stars ranging from Laurence Olivier, James Mason, and Ralph Richardson to Ernest Borgnine, Anthony Quinn, and Claudia Cardinale. The epic, filmed at Ben Ammar's Tunisian studios, was a holy version of Mike Todd's spectacle *Around the World in 80 Days,* but it was very respectful to Jesus, which Italians believed Scorsese's film was not. Smelling the opportunity to promote a clash of the titan *registi*, one tabloid journalist quoted Zeffirelli as saying that Scorsese's film was "a product of Hollywood's Jewish cultural scum." Uh-oh!

Of course Zeffirelli denied he ever said it, and he quickly assembled a panel of international rabbis to attest to what a steadfast
friend of Jews and of Israel the director was. But Hollywood buys
on the rumor and sells on the rumor. Forget the news. In the blink
of an eye, Paramount denounced Zeffirelli and announced it was
not distributing *Young Toscanini*. No other studio dared step into
the breach and pick it up, not even Cannon. Especially not Cannon. How would the Go-Go Boys explain it to the folks back
home in Tiberias, or even the folks back in Beverly Hills at Nate
'n Al's?

At the press screening for the film, which I forwent, preferring
a few Bellinis at Harry's, people literally threw tomatoes at the
screen. In the end, the film, whose cost was upward of $20 mil-
lion and perhaps much more, was shown only in Italy, briefly, and
in France, equally briefly. Even Japan, where Zeffirelli was a god,
wouldn't touch it. You couldn't even find it on video, even in the
most recherché stores. *Toscanini* was a perfect example of why independent film, or at least high-budget independent film, was
not long for this earth.

At around the same time of the Zeffirelli debacle, that other Italian, the lowbrow one, Giancarlo Parretti, was making his big play
to go as mainstream as Zeffirelli could not. Parretti had his sights
on MGM, whose tawny lion had become a tawdry one thanks to
the endless stock manipulations of owner Kirk Kerkorian, whose
interest in movies, at least as art, was basically nil. In 1988, Parretti
bought Cannon Films, after the Go-Go Boys had gotten seriously
reprimanded by the SEC over their Pollyannaish accounting.

Parretti renamed Cannon Pathé Communications after Pathé,
the French movie giant he was also in the process of trying to acquire. He also announced his plans to bail out the bankrupt De
Laurentiis Entertainment Group and the similarly straitened New
World Entertainment. Those last two buyouts quickly fell through,
and the French government blocked the sale of Pathé to Parretti

because of the shakiness of his financing. Still, there was nothing to stop him in America from using the Pathé name, in vain as it may have been. Soon his movie empire would be called MGM–Pathé Communications Company.

At the helm of Pathé USA, Parretti had been able to hire Alan Ladd Jr. for the David Puttnam quote of $3 million a year. Ladd, who barely knew Parretti and almost never socialized with him at Madeo or Tramp, took the job because Dino De Laurentiis vouched for his fellow Italian. At Ladd's side was his longtime friend and fellow executive Jay Kanter, who had been the agent of Grace Kelly and Marlon Brando. The team was as Old Hollywood as could be, and their first announced big project was polished Old Hollywood as well, *The Russia House,* the adaptation of the John le Carré novel by Tom Stoppard and set to star Sean Connery and Michelle Pfeiffer. If Parretti needed to launder his money and his image, Alan Ladd Jr. was Jeeves himself.

But Parretti needed more than a front. He still needed a back, as in backing, and key to this was his new "best friend" Steve Ross, the emperor of Time Warner. Ross was going to enable the MGM buyout from Kerkorian, with a tag of $1.2 billion, by putting up basically half the money in return for the classic MGM library, with the other half to come from Frans Afman's Crédit Lyonnais. Part of the Ross-Parretti friendship was supposedly founded on the two tycoons' mutual interest in art. To that end, Parretti gave Ross the gift of a Picasso said to be worth millions. When Ross decided to hang the Picasso in a place of honor in the Time Warner offices, the company's art appraiser burst Ross's balloon by declaring the painting a fake. Ross, in return, burst Parretti's balloon by pulling out of their deal. It was unclear whether Parretti himself fully understood the provenance of the painting.

With Ross gone, Parretti turned to Italian prime minister Bettino Craxi to lean on Crédit Lyonnais to provide all the money for the sale. The quid pro quo here would be that Italy would buy its new high-speed Eurostar trains from France and not Germany, as originally planned. The deal was then made with France, and Parretti closed his deal with MGM. The tuna canner was now the new lion of Hollywood. However, the roar of creditors quickly drowned out the crowing of the beast. But the new lion really bit itself when Parretti fell into the same trap as had Zeffirelli, being quoted as denouncing the Jews of Hollywood, the ultimate no-no in the film business. In an interview with the Italian newspaper *L'Unità,* Parretti was quoted as having said, "The Jews have ganged up on me," as well as repeating the old canard that the Jews controlled Hollywood, the Christianity of his all-powerful prexy Laddie notwithstanding.

Although he had no rabbinical panel to come to his defense, Parretti, like Zeffirelli, immediately denied having spoken the anti-Semitic rants. "If one Jew can say to me that I am anti-Semitic, put him in front of me," Parretti announced to the press, as usual putting his foot in his mouth. Again, as with Zeffirelli, it wasn't enough. Hollywood believed that the new lion, already a convicted liar, did protest too much. The local Anti-Defamation League denounced him, as did almost all the agency and studio heads, albeit not for attribution.

Soon afterward, Parretti was haunted again by the *L'Unità* reporter who had done the interview over cigars in Parretti's Beverly Hills mansion. The reporter, who happened to be an Italian Jew, claimed that Parretti had now approached him with a job offer of $200,000 if he would disavow his reportage. He didn't snap at the bait. Instead, more of the interview came out, including another "death quote": "The fact is that the Jews don't like the idea that I represent the first Catholic communications network. There doesn't exist a single media holding company in the world that isn't in the hands of Jews." This from the man who had produced *Bernadette.*

Parretti had only two real defenders. One was Jack Gilardi, the former husband of Mouseketeer dream girl Annette Funicello and the ICM agent for such Cannon stars as the "muscles from Brussels" Jean-Claude Van Damme. His biggest Jewish bona fides was his client Don Rickles. The other stalwart in Parretti's empty corner was the man who distributed *Bernadette,* Cannon's Menahem Golan, whom Parretti had bought out for over $100 million, prompting a split with his cousin and numbers man Globus, who had taken his money and run back to Israel. Golan, who also enlisted an encomium from the chairman of the militant Jewish Defense League, declared that Parretti had given Israel much money, not to mention friendship; but no one was listening. Even if they were, they would probably presume the money he gave belonged to someone else.

Now, to get the final financing to close the MGM deal, Parretti had to scramble as he had never scrambled before in a life of scrambling. His desperation took him to the Knights of Malta in New York, a Catholic charitable organization that had no ties other than the name to the ancient order in Rome with the sinister nexus to the Vatican. Parretti was said not to have known the difference. To him, a Knight was a Knight. Through the New York Knights he met the president of an insurance company in, of all places, the Cook Islands in the South Pacific. To get the completion bond he needed to finalize the MGM deal, Parretti pledged the MGM shares he did not technically own until the full $1.2 billion had been paid. Furthermore, the insurance company was outraged that Parretti stiffed them for the $1.75 million fee he promised them for the guarantee. Whether the Cook Islands company was good for the $210 million it was guaranteeing was another matter. In any event, the distant insurance company got a restraining order against the Parretti transaction in a Cook Islands court, which proved to be the final monsoon on Parretti's Hollywood march to power.

By 1991, Crédit Lyonnais itself took control of MGM, removing

Parretti from the chairmanship and precipitating a major fortune in lawsuits in Europe and America. Parretti hit the road, or the air, in his Gulfstream, as authorities in several countries tried to extradite the peripatetic mogul. Alan Ladd Jr. hit the road as well. Despite its pedigree, his *Russia House* was a flop, as were the few other films he struggled to get out in the midst of the scandal. The one exception was *Thelma & Louise,* whose nihilism was appropriate for the dying studio that released it.

Frans Afman, the architect of what added up to be a $5 billion disaster for Crédit Lyonnais in Hollywood, left the once great bank dependent on a humiliating bailout by the French government, in a major cloud of shame. But Hollywood, which has no shame, brought Afman back into the fold as a pivotal vice president, alongside Parretti defender Jack Gilardi, at ICM. Any man who could raise the money Afman did, regardless of its provenance, would always be forgiven any transgressions and guaranteed a seat at the Hollywood high table.

## EPILOGUE
### REQUIEM FOR THE HEAVYWEIGHTS

IT SEEMS as if the only people to mourn the end of the eighties were the totalitarian Communists of Eastern Europe. By 1990, the triumph of capitalism, Reagan capitalism, was utter and complete, as was the triumph of Reagan Hollywoodism. If Woodrow Wilson had made the world safe for democracy, Ronald Reagan had made the world safe for celebrity. America, at least bourgeois America, was flush, flush enough to go out to the movies, and in droves, if the blockbuster were big enough.

After a two-decade identity crisis, the baby boom generation, torn whether to be hippies or yuppies, finally came down decisively for the latter. The incarceration of Mike Milken and Ivan Boesky notwithstanding, the dream job for male boomers was still investment banker or corporate tycoon. In the Reagan age of money, in a decade where the stock market had tripled, Michael Douglas and Richard Gere had made big business look way too seductive to resist. The other dream job, for the biggest dreamers of all, was to be someone who created the dreams of the nation, studio head or megaproducer.

Reflecting the diverse composition of his Hollywood kitchen cabinet, Reagan had redefined what it meant to be elite in

America. His reign as president created an aristocracy of wealth and fame, and not of breeding. In the old days, this would have been dismissed as café society, but now it was Spago society, and everybody was pressed up against the glass and anybody had a gambler's chance to get in.

The end of the WASP aristocracy was symbolized by "read my lips—no new taxes" prevaricator in chief George H. W. Bush, who coasted into the presidency on Reagan's coattails but became a one-term president when the yuppie electorate booted him out for one of their own in Bill Clinton. Yes, they were both Yale men, but Clinton, Yale Law '73, was more a Georgetown man and, most appealingly, an Arkansas man. Similarly, George W. Bush would do at least one masterful job in obfuscating his preppy-Ivy pedigree and playing the dumb-shucks Texas ranch shtick to the hilt.

Unlike W to come, Bill Clinton was also a Hollywood man, beloved of the new kingmakers Spielberg, Katzenberg, and Geffen. He played the sax on *The Arsenio Hall Show,* he engendered delicious Lincoln Bedroom rumors with the godlike likes of Barbra Streisand and Sharon Stone, and he lived the awful truth with tarty wannabes like Gennifer Flowers and starstruck chubettes like Monica Lewinsky that mass America could reflect in and relate to. Bill Clinton turned Washington into his own reality show, before the genre ever existed.

Aside from the überdogs SKG themselves, very few of the locomotives of the eighties kept their big wheels turning into the nineties. The new decade started out for Hollywood presaging more business, big business, as usual. The year 1990 kicked off with a bang, with Matsushita (the maker of Panasonic) acquiring MCA-Universal for over $6.6 billion, in what seemed to be a copycat move, at twice the price, to outdo rival Sony's Columbia deal the year before.

Sadly, for both Japanese conglomerates, Hollywood was anything but the submissive geisha house the tech giants may have thought they were buying. Early on at MCA there was a scandal that reeked like high noon at Tokyo's Tsukiji fish market. Jon Sheinberg, the William Morris agent son of MCA's famously above reproach Sid Sheinberg, was descended upon by the SEC for insider trading, having tipped his father-in-law, his business manager, and another friend to the imminent but top-secret deal orchestrated by Mike Ovitz, the great facilitator. Sheinberg and company had to disgorge over $1 million in stock profits and penalties. If they had been Japanese, seppuku, the samurai suicide by ritual disembowelment, might have been in order.

Matsushita soon had so many flops that even Spielberg's 1993 giants *Jurassic Park* and *Schindler's List* couldn't stop the Japanese from pressing the ejector button, particularly when Spielberg himself defected the next year to co-found DreamWorks. In 1995, the Japanese unloaded the bulk of their investment on Seagram's, whose chairman, Edgar Bronfman Sr., had hooked his son Edgar Jr. on showbiz by "buying" him David Puttnam's first film, *Melody*.

Edgar Jr., for all his billions in paternal indulgence, was a frustrated songwriter and a family rebel, though perhaps less so than his brother Sam, who allegedly organized his own multimillion-dollar ransom kidnapping with an abductor who later claimed to be Sam's gay lover. Edgar Jr.'s rebellion most egregiously manifested itself when he married, to his family's great dismay, a black actress from New Orleans introduced to him by Dionne Warwick, who had recorded one of his songs.

Then again, when your grandfather made his fortune selling hooch during Prohibition to gangsters Meyer Lansky and Longie Zwillman, who were the Bronfmans to tell young Edgar whom to love? Edgar Jr. kept writing flop songs, under the pseudonyms Junior Miles and Sam Roman, and producing flop movies under his own name, the most disappointing of which was *The Border,* a 1982 Tex-Mex modern western that even Jack Nicholson, Harvey

Keitel, and famed British director Tony Richardson couldn't save. Universal released *The Border* in 1982. Now, by owning the place, Edgar Jr. would have the ultimate producer's revenge, doing it *his* way.

Bronfman Jr. was above and beyond revenge, so no personal movies, fueled by whatever demons he may have had, got made at Universal. Furthermore, he was much more interested in music than in movies. He eventually sold the studio to the French conglomerate Vivendi and, perhaps with visions of becoming the next Walter Yetnikoff, purchased the powerful Warner Music Group. Still waiting for his own gold record, Bronfman did make a different kind of headline in 2011 when he was convicted in France for insider trading. He got fifteen months in jail—suspended—and a €5 million fine—negligible. In France, *pace Gatsby,* the rich are even *more* different from you and me.

Back in the States, the nineties saw the dissolution of one of the great brotherly love affairs of the eighties, that of Peter Guber and Jon Peters. Even before they had ascended to their twin thrones at Columbia, tensions were mounting for Hollywood's fun couple.

Jon and Peter actually entered couples counseling together. Their therapist, Margaret Paul, Ph.D., a Mar Vista (West L.A.) celebrity psychologist, was the author of self-help books such as *Do I Have to Give Up Me to Be Loved by You?* and *Healing Your Aloneness: Finding Love and Wholeness Through Your Inner Child.* Assuming naively that brotherly love would conquer all, Jon had no inkling as to how totally alone he would soon find himself.

There were equally big problems at work as there were at home. The huge Sony deal had unleashed Jon's inner interior decorator, and he was going on a wild spree restoring the Thalberg Building on Columbia's new former MGM lot to its deco splendor, as well as redoing his Aspen ranch and stocking its grounds with llamas and reindeer. It also had unleashed Jon's inner flyboy, as he pressured Sony to buy a fleet of private jets to rival that of Steve Ross, the better to send planeloads of flowers to whatever supermodel he might be courting, not to mention keeping the commercial airline–phobic stars and directors happy. And finally, it had unleashed Jon's inner Santa Claus (there was a reason for those reindeer).

Jon built a city of goodwill by hiring, at salaries nearly as inflated as his own, a bloated executive corps of all chiefs and no Indians, where everyone seemed to have the title of president of something, making the new Columbia more top-heavy than Dolly Parton. Jon talked about a Sony resort in Hawaii that would shame the Four Seasons Maui, and about a Sonyland theme park in Santa Barbara that would out-Disney Disney, and about an overall film deal with Michael Jackson that would have impressed an impresario like Cecil B. DeMille.

When it came to the big screen itself, Guber-Peters replaced Dawn Steel with the warhorse Frank Price as chairman of their Columbia division, though Peters was actually using Price as a placeholder until his best buddy Mark Canton could get out of his Warner contract. At Tri-Star, G-P dispensed with Victor Kaufman in favor of Mike Medavoy, the exotic Shanghai-born, Chile-raised Russian Jew who had been the agent for both Coppola and Spielberg and then the studio executive behind such diverse hits as *Rocky, One Flew Over the Cuckoo's Nest,* and *Annie Hall.* In short order, Medavoy signed Spielberg to do the Peter Pan fantasy *Hook,* Warren Beatty to do the gangster chronicle *Bugsy,* and Bruce Willis to do the indescribable *Hudson Hawk.*

With names like that, how could Guber and Peters fail? Easy. Even in a world gone mad for celebrity, if the celluloid chemistry was wrong, a big name was no sure immunity from a big disaster. On *Hook,* for example, the supposed sure thing, Tinker Bell was played by Julia Roberts. Close to a breakdown after her split from Kiefer Sutherland, America's sweetheart was plagued by drug rumors, particularly one that had Spielberg finding her passed out in a bathroom on the set. Despite Roberts's vehement denial of all the drug rumors, soon the movie became lampooned in Hollywood, and beyond, as *Hooked*. The film wasn't a bomb, but it wasn't the Spielberg blockbuster the boys in Tokyo had been promised.

The true bomb, a nearly $50 million loser, was Jon Peters's pet project about child abuse, of which he knew a lot, *Radio Flyer*. This was Columbia's first "go" picture, and it certainly "went" south, deep, deep south, in a bigger nosedive than *Ishtar*. Undeterred, Peters stood behind his *next* child abuse pet project, *The Prince of Tides*, to star and be directed by none other than Barbra Streisand. Jon may have owed his career to Barbra; the Japanese owed themselves to begin watching their bottom line. Japan was going into a recession that would have no end. The yen was losing its previous buying power. Barbra Streisand was one brandname status symbol that Sony would have to forgo.

About to turn fifty in 1992, Barbra was no longer perceived as entertainment's Wonder Woman. Her previous stint behind the camera, *Yentl,* nearly a decade before, was attacked by some reviewers as a vanity flop better suited to the Yiddish theater than the cineplex. Barbra's long absence from the screen had made Hollywood's heart grow not fonder, but rather much more cautious. She might have been enshrined as a cultural icon, the female Frank Sinatra, but at fifty even Sinatra was washed up in cinema. It was at this point that Sony decided to act upon their many second thoughts about their "Tiger-san."

In May 1991, the ax fell on the studio head of Jon Peters, in a reign over Columbia even briefer than that of David Puttnam. The beheading took place in New York, where Jon was blindsided by Sony's axman Mickey Schulhof. Peter Guber, at the last minute, missed the Sony jet for the trip Jon had assumed would be a solidarity mission. Just as Jon had given the Sony-axed Walter

Yetnikoff the Tokyo swerve, now Peter Guber turned Japanese on his "brother" and did not return Jon's phone calls.

Some in Hollywood blamed Peter's breach of brotherhood on his wife, Lynda. Others blamed the old Columbia lion Ray Stark, forever pulling that studio's strings, wreaking revenge on Jon for having replaced Stark in Barbra Streisand's heart and mind. The most likely explanation was that the ham radio waves that drew Guber and Schulhof together, plus their shared upper-bourgeois Jewish suburban backgrounds, were stronger than the New Age vibes that Jon was channeling through Margaret Paul.

Those radio waves lasted only three more years, until Schulhof finally axed Guber, who, notwithstanding his ability to talk the fastest game in Hollywood, never gave Sony the *Batman*-type blockbuster for which they had squandered billions on him and Jon Peters. Guber could claim hits like *Basic Instinct* and *Terminator II*, but he was just distributing those films for the producer Carolco, which raked in most of the worldwide grosses. More, and sadly, to the point were monster flops like *The Last Action Hero,* which may have convinced Arnold Schwarzenegger to consider politics as a backup career. The most painful lesson learned was that unlike in the 1980s, when Eddie Murphy could have turned *Roget's Thesaurus* into a smash, in the 1990s no star alone could guarantee a gross.

By 1995, both Akio Morita and Norio Ohga had fallen on their swords corporately and resigned, followed by Schulhof himself. The once mild-mannered scientist had mutated, under Guber's influence, into a free-spending nutty professor. He gave big parties, western hoedowns, tropical luaus, but his biggest extravagance was taking his ham radio obsession to its outer limit by buying his own radio station in the Hamptons, an unseemly large percentage of whose advertising came from Sony, as noted suspiciously by *The Wall Street Journal.* It was all too much for headquarters in Tokyo, which ended up writing off nearly $3 billion in losses stemming from its tragic romance with Walter Yetnikoff, who wanted to rock and roll again but never could get his Columbia groove back.

Other than their own, there were no tears shed for either Jon Peters or Peter Guber, whom Sony had enriched beyond greed for the rest of their lives. Both got kiss-off eight-figure independent production deals at Sony. Neither man ever had another monster hit, though Peters, forever swinging for the fences, did get a producer credit on *Batman Returns* in 1992 and *Superman Returns* in 2006. Jon's perpetual swinging also got him in deep legal trouble with several sexual harassment lawsuits by former employees, and not only from the big blondes that were his trademark as much as they were Helmut Newton's, but also from one of his male assistants. The macho-manqué Guber became an éminence grise (or éminence orange, given his forever young and cool hair coloring) of the film business, holding forth on every TV show that would have him, as did Walter Yetnikoff on the state of pop music.

Peter Guber's biggest passion is his newest toy, for the mogul who has had everything, his own NBA team, the Golden State Warriors. He and Peters have never reconciled. In a major irony, Sony Pictures Entertainment, as Columbia is now known, in the long run has done better than Guber and Peters have. The Japanese stayed the course, as movies and television continued to become bigger, if not better, than ever. Their investment in Columbia, ridiculed in its time as the raw deal of the century, in hindsight looks like a brilliant bargain.

Poor Don Simpson. His unspoken rival Jon Peters was always driving him crazy. So jealous of the huge deal Peters had made at Sony, Don took out full-page ads in *The New York Times* and *L.A. Times* trumpeting Simpson-Bruckheimer's own new deal with Paramount, their "visionary alliance," as they called it, worth (off the record) anywhere up to $500 million, if you could believe Don. But nobody really believed Don, or Jon, for that matter, despite their awesome string of successes. The point here was to make the world know that Don's deal was bigger than Jon's deal. Photographs of Don and Jerry were everywhere in the press, two men in matching black Italianate coolness on their backs, with matching Ferraris on the ground. In terms of image, Guber-Peters couldn't touch the swagger of Simpson-Bruckheimer.

And then Don's string snapped. He was the first superproducer to learn, the hard way, of the limits of stardom, when Tom Cruise did not bring home the box office bacon on 1990's *Days of Thunder,* the first release under the "visionary alliance," which was supposed to be *Top Gun* at NASCAR. In the film, Don (slimmed down after a kamikaze diet at Canyon Ranch) gave himself a narcissistic cameo as an Italian race car driver. He put his plastic-sculpted, chin-implanted face on the line for this film, and he got mud in his eye. *Thunder* wasn't a disaster, but it got blown off the screen in its second weekend by *Die Hard II.* Such was the disappointment that Paramount lost its vision in the alliance, and Simpson folded his tent and trekked over the Hollywood Hills with Bruckheimer to reunite with his old Paramount partners Eisner and Katzenberg, who had enjoyed such a smashing start running Disney.

Alas, the arrogant, freer-spending, *Dick Tracy*–ish Disney of the 1990s couldn't come close to the tight-ship *Ruthless People*–ish Disney of the 1980s, and Don Simpson could never resume his trademark swagger. Instead, he drowned his sorrows in a whirlpool of drugs and hookers. On the sex side, his chief enablers were Madam Alex and her disciple, Heidi Fleiss, whose legal bills Don was said to have helped defray when the Jewish princess "junior madam" was busted in 1993 on pandering and cocaine charges at the Benedict Canyon aerie she had bought from Michael Douglas with her wages of sin. In the aftermath of the bust, rumors of the imminent leakage of Heidi's "black book" created massive paranoia throughout the movie elite. Don didn't care. Everyone *knew* that he was a superjohn. The studio with the most to lose was Sony, where several of Peter Guber's chief lieutenants got their names in the papers as persons of interest, as did the producer of *The Last Action Hero,* whose failure was causing enough injury by itself without the insult of a sex scandal.

About the only consolation the Japanese could take was that they didn't have Don Simpson on their lot. Not that Don was on the Disney lot very much, either. Instead, he was holed up in his Coldwater Canyon designer home, taking more drugs than Elvis ever had and with the same sad results. In early 1996, Don died on his toilet, not long after his personal live-in physician had also died of an overdose in Don's pool house and the very uptight, upright Jerry Bruckheimer had severed their seemingly immutable visionary alliance. Another loss, perhaps nearly as painful for Don, was the 1995 death, at sixty, of Madam Alex, herself now a diabetic with a cocaine habit, a fatal combination. Alex had become Don's mother confessor, his closest confidante, as well as his sexual enabler. They spoke on the phone for hours in coke-fueled reveries. He simply couldn't live without her. Don was fifty-two.

Without Don, most people in Hollywood assumed that the self-effacing Bruckheimer would simply self-efface and fade away. In this case, however, the meek inherited the earth. Bruckheimer had discovered Michael Bay, a young director who had come out of Wesleyan, and turned him into the DeMille of demolition. With Bay at the helm, Bruckheimer reinvented the blockbuster, with smashes like *Armageddon* and *Pearl Harbor.* Nor was Bruckheimer putting all his eggs into the Bay basket, as he had seemed to do with Simpson. He also created the *Pirates of the Caribbean* franchise, not to mention such television cash cows as *CSI* and *The Amazing Race.* But he may be the quietest, dullest mogul to ever make it this big; the man makes movies, not copy.

The only other eighties star producer to similarly enlarge his footprint in the nineties and into the new millennium was Joel Silver, of the *Lethal Weapon, Die Hard,* and *Matrix* franchises. Unlike Bruckheimer, however, Silver has been a volume producer with far more flops than hits and a very low batting average. Like Bruckheimer, Silver hasn't made much copy, other than for his collection of Frank Lloyd Wright homes. The fat, bearded, unrepentantly nerdy Silver, the most Mephisphelean-looking man in Hollywood, was once dubbed by *Premiere* magazine the "Selznick of Schlock" and was given the ultimate tribute in *Variety*: "Silver would even stab *himself* in the back to close a deal."

Probably the reason for his low profile was that Silver's most egregious excesses involved screaming at his assistants, one of whom he has been married to, without scandal, for years. In his bachelor days, Silver would be seen at Spago with starlet types he would meet through Playmate wrangler Melissa Prophet, but he never scaled the pulchritudinous heights of Jon Peters, nor did he ever plumb the distaff depths of Don Simpson. Hence he has missed becoming a legend. In terms of mystique, a producer without sex is like a director without a camera. Silver may have given the public the spectacle they demanded on-screen, but not in his real life. By not living up to the expected showbiz high-wire act of women, drugs, and general excess, Joel Silver will remain outside the pearly gates of the producer pantheon, an Olympus of infamy whose rolls were basically closed when the eighties ended. On the other hand, on the plus side, he's still alive.

The producer-moguls with the mystique have almost all died off by now, none more ignominiously than the one who got more copy than all the others combined: David Begelman. Begelman seemed like the crook with nine lives. He had bounced back from his scandal at Columbia to run MGM, and when he was bounced out of there in 1982, he bounced into his own production company, lavishly funded in complicity with a young crook after his own heart, Bruce McNall, a dealer in antique coins and other ancient treasures (which, it was later admitted, had been smuggled out of foreign countries) who pretended he had gone to Oxford in the way Begelman pretended he had gone to Yale.

While McNall was bringing in money from one of his fat-cat clients, Texas oil tycoon Nelson Bunker Hunt, Begelman was kneeling at the foot of the patron saint of independents, the banker Frans Afman of Crédit Lyonnais, whom Begelman secretly put on his payroll to ensure the necessary multimillion-dollar lines of credit an ambitious film company would need. In one of the most celebrated quotes about film financing, Afman told *Forbes,* "Bankers should avoid working with crooks and ignorant people. But if you have a choice, I'd rather work with a crook because he can steal from someone else to repay his bank." Afman knew full well that Begelman was the showbiz master of robbing Peter to pay Paul, or Frans, as this case turned out to be.

McNall lied as big as Begelman and lived even larger. He had a palace in Holmby Hills, owned a string of Thoroughbred racehorses as well as the L.A. Kings hockey team. The pair entertained lavishly at the Cannes Film Festival and in L.A. at the Begelman-financed Drai's, run by Begelman's Moroccan playboy pal from Ma Maison, Victor Drai, who had produced a few films but had segued into hospitality. Drai's had entered the Spago-Morton's pantheon as one of the high tables of the film business. Armed with money, cachet, and haute cuisine, Begelman produced a number of big, star-filled films, some hits like *WarGames, Blame It on Rio,* and *Mr. Mom,* and one megaflop, *The Sicilian,* Mario Puzo's *Godfather* follow-up, directed by *Heaven's Gate's* poster child of fiscal waste, Michael Cimino.

Begelman ran into trouble once again when he tried to fleece the major New York *garmento* Sidney Kimmel, who owned Jones New York and had bought Charles and Robert Evans's Evan-Picone. Foolishly trying to kid a kidder, Begelman pulled another Cliff Robertson when he stiffed the Forbes 400 member

Kimmel out of $3 million in profits from *Blame It on Rio*, a sum that no number of Drai's dinners with such glamorous Begelman friends as Billy Wilder, Walter Matthau, and Michael (call him Mr.) Chow could charm Kimmel into forgiving and forgetting. Kimmel sent his corps of lawyers after Begelman. The master-mind producer was also snared in the net of the FBI, who would eventually corner McNall and send him into bankruptcy and into prison for five years for sundry fiscal frauds.

Always a courtly ladies' man, Begelman had remarried after the death of his Manhattan socialite first wife to the beautiful TV producer Ann Weston. But Begelman, a compulsive gambler who had run up poker debts of nearly $500,000, also gambled with conjugality and maintained a torrid romance with Sandi Bennett, the Louisiana model ex-wife of Tony Bennett and ex-girlfriend of Gene Kelly. It was Bennett who discovered Begelman's body in a room at the Century Plaza Hotel, with a bullet from a .38-caliber pistol in his head. In his suicide note, Begelman, who was loved for his ironic sense of humor, wrote to leave his ashes to his rival in poker and producing, Elliott Kastner, who, if only to goad Be-gelman, had bought the film rights to *Indecent Exposure*. "Just kid-ding," Begelman had amended his missive, laughing all the way to the bitter end.

The end also came, and was invariably bitter, for all of Begel-man's fellow agents—Kastner, Fields, Beckerman—who had be-come the swashbuckling producers of their generation, an era that ended with the eighties. Hollywood was no country for old men, except perhaps Ray Stark, who kept relentlessly pulling strings and breeding Thoroughbreds (equine, not Streisandoid) until he was felled by a stroke in his eighties. He died in 2004, leaving his $750 million sculpture collection to UCLA. The Italian Ray Stark, Dino De Laurentiis, also lived long and powerfully, passing away in 2010 at ninety-one. De Laurentiis's death was something of a coup de grâce to independent film, which received a symbolic double blow in 2011 when its candy man, and Dino's chief lender, Frans Afman, passed away after a long illness. The days of funny money, easy money, Parretti money, were gone and sorely missed, not least by Parretti, still at liberty and probably still in his Gulfstream, notwithstanding a four-year in absentia French prison sentence and a raft of unresolved securities violation charges in America and Italy. He is the airborne Italian version of the Kingston Trio's hymn to perpetual motion, "The Man Who Never Returned."

Those godfathers of the B-picture Golan and Globus again became kissin' cousins after their post-Parretti internecine fallout. They both are back in Israel, making Cannonesque films like still another sequel to *Lemon Popsicle* and other efforts that may be playing in Albania or Bangladesh. Conversely, those godfathers of the action spectacle Vajna and Kassar have kissed and made up only once, in hopes of resurrecting their *Terminator* franchise. They are still wishing and hoping. Where is Rambo when they really need him? Mark Damon, nearing eighty, has become the toast of the lecture circuit, an oracle of independent cinema, preaching the gospel of foreign presales and still practicing what he preaches, financing movies as a name game in a world with an infinitely expanding, if infinitely inflated, pool of celebrities.

Another unexpectedly sorry end came for the (literally) biggest of the big-money players of the eighties, Marvin Davis. In 2004, when he died at seventy-nine, the behemoth Davis, the man who brought his own throne to Spago, had lost 130 pounds. He had heart disease, diabetes, pneumonia, spinal tumors, just about everything a man who ate like a trough of pigs could acquire in this life. But he had lost more than weight. The wildcatter who had flipped Fox to Rupert Murdoch, who had flipped the Beverly Hills Hotel to the sultan of Brunei, who had flipped Pebble Beach to the Japanese, who in 2002 had talked up a $20 billion offer for Vivendi Universal, the new French master of MCA, had long before run out of money. He died broke. The big bids for Vivendi and so many other companies were a huge sham. Davis was a true Hollywood billionaire: a fake one.

In a lawsuit filed by one of his daughters, Davis was accused of living high on the hog by looting his children's trusts. The emperor truly had no clothes. He had gone the way of David Begelman, minus the bullet. After his interment at Westwood Memorial Park, down from the crypts of Marilyn Monroe, Dean Martin, Jack Lemmon, Walter Matthau, and Truman Capote, two of his frequent Spago-fest guests, Stevie Wonder and Carol Bayer Sager, wife of Warner chief Bob Daly, sang "That's What Friends Are For." Despite the grand illusion of his billions, Marvin Davis, who lived like a star, died like one as well. Meanwhile, his former partners in slime, Marc Rich and Pincus Green, are still living the fugitive high life in Switzerland, happily ever after.

If the Davis charade was unadulterated soap opera, the Disney donnybrook was sheer Greek tragedy. It was all about hubris, overreaching, arrogance. Disney was something of a movie version of the clothier Barneys, originally a discount operation that grew and grew until it got too big for its Armani britches. In a sign of the changing times, following the huge success of 1987's *Three Men and a Baby,* the studio's master of parsimony Jeff Katzenberg somehow became deluded that TV star Tom Selleck needed to be paid like a movie star on the 1991 sequel, *Three Men and a Little Lady.* Otherwise, Katzenberg feared, he would lose Selleck's next picture.

Disney's financiers Tom Bernstein and Roland Betts, whose Silver Screen "dumb dentist" consortiums had raised $1 billion for the studio, disagreed. They also foresaw the specter of blockbuster bloat with Katzenberg's eager acquisition of E. L. Doctorow's Dutch Schultz–inspired novel, *Billy Bathgate,* as a vehicle for the notoriously profligate Dustin Hoffman and Bruce Willis. This seeming betrayal of the Disney formula of small actors, big stories led Bernstein & Betts to bid adieu to Eisner & Katzenberg and abandon the movie business in favor of real estate. The monument to their perspicacity is the enormously successful Chelsea Piers sports complex on the Hudson River, not to mention Betts's pivotal role in the election of George W. Bush as president of the United States. DKE rules!

One of the greatest ironies of the Ivy League technocrat invasion of the entertainment world in the eighties is that it made movies businesslike—that is, more quantifiable and predictable than ever before. The case could be made that in so doing, the movies got even worse than they were. After the eighties, with all the colorful independents and the remaining iconoclastic producers pushed to the sidelines, all that big business has made Hollywood a relatively dull place. Seeing Yale lawyers and Harvard M.B.A.s in the executive suites was no longer a special occasion, but par for the course, so par that Hollywood lost a lot of its mystique as a job destination. Sequels and comic book adaptations were pretty hard to get excited about. Yes, there was big money in blockbusters, but there was bigger money, a lot bigger, at Goldman Sachs. If money was going to be its own reward, the Ivy Leaguers preferred to go for the gold where the gold was buried, on Wall Street.

Back in Burbank, the plot thickened with the death in 1994 of Eisner's number two man, Frank Wells, in a helicopter crash on a skiing holiday. Number three Katzenberg had always assumed that if anything ever happened to Wells, or Eisner, he would move up to the second slot. But Katzenberg, who seemed the ultimate team player, had been making unseemly waves. In the midst of Disney's first real slump in 1990, Katzenberg, realizing the error of having deviated from the path of penury, wrote a widely disseminated memo that proved to be a page from the David Puttnam foot-in-mouth playbook.

In the document, Katzenberg singled out the Warren Beatty

had to run deep. In the end, Katzenberg couldn't be number two. Instead his number was up. Out he went.

Not that the golden retriever ended up in the Hollywood doghouse. Instead, he teamed up with Dive! partner Spielberg and Big Brother figure David Geffen, a billionaire from selling his record company to MCA, to form DreamWorks, where he found his true passion in animation. At the same time, Michael Eisner showed the world just who was talking when he *hired* the supposedly most powerful man in Hollywood, Mike Ovitz, as his new number two, the president of the Walt Disney Company. Ovitz resigned from CAA to take this supposed dream job, which turned into his worst nightmare. The move made it clear that Eisner was the true king of the entertainment jungle, the most powerful man in the world of showbiz. The point was rammed home even harder when, barely two years later, Eisner *fired* his former best friend and tablemate. The lord giveth, and the lord taketh away.

Michael Eisner retired from Disney in 2005 at age sixty-three, but he has never stopped being a player, dabbling in numerous new media ventures. In 2007, he bought control of the very old-fashioned Topps, the bubble gum trading card giant. Mike Ovitz has not fared as well. His attempt to revisit his CAA power as a seller rather than a studio buyer, by founding the Artists Management Group, was another bitter disappointment. The most fear that Ovitz inspires today is whether or not he will give you a table at Hamasaku, the minimalist Japanese restaurant he owns in a strip mall near the scenes of his youthful triumphs at UCLA, whose hospital he has majorly endowed. He's not exactly the maître d', a move that would have been evocative of Erich von Stroheim in *Sunset Blvd.*, but he's often there minding the store.

At least Ovitz is still among the living. Given their propensity to court prestige medicine with huge donations like that of Ovitz or, in Eisner's case, production deals, it is curious how many of the producers and moguls died before their time, which, had it been up to them, would have been never, life at the top being as sweet as it is. Steve Ross of Time Warner died of prostate cancer at sixty-five. Those seemingly forever young musical chairs multiple-studio heads Ned Tanen and Dan Melnick both shuffled off at seventy-seven, surprising since both were on the Toscana Eisner Italiana meal plan and were always seen with beautiful women a fraction of their age, which no one might have guessed until the bitter end. Dawn Steel went much sooner, at fifty-one, of a brain tumor. Richard Zanuck, who eschewed all his father's vices and was an ascetic fitness fanatic, still died of a heart attack at seventy-seven. His sudden passing in 2012 made the wannabe Methusalehs of Hollywood very nervous.

But Barry Diller, seventy, continues to move and shake like a Young Turk. As does Bob Wachs, now seventy-two and freed of Eddie Murphy, who returned to New York to run his Comic Strip and produce an off-Broadway musical about a discotheque. He remains committed to staying far from Paul, Weiss and his Harvard education. Robert Evans is eighty-three, bowed by a stroke but hardly broken and, while not in production, ever the babe magnet. Rupert Murdoch, also eighty-plus, will never go gently into any good night. Sherry Lansing is still around, the toast of the A-tables, as are the once golden boys Alan Ladd Jr. and Richard Zanuck, now in their golden age.

And so is David Puttnam, for whom outliving his nemesis, the *Terminator*-like Raymond Otto Stark, may be sweet revenge. Puttnam is living proof of life, a wonderful life, after Hollywood. Although he barely made any more pictures after ignominiously leaving Columbia, he became a star of Britain's Labour Party and now sits grandly in the House of Lords. Lord Puttnam. Hail, Britannia, Ray, and *requiescat in pace,* if that is possible for a perpetual motion Hollywood mogul.

# *APPENDIX*

A Studio-by-Studio Timeline of Hits, Flops, and
the Executives Behind Them

### Columbia

| | |
|---|---|
| Owner | Allen & Company (late 70s) |
| | Coca-Cola (1982) |
| | Sony (1989) |
| | |
| Key Executives | David Begelman, Dan Melnick, Alan |
| | Hirschfield (late 70s) |
| | Frank Price (1980) |
| | David Puttnam (1985) |
| | Dawn Steel (1987) |
| | Peter Guber, Jon Peters, Frank Price (1989) |
| | |
| Hits | |
| (> $100 million | |
| domestic gross) | *Stir Crazy* (1980) |
| | *Tootsie* (1982) |
| | *Ghostbusters* (1984) |
| | *Rambo* (1985) |
| | *Karate Kid II* (1986) |

Flops
(> $20 million loss)   *One from the Heart* (1982)
*Ishtar, Leonard Part 6* (1987)
*The Adventures of Baron Munchausen* (1989)

## Twentieth Century Fox

Owner   Publicly held (late 70s)
Marvin Davis, Marc Rich, Pincus Green
  (1982)
Rupert Murdoch (1984)

Key Executives   Dennis Stanfill, Alan Ladd Jr. (late 70s)
Sherry Lansing, Alan Hirschfeld (1980)
Larry Gordon (1982)
Barry Diller (1984)
Joe Roth (1989)

Hits
(> $100 million
domestic gross)   *The Empire Strikes Back, 9 to 5* (1980)
*Porky's* (1982)
*Return of the Jedi* (1983)
*Big* (1988)

Flops
(> $20 million loss)   *Rhinestone* (1984)

## Paramount

Owner   Gulf + Western (Charles Blühdorn) (late 70s)
Gulf + Western (Martin Davis) (1983)
Sumner Redstone (early 90s)

Key Executives      Barry Diller, Michael Eisner, Jeffrey
Katzenberg (late 70s)
Frank Mancuso, Ned Tanen, Dawn Steel
(1985)
Sid Ganis (1988)

Hits
(> $100 million
domestic gross)      *Raiders of the Lost Ark* (1981)
*An Officer and a Gentleman* (1982)
*Terms of Endearment* (1983)
*Beverly Hills Cop, Indiana Jones and the
Temple of Doom* (1984)
*Top Gun, "Crocodile" Dundee, Star Trek IV*
(1986)
*Fatal Attraction, Beverly Hills Cop II* (1987)
*Coming to America* (1988)
*Indiana Jones and the Last Crusade* (1989)

Flops
(> $20 million loss)      *Popeye* (with Disney) (1980)

## Disney

Owner      Disney family (late 70s)
Sid Bass, et al. (1984)

Key Executives      Ron Miller (late 70s)
Michael Eisner, Jeffrey Katzenberg, Frank
Wells (1984)

Hits
(> $100 million
domestic gross)      *Three Men and a Baby; Good Morning,
Vietnam* (1987)

*Who Framed Roger Rabbit?* (1988)
*Honey, I Shrunk the Kids; The Little*
    *Mermaid* (1989)

Flops
(> $20 million loss)    *Popeye* (with Paramount) (1980)


## MGM/UA

Owner                    Kirk Kerkorian
                         Ted Turner (1985)
                         Kirk Kerkorian (1986)
                         Giancarlo Parretti (1989)

Key Executives           David Begelman,
                             Dan Melnick (1980)

Hits
(> $100 million
domestic gross)          *Rocky IV* (1985)
                         *Rain Man* (1988)

Flops
(> $20 million loss)     *Heaven's Gate; Inchon; Yes, Giorgio* (1980)
                         *Shanghai Surprise* (1986)


## Universal

Owner                    Public (Jules Stein, Lew Wasserman)
                             (1980)
                         Matsushita (early 90s)

Key Executives        Sid Sheinberg, Ned Tanen (1980)
                      Frank Price (1986)

Hits
(> $100 million
domestic gross)       *On Golden Pond* (1981)
                      *E.T.* (1982)
                      *Back to the Future* (1985)
                      *Twins* (1988)
                      *Parenthood* (1989)

Flops
(> $20 million loss)  *Howard the Duck* (1986)

### Warner Bros.

Owner                 Steve Ross (1980)
                      Time Warner (1989)

Key Executives        Bob Daly, Terry Semel, Frank Wells (1980)

Hits
(> $100 million
domestic gross)       *Superman II* (1980)
                      *Gremlins* (1984)
                      *Batman, Lethal Weapon II,*
                          *Driving Miss Daisy* (1989)

Flops
(> $20 million loss)  none

## Surprise Smashes

Cost
(< $10 million)        *Airplane!* (Paramount) 1980
Grosses                *Arthur* (Orion), *Porky's* (Fox),
(>$60 million)             *Stripes* (Columbia) 1981
                       *Flashdance* (Paramount) 1983
                       *The Karate Kid* (Columbia) 1984
                       *Platoon* (Hemdale), *"Crocodile" Dundee*
                           (Paramount) 1986
                       *Dirty Dancing* (Vestron) 1987
                       *The Naked Gun* (Paramount) 1988
                       *Driving Miss Daisy* (Warner Bros.) 1989

# SELECTED BIBLIOGRAPHY

Daniel Ammann. *The Prince of Oil*

Steven Bach. *Final Cut*

Alex Ben Block. *Outfoxed*

Connie Bruck. *Master of the Game*

———. *The Predators' Ball*

Bob Colacello. *Ronnie and Nancy*

Frederic Dannen. *Hit Men*

Bernard Dick. *City of Dreams*

———. *Engulfed*

John Gregory Dunne. *Monster*

Joe Eszterhas. *Hollywood Animal*

Robert Evans. *The Kid Stays in the Picture*

Ivan Fallon. *Billionaire*

Charles Fleming. *High Concept*

Natasha Fraser-Cavassoni. *Sam Spiegel*

Nancy Griffin and Kim Masters. *Hit and Run*

Kitty Kelley. *Nancy Reagan*

Tullio Kezich and Alessandra Levantesi. *Dino*

Charles Kipps. *Out of Focus*

George Mair. *Inside HBO*

Kim Masters. *Keys to the Kingdom*

David McClintick. *Indecent Exposure*

Mike Medavoy. *You're Only as Good as Your Next One*

Joyce Milton and Ann Louise Bardach. *Vicki*

Linda Obst. *Hello, He Lied*

Pierce O'Donnell and Dennis McDougal. *Fatal Subtraction*

Julia Phillips. *You'll Never Eat Lunch in This Town Again*

Stephen Prince. *A New Pot of Gold*

Frank Rose. *The Agency*

Linda Schreyer and Mark Damon. *From Cowboy to Mogul to Monster*

Dawn Steel. *They Can Kill You but They Can't Eat You*

James B. Stewart. *Disney War*

John Taylor. *Storming the Magic Kingdom*

Walter Yetnikoff with David Ritz. *Howling at the Moon*

Andrew Yule. *Fast Fade*

————. *Hollywood a Go Go*

# *ACKNOWLEDGMENTS*

Many thanks to: Peter Bart, Carol Baum, Janis Beckerman, Nicolas Bernheim, Michael Bessman, Irving Blum, Mel Brooks, Marty Caan, Lewis Chesler, Joe Cohen, Robert Evans, Adam Fields, Michael Fuchs, Peter Graves, Allen Grubman, Alan Ladd Jr., Sandy Lieberson, Paul Maslansky, Rospo Pallenberg, Jon Peters, David Puttnam, Marty Ransohoff, Eddie Redstone, Bebe Reed, Carl Reiner, Matt Tabak, Richard Tuggle, Andy Vajna, Dimitri Villard, Bob Wachs, Sandy Whitelaw, Ronald Winston. Special appreciation to my agent, Dan Strone, and his assistant, Kseniya Zaslavskaya, and to my editor, Elizabeth Beier, and her assistant, Michelle Richter.

# INDEX